The Sound Production Handbook

Don Atkinson
Audio Consultant, Leeds, UK

With contributions by
John Overton
and
Terry Cavagin

BLUEPRINT
An Imprint of Chapman & Hall

London · Glasgow · Weinheim · New York · Tokyo · Melbourne · Madras

Published by Blueprint, an imprint of Chapman & Hall, 2–6 Boundary Row, London SE1 8HN, UK

Chapman & Hall, 2–6 Boundary Row, London SE1 8HN, UK

Blackie Academic & Professional, Wester Cleddens Road, Bishopbriggs, Glasgow G64 2NZ, UK

Chapman & Hall GmbH, Pappelallee 3, 69469 Weinheim, Germany

Chapman & Hall USA, 115 Fifth Avenue, New York, NY 10003, USA

Chapman & Hall Japan, ITP-Japan, Kyowa Building, 3F, 2-2-1 Hirakawacho, Chiyoda-ku, Tokyo 102, Japan

Chapman & Hall Australia, 102 Dodds Street, South Melbourne, Victoria 3205, Australia

Chapman & Hall India, R. Seshadri, 32 Second Main Road, CIT East, Madras 600 035, India

First edition 1995

© 1995 Don Atkinson

Typeset in 10/12pt Photina by Saxon Graphics Ltd, Derby

Printed in Great Britain at the University Press, Cambridge

ISBN 1 85713 028 6

A catalogue record for this book is available from the British Library

Library of Congress Catalog Card Number: 95-77016

Don Atkinson has spent 30 years in broadcasting, mainly in Independent Television. He has experience in all fields of broadcast audio and particular expertise in location audio. He also spent three years as a VTR dubbing mixer on the half-inch Betacam equipment – now the industry standard. He is currently involved in sound training for the broadcasting industry and universities. His credits include *Whicker's World, The Outsider, The Professional* and *Johnny Come Home.* He has been nominated for a BAFTA craft award for location studio.

John Overton has had 34 years' broadcasting experience, with special knowledge of studio audio, culminating in his appointment as Head of Sound for Tyne Tees Television. He is currently a senior tutor at the European Media Training Centre in Newcastle upon Tyne and operates also as a freelance sound supervisor.

Terry Cavagin has spent over 30 years in broadcasting, mostly as Senior Dubbing Mixer for Yorkshire Television. He was Head of Film and Sound for Yorkshire for many years. He now lectures in Film and Television Production at Cleveland College of Art and Design. During his broadcast career he was twice nominated for BAFTA craft awards for film sound.

The Sound

This book is to be returned on or before
the last date stamped below. Overdue
charges will be incurred by the late
return of books.

UПIVERSITY COLLEGE
CHESTER

Contents

Introduction   **xi**

Acknowledgments   **xii**

1 Basic sound principles required in the industry   **1**
    Basic acoustics   1
    Fidelity   3
    Analogue audio   4
    Digital recording   6
    Distortion   10
    Phase   13
    Sound volume and the human ear   17
    Signal-to-noise ratio   19
    The balanced input system   20

2 Measuring and monitoring sound   **23**
    The decibel   23
    The dynamic range in broadcast sound   26
    Metering and controlling levels   28
    Controlling sound levels and quality   34
    Recommended PPM levels within broadcast television   36

3 Microphone types   **38**
    Directional responses of microphones   38
    Hypercardioid microphones   45
    Pressure zone microphones   46
    Personal microphones   47
    Artistic and physical restrictions on microphone placement   48
    Special-purpose microphones   49
    Dynamic microphones   50
    Capacitor microphones   50
    Choosing the right microphone   54

4 The audio mixing console   **57**
    The basic studio analogue mixing console   57

Impedance and source matching   62
Limiters and compressors   63
Interfacing domestic equipment and professional equipment   67
Use of equalization   69
The audio jackfield   73
Distributing the audio signals   74
Digital mixing consoles   76

5   Balancing audio levels in the studio   79
Monophonic productions   79
Drama   80
Music   81
News and current affairs   84

6   The studio floor   86
Wall box facilities   86
Rigging the studio   86
Providing playback of audio   87
Boom operation in the studio   88
Microphone positioning   89

7   Stereo operations in the studio   93
Technical requirements for stereo   93
Conservation of the polarity of audio signals   95
Choice of programme material for stereo   96
Boom operation for stereo   97

8   Editing techniques for audio   98
Quarter inch editing   98
Digital hard disk editing   98
Using the Audiofile system   99
Optical disk editing systems   103

9   Dubbing   104
Dubbing a video programme   104
Dubbing a film production   106

10 The roles and responsibilities of the sound supervisor   108

11 Radio microphones   110
Setting up radio microphones before use   111
Common problems with radio microphone systems   111
Suitable personal microphone heads   112

Radio mics in the studio   113

12 Location recording   **114**
The art of location sound recording   114
Microphones suitable for general location work   117
Suitable portable consoles for location work   119
Location recording preparation   122
Mixing sound on location   123

13 The Nagra recorder on a film location   **125**
Nagra IV-S timecode recorder: simplified operating instructions   128
Synchronization with video on location   129
Using the Nagra IV-S TC with video   130
Working with a cable link with one or more cameras   131
Using the Nagra timecode recorder for sync playback   132
Timecode clapperboards   133

14 Working with video equipment on location   **135**
Line-up and use of Sony Betacam equipment   137
Locking cameras with timecode on location   139
Suitability of the camera microphone provided on camcorders   140

15 Relationships on location   **141**
The sound recordist's relationship with the cameraperson
    and director   141
Crew relationships with artistes and the general public   144
Informing interested parties of problems   145
General location discipline   146

16 Location considerations for audio productions   **147**
Drama production   147
Location acoustic considerations   151
Documentary and current affairs production   152
Planning and location surveys   153
Hiring equipment   155

17 Stereo location production for television and film   **157**
Location recording for stereo   158
The sound recordist on location   158

18 Technical considerations for stereo studio and location productions   **163**
The A/B stereo system   163
The M/S stereo system   165

Establishing the stereo mode of operation 167
Post-production considerations 168
Using RDAT recorders on a production 168
Using RDAT recorders on location 171
Advantages of using RDAT as a location source 173
Supplying wildtracks or buzz tracks 174

19 Leaving the nest **177**
Purchasing equipment 177
Pricing your product 178
Accounting and billing 179
Finding the work 179
Keeping up with standards outside the broadcasting industry 180

Appendices
A Further reading 183
B Glossary 184
C Television organizations and manufacturers 190
D Audio formats with video 196
E Current technical requirements for broadcast location stereo input
  to companies 199
F Digital sound editing tools 205
G The licensing of radio microphones in the UK 210
H Film dubbing chart 213

Index **215**

Introduction

This book is written with the express desire to make sound engineers and recordists, new to the studio and location, aware of the pitfalls and technical requirements for broadcast and corporate work.

The author and co-authors have worked within the broadcast industry for 35 years to date. With the service in broadcasting, experience has been gained in all types of sound recording and transmission as well as personnel management, and much change has been observed in general operation practices from a technical and manning point of view.

Although this book contains technical information, it is not intended to be an absolute technical manual, nor does it contain a high degree of technical data that a newcomer cannot absorb. Indeed, it is designed to give as much information to the reader as possible, and point out relevant differences between studio and location sound operations. There seems to be a general opinion that location work and studio work are the same thing from a sound and picture point of view. Although they are similar they are far from identical; special skills apply on both fronts.

The desire for faster operation and cost saving on location has tended to cause broadcast companies and independent companies to seek much more multiskilling. This has resulted in operators having to play dual roles, often without full training for their new roles prior to operating on location or in the studio. The new National Vocational Qualifications may redress the balance on the minimum training requirements within broadcasting, and this book will take into account all aspects required for such qualifications.

It is the author's hope that the information within this book will be simple enough for the newcomer to understand, but it does require a little prior knowledge of physics and acoustic techniques. Suitable further reading material is listed at the end of the book.

Acknowledgments

Extracts from Granada Television's *Technical Aspects and Transmission Requirements* are included by kind permission.

I should like to thank the following broadcast organizations and companies for their valuable assistance in writing this book: AKG Acoustics plc; Ambient Recording GmbH; AMS Industries plc; Audio System Components Ltd; Audio Developments Ltd; Audio Ltd; BBC Television Network; Border Television Ltd; Canford Audio plc; Central Broadcasting Ltd; Dennis Craven, Technical Consultant; Filmtech TV and Film Equipment; Fostex (UK) Ltd; Granada Television Ltd; Nagra Kudelski (GB) Ltd; S4C; Script to Screen Ltd; Sennheiser (UK) Ltd; Soundcraft Electronics Ltd; SQN Electronics Ltd; Sync Facilities Ltd; Studio Audio and Video Ltd (SADIE); The Institute of Broadcast Sound.

CHAPTER 1

Basic sound principles required in the industry

BASIC ACOUSTICS

Sound is a form of energy similar to light, which travels from one place to another by alternately compressing and expanding the medium through which it travels. This is known as **wave propagation**.

If you throw a stone into a pool of water, the stone will cause a ripple or wave extending outwards from the disturbance. If an object such as a cork is on the edge of the pool, you will see it bob up and down, showing that energy has been transmitted through the water by means of waves. In this case the medium through which the energy has travelled is water. The distance between the ripples is called the **wavelength**; the height of the wave is called the **amplitude**.

Consider the analogy of a pendulum. Attach a weight to a thin cord, suspend it from above and allow it to swing freely. If you attach a pencil to the weight, pointing downwards, and draw a piece of paper across the path of the pendulum in contact with the pencil, it will trace out a record of the path of the pendulum. The rate at which the paper is drawn past the pendulum determines the 'time-base' against which the swings are being examined. If this is one centimetre per second (1 cm/s), and the pendulum is swinging at one swing per second, an oscillation of the pendulum will 'draw' one waveform every centimetre.

Examination of these regularly occurring waveforms will reveal:

- that they are equally spaced, i.e. that the pendulum is swinging at a constant speed;
- that the picture made on the paper is the path of the pendulum with relation to time, and has a particular shape. This is known as a **sinewave**. It represents the simplest form of regularly recurring motion occurring in nature.

Sound waves are generally caused by a sound source vibrating and sending its vibrations into the air. Sound is transmitted by air, and by other substances such as water, wood and metal. Some examples of sources of sound that can be felt *without* using the ears are bells, loudspeaker cones, explosions, and tuning forks. Sound cannot pass through a vacuum; this is because the physics of sound dictate that sound propagation depends on vibrations alternately compressing and rarefying the medium between the source and the receiver.

The human ear acts as a receiver or detector for the minute air pressure variations produced by the transmitted sound waves, which cause sympathetic vibrations in the eardrum. The received vibrations are transmitted through a complicated set of delicate bones to the inner ear, where they excite nerves that translate the sound waves into brain impulses or minute electrical signals. This mechanism is described in more detail later in this chapter (p. 17).

Frequency

The number of times that a sound wave occurs per second is known as its **frequency**. It is generally expressed in cycles per second, or hertz, abbreviated to Hz. A musical note of 1000 cycles per second, travelling through air at 340 metres per second, will have a distance between each cycle of 340/1000 = 0.34 metres or 34 cm.

Wavelength

The physical distance between cycles of sound travelling through air is called the **wavelength**. Sounds of long wavelength are of low frequency and are heard as deep in tone; sounds of short wavelength are of higher frequency and are heard as high or shrill. The number of cycles per second, or frequency, of a sound determines its pitch:

$$\text{Wavelength} = \frac{\text{Velocity}}{\text{Pitch}}$$

Reflection

Sound can be reflected by hard surfaces or absorbed by soft surfaces. The quality of the wall, ceiling and floor surfaces of a room or studio determines the way a sound can be reproduced. Hard walls will reflect the sound to produce reverberation; if the reflections of the sound can be distinguished separately from the original sound they are known as echoes. The science of treating rooms for sound is known as **acoustics**.

Sound quality

The quality of sound depends upon the way it is generated. Musical notes of the same pitch or frequency can sound different, depending on the musical instrument that they are played on. Although the notes may be of the same identical basic frequency, they contain overtones that determine their quality or **timbre**.

If a musical instrument plays a note with a pitch of middle 'A', it will have a fundamental frequency of 440 Hz. The note will also contain frequencies of twice, three times, four times and so on of the fundamental frequency, i.e. 880, 1320, 1760 etc., up to the limits of audible frequency. The overtones, which are always multiples of the fundamental frequency, are present in varying ratios of amplitude; it is these, and their proportions, that determine the timbre of the sound. They are called **harmonics**.

It is the harmonics that give individual instruments their unique sound, and help to explain why electronically created instrument sounds do not quite match their real-life counterparts, unless they are an accurate digital sample. Another major aspect in the sound that instruments make is their physical construction and the materials from which they are made.

FIDELITY

Audio systems are usually called **chains**, and each component of a system forms part of this chain. We use the term **fidelity** to mean the degree to which a chain approaches its perfect state.

High fidelity is the term that first applied to our home systems when quality was dramatically improved, and it has stuck there since. In general it means that the system will reproduce an exact copy of the original sound waves, without coloration due to any form of distortion. High fidelity is only a purely relative term; recording techniques and equipment design have improved considerably since the term was introduced. It is not unusual in the 1990s to have domestic equipment outperforming professional equipment from a recording point of view.

No two people can agree on what constitutes good, faithful sound reproduction: it is a matter of choice. Everybody's hearing is different: one person will decide that a certain recording has too many high frequencies, while another may decide that this is not so. People also get used to their own particular room acoustics. In addition, men and women hear sound differently. A woman has a better response at high frequencies, and a man has a slightly better one at low frequencies. In tests that we conducted for a training film we were able to feed audio tones to a selection of male and female volunteers and came out with results that bore out the hearing differences of our sample at certain frequencies.

All this makes it more difficult for the audio engineer to assess the overall tonal balance, and means that there is generally only one yardstick that can be applied: the recording must cover the overall frequency range in an even manner. You must assume that all equipment in the chain has a 'flat' frequency response: this means that all equipment should give a true response at all frequencies, with no peaks or lows in particular areas.

You should expect the equipment within broadcasting to have a flat frequency response between 20 Hz and 20 kHz (1 kHz = 1000 Hz) and not to

deviate much more than about 2 dB at all frequencies. (The use of the decibel –
dB – to measure sound is explained in Chapter 2.) This is now fairly easy to
obtain with the new digital equipment, but it is not so easy on analogue equipment, as a constant watch needs to be kept on equipment technical line-up.

Most domestic equipment is capable of the type of fidelity that we require for
our broadcast audio. However, there are limitations with loudspeaker sizes, and
also with the manufacturers' previous reluctance to place any importance on the
audio side of a television transmission. This situation has improved with the
introduction of Nicam digital audio to the television system: not only does Nicam
give an almost 100% digital path for audio from the studio transmission centre,
but it has also encouraged manufacturers to pay more attention to the audio side
of the television set's receiving and reproducing system.

The difficulty for the broadcast audio engineer is that there are still millions
of viewers who are listening to their audio on inferior systems that do not give
the transmitted quality its true fidelity. How can you deal with a system that
requires on the one hand a full bandwidth to reach a minimal audience in stereo,
while on the other hand still has a maximum audience only capable of listening
in lower fidelity? There is really only one answer, and that is to aim to achieve
the highest possible overall standard all the way down the chain. In this way you
can satisfy all the listeners.

Before the introduction of the Nicam stereo system to broadcasting it was
possible to restrict certain areas of the frequency range and dynamics to take
account of the poorer listening environment in the home. Now it is much harder
to decide how to use a broadcast stereo system to its true advantage. You have to
consider the majority of monophonic listeners who for a long time will be your
main audience. This brings to mind the classic snooker commentary that
occurred in the early days of colour television, when the commentator referred to
the colour of the balls, forgetting that most of the viewers would still be watching
in black and white.

ANALOGUE AUDIO

Much of what we record in television and audio is in the analogue domain. At
the heart of the distinction between analogue and digital are the ideas of change
and measurement. In our daily life we function in an analogue way. We perceive
and react to all kinds of events and situations that change over time in a more or
less continuous way.

Consider water running from a tap in a continuous stream. You could measure the rate of flow continuously with some sort of flowmeter. If this meter could
give you a readout it would probably be in the form of a graph or continuous
moving pointer indicating the continually changing flow.

The devices used to measure and record continual change can be regarded as kinds of computers, as they convert an analogue signal, mostly by mechanical means, to give a display that we can understand and often calculate in one way and display in another. A flowmeter rising and falling, a clock's pointers moving, indicating the passing of time: such devices present analogues of something that we cannot perceive accurately otherwise.

Electricity can travel very great distances. If you can make an electrical analogue of the sound that you want to convey over a long distance, you can use that instead, provided you can reverse the process and reproduce a sound analogue from the electrical analogue at the far end. Much of the technology that we take for granted works in just this way. The mechanical change when you put your foot down in a car is translated into a different mechanical change as the car accelerates. The mechanical change of turning a volume control on your radio is translated into an equivalent electrical change, which in turn is translated into a change in sound level, and so on. In all cases, you are turning one form of energy into another, as many times as you need to do a useful job. The ability to change from one form of energy to another is therefore a useful means to an end. But there are some snags, especially when it comes to using these analogue chains to carry information.

Consider the basic example of picking up some simple sound within a room. The first link in the chain will be the microphone. The electrical impulses that it generates will then be fed into a mixer unit. This will entail two conversions: the first is from a sound wave to an electrical wave, and the second is from a low-level electrical signal to a higher electrical signal. To hear the acoustic analogue, the third conversion is through a sound wave transducer in the form of either a set of headphones or a loudspeaker. This assumes the minimum of conversion and does not carry the product any further down the line. But already there have been three conversions of standards – more if the mixer unit incorporates devices to alter the levels of particular frequencies.

Each of these conversions will include some form of unwanted modification of the signal. It may be a mechanical imperfection within the microphone; it may be the addition of noise within the amplifier circuits; or it may be a mechanical imperfection within the headphone circuit or loudspeaker circuits. In addition, the acoustics of the area where the audio was recorded could cause further modification of the original sound.

So far, this is quite a simple situation. If you then want to take the product even further, you have to record the information onto tape, which again is a conversion of the signal. Once recorded onto tape, the signal must then go through many more processes until you have a final product for transmission. Clearly, every stage until the final transmission will degrade the product in some way.

Training within the BBC and most broadcast companies clearly points out to newcomers that they should strive for the highest possible quality or fidelity in the first instance, as the product will be downgraded as it goes further down the chain. This applies to the choice of microphone, equipment and tape stock on which the signal is recorded.

In the new multiskilling environment a less careful watch is kept on equipment, with it passing through many (often less experienced) hands. Technical problems on equipment may not be noticed; equipment may be adjusted for specific reasons and not then returned to its original correct line-up. And even with perfectly lined up analogue recording equipment, running at the highest possible speeds (as audio quality is dependent on tape speed), some downgrade is inevitable.

Studios generally maintain a tight control of their audio standards, and have maintenance departments who keep on top of technical problems. This is often not so with equipment that is continually being used in the field, particularly with 'pool' equipment issued successively to a number of operators. All audio operators must keep a close watch on analogue equipment and its line-up, as any imperfections may not only detract from the excellence of the final product, but may also affect the reputation of the individual.

When a problem occurs on a particular production with audio equipment, it is rarely the equipment that is at fault. There are so many interchanges along the way that at any one stage a modification of quality may have occurred. For example:

- incorrect line-up of equipment;
- poor matching of equipment to systems;
- inadequate monitoring facilities;
- variable frequency response on analogue equipment;
- incorrect matching of tape stock to equipment.

How can you can get round some of these problems? The answer is in the next section.

DIGITAL RECORDING

Since the early introduction and use of PCM (pulse code modulation) by the BBC in the 1970s, digital recording has now become commonplace. With the introduction of the lower-priced 16-bit digital recording systems like RDAT and Hi-8-based systems, plus other higher-priced studio equipment, the use of digital in some form is now common practice in broadcast audio.

A brief description of the digital process follows, which generally covers most systems in current use in the processing form. The main difference between systems is in the way the digital information is stored: some systems use optical disks or floppy disks, while others use magnetic tape. The newer PC- and Macintosh-based editing and recording systems often use the computer's hard disk system, or external storage units of a similar nature.

Sampling

Consider the example of the tap and the flow of water again. This time the tap is just dripping. In the digital way of things, you assume that each droplet contains the same amount of water, so you can compute the total amount of water falling in, say, 30 seconds by counting the drops and doing some mathematics.

Compare this with the analogue method, using a flowmeter. To convert a continuous flow to a set of discrete data, you can 'digitize' the measuring process by taking readings at intervals. This is called **sampling**. Sampling produces a list of readings to constitute a record of the analogue flow. The product of sampling is therefore **discrete data**. Once you have discrete data, you can make calculations about the flow. But in audio, you do not want to do calculations: you want to make, send and receive sound signals. Computers may be better at calculating than we are, but, used as the front end of audio systems, can they help to make better audio recordings?

By converting the analogue electrical current or signals that represent the sounds into a stream of discrete data, you can greatly improve the audio fidelity. This conversion is done in much the same way as in the tapwater example, but the computer does it more rapidly. Within the computer, there are only two states of data: on and off. Current either flows, or it does not. This means that what comes out is exactly what goes in. You cannot have unwanted gains or losses in the signals: they are either there, or they are not. As long as the signals that represent the audio are in digital form, fidelity is 100%.

Computers can only deal with discrete data consisting of two states. If you assign meanings to each state, you can do a great deal more than simple arithmetic. By assigning ones and zeros to each state, you can string them together to form longer patterns (called **code**), which can represent almost anything you like. This is how computers do things like representing the words in this book: each character (letter, number, or sign) has its own unique pattern of ones and zeros.

As well as helping you to record your audio better, going digital enables you to do some things that are simply not possible otherwise.

Digital processing

Once you have turned your signals into numbers, you can perform all kinds of tricks on them by programming the computer to do different calculations. This kind of operation is called **digital processing**. Digital processing is a powerful toolbox these days, and new tools are arriving every month. You can edit audio alongside pictures, stretch audio lengths without altering pitch, synchronize audio and pictures, and perform many other operations. You can move pieces of audio in chunks without altering your original recording, giving **non-destructive editing**.

Computers need discrete data. The keyboard that was used to type this book is an example of an **input device**. It converts human actions into discrete data. The computer screen of the word processing system and the printer used to create the typescript for the publisher are examples of **output devices**, which convert the data back into analogue form, so that you can make use of it. For audio signals the equivalent input device is known as an **analogue-to-digital converter** (A to D); as an output device it performs the reverse function on the digital signal by becoming a **digital-to-analogue converter** (D to A).

The audio signal on the input of the digital system is converted to a digital train of pulses by the analogue-to-digital converter. These pulses are sampled at around 44.1 kHz in professional equipment and at 48 kHz in domestic equipment. This allows digital equipment to have a bandwidth of around 20 Hz to 20 kHz. Within the digital system the analogue signals are converted to binary codes, the information being recorded as a series of digital pulse trains of equal amplitudes. On playback, all that has to be done is to discriminate between the presence and absence of pulse. The quality of the recording does not depend on the characteristics of the heads or tape, except perhaps for any creasing or dropout on the tape itself, which can cause problems.

The number of digits or **bits** used to code each amplitude of the analogue signal sampled has to be high enough to give very small differences in the levels that can be accurately coded. (Bit is the abbreviation for **binary digit**.) High-quality music requires more resolution to avoid the noise in digital systems called **quantization noise**, which the use of too few bits would produce. Sixteen bits are currently used in most systems, which gives 65 536 levels, resulting in the greater accuracy required for quality music reproduction. Higher bit rates are gradually being introduced, mostly in the audio editing areas and music mastering studios, for even higher quality. The bit rate of a digital recorder without additional error correction is about 1 500 000, which requires a wide-band recording system: hence the use of videotape or rotary head systems.

The basic quality of a digital system is dependent on the analogue-to-digital converters. Usually, the distinction between broadcast and domestic equipment is the quality of these converters, as well as the mechanical robustness of the equipment. Certainly the broadcast equipment will have more carefully designed electronics and more comprehensive input and output facilities. However, it would be difficult even for an expert to tell the difference audibly when monitoring the audio quality by ear.

In conventional analogue recording the quality of the sound reproduction depends upon the quality of the mechanical construction, electronics, magnetic tape and its heads. Even with metal tape and higher-quality electronics it is virtually impossible to bypass the inherent limitations of analogue recording, including its dynamic range and frequency response and its associated distortion and noise, even on the highest-quality equipment. Other factors in analogue equipment, such as noise-reduction systems, have their own intrinsic problems. With a digital system a noise-reduction system becomes unnecessary, provided extremely high-quality electronics are used prior to the digital conversion and after the digital processing.

It is of little use to feed signals into a digital system from a mixer unit or microphone that itself had a poor signal-to-noise ratio (see p. 19); both will add noise to the recorded signal. A digital system will faithfully record and reproduce a transparent copy of the original. If the signal is kept totally within the digital domain the exact copy of your original recording will be preserved, provided the digital-to-analogue conversion circuits are accurate.

When considering other advantages of the digital system, transferring material at digital levels offers no reduction in audio quality or modification to the original signal as in the analogue system; only digits are being transferred, which are only a train of 'on and off' pulses. There are no head alignment problems to worry about, nor tape set-ups to be done. Overall, the advantages of digital systems are the ability to make a transparent copy, which adds no further noise to a recording, and the overall lack of distortion within the recording system.

It would be prudent at times on RDAT equipment to check tensions on the mechanical tape path of the machine. The only real areas of problems are in either mechanical or tape quality, which could affect overall performance. Even with the new DAT machine designs and their advantages, on current professional models the problem of battery consumption still remains. It is relatively easy to supplement domestic recorders with external batteries of the Sony NP1 or other types and run up to 4 hours on one charged battery. This still falls short of the capability of the Nagra analogue recorder, which can happily record all day on one set of batteries, and was seen as an industry standard.

With a suitable front-end mixer like an SQN or similar unit, most domestic digital DAT systems can be used, with a little care. However, they do not contain the four-head **off-tape monitoring** of their bigger professional sisters. This requires the recordist to do constant checks on the condition of the heads when recording on location, to avoid any tape head clogs or tape 'dropouts' on the recorded audio signal. A digital flag applied by domestic RDAT machines called **SCMS** (serial copy management system) can be problematic, as it applies a 'one copy only' restriction on the system. This is to prevent pirate copies of recordings, and was meant to prohibit the recording of CDs and such like. Electronic units are available to remove this digital flag for professional copying purposes.

Most digital studio edit systems, such as Audiofile (see Chapter 8 and Appendix F) would require you to record at the professional sample rate of 44.1 kHz to enable a pure digital transfer; otherwise the transfer would have to be done in the analogue domain or via a digital converter. The availability of new digital standards converters and modifications in software will perhaps help in these matters.

It has been found in practice that digital systems should be lined up at different levels for reasons of headroom safety. For 16-bit recordings the EBU recommendation is to line up at −18 dB with reference to peak level. This puts analogue peak at −10 dB with reference to digital peak level. These recommendations have been adopted by the BBC. Experience has shown sound engineers that it is advisable to line up at lower levels, as recommended above.

Many new systems have evolved based around the RDAT system. The main ones are an ADAT machine by Alesis and Fostex, with eight-track capability, and a similar machine using Hi-8 cassettes by Tascam. Both these machines can be 'daisychained' together to give further track expansion for music recording or dubbing. The Alesis machine is based around a VHS format cassette, while the Tascam machine is based around a Hi-8 cassette. Both machines have similar maximum running times, with about 110 min being the maximum recordable time. There is no dedicated track needed for timecode (required for synchronization with video), so both the above machines have a full eight tracks of digital audio available for recording.

A further newcomer on the digital scene is the Nagra digital recorder (Nagra D). This is equipped with rotary heads, but has four-track audio capability, which will give distinct advantages for film and video locations. However, this machine is not very portable, and would require the location recordist to have a suitable trolley available to support the machine; also, adequate power supplies should be made available.

Sony have introduced a floppy disk recording system, used commercially in 1993. At the time the system did not seem to have a wide enough bandwidth for broadcast use. However, these units are now appearing as broadcast units suitably cased and modified for broadcast purposes. Classic FM, the independent radio network commercial music channel, and other radio stations are using such minidisk systems for broadcast purposes without any complaints from listeners. Other new uses are being found for the system on location, so the early technical doubts about this system are being removed.

A similar system of digital recording, but with reduced running times, is available from Audio System Components, called Dart. The Dart system is fast replacing tape cartridge machines for playing music and jingles on programmes. It is a pure digital system but with less overall running time than the minidisk system.

Other systems of digital recording, which are discussed later in this book, are generally used in post-production.

DISTORTION

When an audio engineer goes beyond the limits of the dynamic range of the equipment and modulates beyond the 100% limit, **distortion** will become evident. There are many forms of distortion; perhaps the first one noticed is overload distortion, but any modification of the original sound, or anything added to or taken away from the original sound, constitutes distortion.

Harmonic distortion

Although the ear is very critical of quality changes in reproduced sound, it soon accepts poor-quality sound if subjected to it over a period of time. Harmonic distortion is caused by the non-linearity of the input-to-output characteristic of a recording chain or reproducing chain. The chain may introduce harmonics that were not present in the original signal, or alter the original harmonics by suppressing them. The resulting sound will not be like the original sound if the harmonics are suppressed or altered in any way.

Frequency distortion

This is generally caused by the unequal amplification of frequencies in the audible range and, indeed, at times the omission of certain frequencies. This form of distortion is always present on all recordings to some degree. No microphone or analogue device can really be accurate enough. However, large changes of balance in the bass or treble frequencies, in either their level or their frequency range, will make this form of distortion detectable. No recording with a wide frequency range would be acceptable unless all forms of distortion were at a minimum.

Intermodulation distortion

When two sounds of different frequencies are superimposed upon each other, this can result in a modulation of one frequency by the other, producing unwanted 'beat' frequencies and combination tones. For example, this problem might occur on location, where a microphone may be modulated by the wind, but be recording a choir or musical instrument with much higher frequencies. The movement of the microphone diaphragm by the lower unwanted frequencies can affect the wanted higher frequencies, because the lower frequencies have more power. In this case windshielding or low-frequency compensation could effect an improvement.

A similar problem can occur in a single loudspeaker circuit where one speaker is handling differing levels across the whole frequency range: hence the multispeaker arrangements in current speaker systems.

Transient distortion

This is usually the result of some part of the reproducing or recording system not being able to copy faithfully the steep wavefronts in the original sound waveform. It is often caused by inertia in equipment that transfers energy from one medium to the other, such as microphones and loudspeakers. When a particularly high transient hits either the microphone diaphragm or the loudspeaker cone it is unable to recover quickly enough and continues to ring, or 'hang over', before assuming its normal rest position. This is probably caused by a combination of inertia and resonance.

Spatial distortion

This is generally known as the 'hole in the middle effect', and is peculiar to stereo recordings. It is often caused when using a spaced microphone pair: sounds in the middle of the listening field can be lost because of phasing effects due to the arrival time of the signal at each microphone, thus cancelling out some of the information. The result is that sounds moving between the microphones seem to increase off the centre line. The problem can usually be cured by using directional microphones placed in the centre angled inwards, with the left-hand microphone angled towards the right-hand side of the audio field and vice versa. (See the description of the A/B recording system on p. 163.)

Another aspect of spatial distortion is that the image can often appear wider or narrower than the original, so great care must be taken in placing microphones under these circumstances.

Volume distortion

Also known as **scale distortion**, this is usually caused by listening at different levels from the original recorded sound on a loudspeaker or headset. The distortion exists and is usually accepted by the human ear. It would be wrong to listen to an orchestra in the home at the same sound level that it would create in a concert hall. Very low-volume speech, however, is often reproduced at a higher than normal level to create a more constant overall balance. This sounds perfectly acceptable to the ear, and is an example of an occasion when the audio engineer can sensibly alter the dynamic range to the advantage of the listener.

Resonance

Sound waves are caused by vibrating air particles, and are capable of causing anything in their path to vibrate in sympathy. Any item that has mass or stiffness will vibrate more freely at one particular frequency than any other. This effect is known as **resonance**. If you move your dampened fingers slowly around the rim of a wineglass, it will emit a sound at its resonant frequency. A low-humming generator will have the same effect on certain objects around it. You may have noticed when playing your audio system that some objects rattle in sympathy with certain frequencies as their own resonant frequency is reproduced.

Rooms contain pronounced resonances, due to sound waves being reflected from the different parallel walls and surfaces that are half a wavelength apart, or multiples of half a wavelength. The build-up of such resonances into a continuous wave motion is called a **standing wave**. Standing waves are a big problem at low frequencies, and can cause **coloration** of the sound quality in small untreated rooms.

When recording on location and in the studio it is apparent that some form of acoustical damping must be applied to reduce these reflections and stop standing waves occurring. This is no problem in the studio, as studios are normally acoustically treated, but many locations are now being used to simulate a studio situation and often have poor acoustics. See the section on location acoustic considerations (p. 151) for a discussion of the steps that you can take to improve acoustics on location.

Microphones and loudspeakers also have mechanical resonances; the exact resonance depends on the stiffness and mass of any of the moving parts: the greater the mass, the lower the frequency; the stiffer the mass, the higher the frequency.

You can arrange capacitors and inductors in certain configurations in an electrical circuit to resonate at certain frequencies. This enables you to construct circuits that become your equalizers used for frequency correction within recording and transmission systems.

PHASE

Look at the two identical sound waves in Figure 1.1. They have equal amplitude and frequency, but are displaced relative to each other. The two waves are said to differ in **phase**.

Phase is the term used to describe the actual point reached by a sound wave in its cycle of movement. Phase is always measured in degrees of a circle; 360 degrees corresponds to one cycle of movement. In Figure 1.2 you can see that the start of any one wave is exactly 360 degrees away from the end; all crests will be said to be in phase with each other. All valleys are separated by 360 degrees, so they too can be said to be **in phase**. The crests are said to be **out of phase** with the valleys, as their phase relationship differs by 180 degrees.

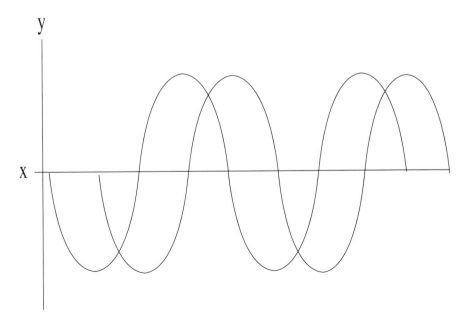

Figure 1.1 Two sinewaves differing in phase.

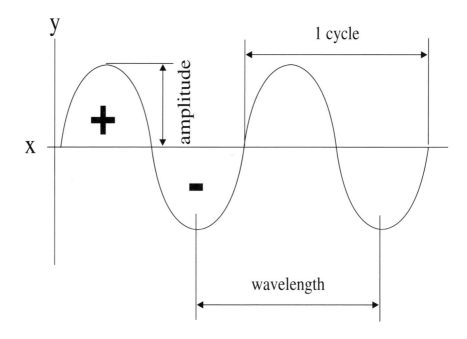

Figure 1.2 Simple sinewave.

A problem may occur when two signals very similar in form but different in phase are combined. If two equal pure tones in antiphase were fed into a channel or input and added together the result would be zero, as in Figure 1.3. Sound patterns are normally so complex that using microphones that are sufficiently far apart on the same location will present no problems if their outputs are mixed. Differences of phase will have little noticeable effect.

The ear is generally not too interested in phase. In reality the ears do not know of the 'out of phase' signal, as it is impossible for the ears themselves to be 'out of phase'. Sound waves can be added together with all sorts of complex waveforms, which all sound the same to the ear. This is quite important when we come to the issue of microphones and their design and use. It does not matter whether the microphone measures pressure, as the ear does, or pressure gradient, which is 90 degrees out of phase with it. The output of both types can be mixed together quite happily.

As far as sound is concerned, it is of extreme importance that the waves are in phase for the following reasons: waves that are out of phase tend to cancel each other out; waves that are in phase reinforce each other.

Sinewaves are almost unknown in the natural world. You can, of course, generate sinewaves electronically for test purposes, and they form the standard test references. Sound that you hear has much more complicated waveforms, which vary with the sound emitted.

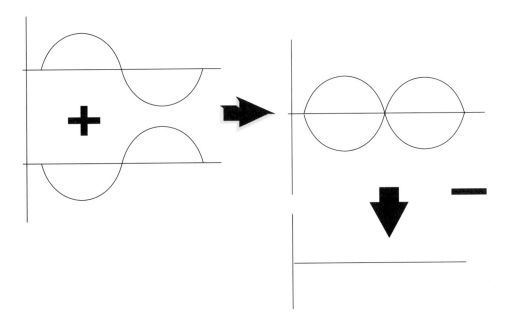

Figure 1.3   Illustration showing effect of two sinewaves in phase and antiphase.

Phase in stereo

Phase becomes much more important when applied to the stereo operation, as you can end up with some rather strange results if the phasing is wrong. One of the main problems that you have to watch for is the phase of your cables, as you will generally be using balanced cables, which feed into a phase/antiphase input on the mixer unit. Most problems will not show up in mono operation, but will show up drastically when recorded in stereo and converted to mono for transmission or distribution.

In mono operation the most likely time that phase will show on microphone inputs is when two microphones working very close together are fed into a mixer and the inputs are summed. There will be a distinct reduction in bass response due to the cancelling-out effect when two similar signals are out of phase. This technique is used to great effect on the design of balanced high-level or microphone input channels to reduce interference from outside sources on mic lines or signals.

Reversing a wrongly phased cable will restore the low-end response, and no phasing effects will occur. Built into the input stage of modern mixer units is the facility for phase reversal by a simple switch. This avoids the need for inserting phase reversal plugs on the input cabling.

As most companies have operated in mono for a long time there may well be a few cables within the system that could have a phase reversal problem. A location recordist, on commencing stereo operation, should do a complete phase check on all cables within the kit supplied, to avoid phase problems. Indeed, it would be prudent for all companies to spend time checking all balanced cables within a system for phase integrity. It is unlikely that microphones will have a phase problem within themselves or that equipment will be supplied with a phase reversal on their inputs and outputs.

During the stereo sound mixing operation the sound engineer should make occasional phase checks on the output by switching the stereo output monitor circuits to mono. If a reduction in the bass response is evident, then there may be a phase reversal.

The recently introduced **EBU tone** will give an indication of absolute phase when merged to mono, as it consists of two 'in phase' sinewaves, one interrupted by 0.25 s every 3 s. On merging this tone to mono, if the signal lowers when both tones are present then the output of the mixer is out of phase, which in this case points at an output lead reversal or a phase reversal within the equipment. As two symmetrical waves in phase at zero level should give about 6 dB lift in signal, any drop in the signal level indicates a phase reversal. The EBU tone within the mixer will only give an indication of the phase within the mixer or the phase of the recorded signal. The operator should ensure that all incoming signals are in phase.

At the studio end an indication of phase can be obtained by M/S metering; some units have a monitor within their PPM units for the side signal, which will indicate phase reversals. This is covered later in the section on M/S meter indications (pp. 32–33). Other suitable phase indications are available using either a cathode-ray tube display or bar-graph display and mechanical meters.

It is possible, by having a 180 degree phase reversal, to lose the centre image portion of the signal completely and remove, say, a vocalist set in the centre of the image. The indications when listening in stereo are of a rather unsure centre image but little more: perhaps a 'pulling' of the image within the ears one way or the other. It is interesting to note that as an 'out of phase' signal is unnatural to the ears, constant listening to such signals can cause headaches.

The main points to watch on phase are as follows.

- Check all cables for phase.
- Check your mono output regularly for phase reversals.
- Use EBU or GLITS tone (where available) on all stereo tapes and check phase in mono. A description of BBC GLITS tone can be found in the glossary (Appendix B).

Remember that when recordings are made in twin mono (mono on both tracks) phase is just as important; the output leads on the mixer or player should be in phase. The same problems that occur in stereo with phase can happen in the twin mono situation, when a merge of tracks may occur.

Phase and processors

Care must be taken with the use of limiters and compressors, and indeed any processors such as echo units and other effects units, as they have a processing time built in, which can cause timing or phase errors within a stereo system. It is important in stereo operation that the delays are the same in each stereo leg, which dictates that a twin effects unit should be used, with a stereo ganging control available within the unit. With limiters and compressors the trigger for the unit should be ganged and worked from an average of the two inputs. This will avoid any 'weaving' of the stereo image from side to side.

SOUND VOLUME AND THE HUMAN EAR

The part of the ear that senses sound is a tiny spiral structure called the **cochlea**. Sound enters the ear via the outer ear and auditory canal. The channel has a resonance peak of about 3–6 kHz. At the end of the auditory canal is the **eardrum**; this vibrates in sympathy with the incoming sound but is not too good at following low-frequency signals. Three small bones carry the vibrations from the eardrum, forming a sort of impedance-matching device, converting the acoustic energy of the air to a form more suitable for transmission through the fluid of the tiny channels of the inner ear (Figure 1.4).

The middle ear contains air, which permits the free vibration of the eardrum, and avoids excessive damping of the movement of the small bones. Air pressure is

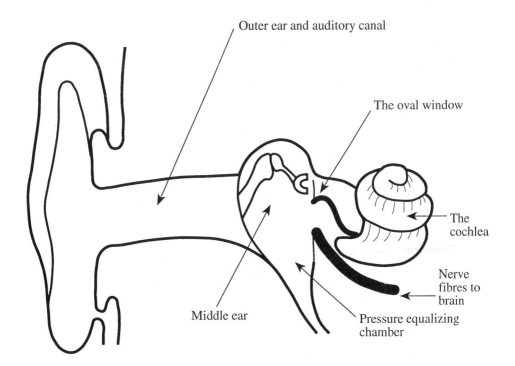

Figure 1.4   The human ear and its component parts.

equalized by the **Eustachian tube**, a channel in the nasal cavity. The inner ear is a shell-like structure. There are two channels along the length of it, narrowing where they join at the end. Along the upper channel are fine hairs, which respond to different frequencies; when the hair is bent, a nerve impulse is emitted. The further down the canal you go, the lower the frequency recorded. Approximately 4000 nerve fibres or sensors carry the impulses to the brain, which, like a computer, decodes the information.

The ear measures sound in a **logarithmic** way for both frequency and volume, with the perception of sound volumes and frequencies in ratios rather than a linear scale. The growth of sensation doubles at equal intervals. When the ear handles such inputs they are perceived in a manner similar to the musical scale, and increase numerically in the following manner: 1:2:4:8:16:32:64, and so on. The logarithms of these numbers can be simply expressed as 0:1:2:3:4:5:6:7, and so on. This is exactly how we perceive the musical scale.

The ear's reaction to mid and high frequencies is better than to lower frequencies with regard to changes in volume. The normal range of hearing is approximately 20 Hz to 20 kHz for a younger person, but the upper end of the range falls off with age to 10 or 15 kHz. The ear's sensitivity is at its best from 1 kHz and above. The auditory canal has a broad resonance at around 2–6 kHz, which helps at these frequencies. These frequency areas are used to give audio extra **presence** when using electronic equalization. In reality you would expect a young person to be able to hear a frequency of up to 17–18 kHz. The lowest frequency generally heard would be around 16 Hz.

The trained ear can detect a change of about 1 dB in level. The ear's natural resonance means that it needs more intensity in the sound at the lower and higher frequencies. The lower limit of hearing is called the **threshold of hearing**, and is generally referenced at 1 kHz as zero on the decibel scale. This should not be confused with broadcast 0 dB reference level. There is actually no real natural zero, as this would be infinitely low on the decibel scale. The upper limit of hearing is set where sound can be *felt* rather than heard. It is often called the **threshold of pain**, and is between 100 dB and 120 dB above 'zero' level.

Equipment and equipment chains are designed to take into account the human hearing range of 20 Hz to 20 kHz. It is of little use to design above this frequency range as it would only be heard by certain animals, such as bats. Manufacturers usually quote their frequency resonances based around the human hearing range and slope off the frequency range beyond 22 kHz, as there is the possibility that oscillations outside the human hearing range could cause damage to some equipment.

Sense of direction only starts to come into play around 1 kHz, as the ear responds to lower frequencies with an out-of-phase effect. This is because the signal reaches one ear at a different point in its waveform from the signal reaching the other ear. Above 1 kHz the distance between the ears is greater than the wavelength, so the signal heard in each ear is in phase, occurring at the same point on the signal wavelength.

The mass of the head has a shielding effect, which causes each ear to receive the signal in phase but at slightly different volume. By turning the head and equalizing the signal level we get our sense of direction. Obviously we get our sense of direction from the higher-frequency signals and their **time of arrival** (TOA). This effect will be discussed later in the section on the A/B stereo system (p. 163), as arrival time at the ears is the main effect that allows us to perceive sound in stereo.

SIGNAL-TO-NOISE RATIO

The signal-to-noise ratio of a system or individual piece of equipment is the ratio between peak programme and the peaks of noise. The figure is always quoted in decibels (see Chapter 2). In general terms, the higher the decibel figure the better the signal-to-noise. The general problem with all audio equipment in the past has been to maintain a good signal-to-noise relationship: equipment electronics had to be extremely well designed to keep the noise figure down to acceptable levels.

System noise on its own is not the only form of signal-to-noise ratio to consider. In the same way as hiss or noise would be annoying on the recorded or live audio signal, so would any noise that was not the noise we wished to hear, such as traffic or drills. When considering a recording made outside on a location with heavy traffic, the traffic level may be at such a ratio that it confuses the main signal, which might be a person playing a part in a drama or just making a statement to camera. These interferences to the sound we require to transmit or record are unwanted noise, which it is desirable to reduce to the minimum. The ways of dealing with these problems will be discussed later in the section on location recording (p. 114). See also the section on audio acceptability levels on p. 160.

As noise is generally additive, with all sorts of equipment in the chain creating their own form of noise, the highest possible signal-to-noise ratio must be maintained on all the components down the chain. Modern microphones have improved noise figures, as have the microphone amplifiers and the audio equipment that follow in the chain. Digital equipment, by its very design, can achieve noise figures of up to 94 dB, which is a figure at which we would not perceive any problem. Unfortunately, not all systems are digital, and the old analogue equipment still has poor noise figures. Magnetic tape adds another noise problem, as does the tape used in videotape recording, which is formulated to favour the video signal rather than the audio signal (recorded on a separate track alongside).

Electronic noise-reduction circuits such as Dolby C and Dolby A, and other similar systems, help to reduce tape noise by their own particular compression of frequency ranges during recording and expansion of these bands on replay. However, no noise-reduction system can reduce noise that is there as part of the audio signal being introduced to the mixer input circuit. Nor can a noise-reduction circuit help if the microphone itself is generating some noise.

In the near future it will be possible to go 100% digital, with location and studio video recorders having their own dedicated digital tracks. Further transmission of the audio signal can be handled digitally, keeping the whole process from the original to the actual transmission totally within the digital domain.

Most current high-quality microphones now have a signal-to-noise ratio of about 74–84 dB, so little problem will be found there. However, these are the newer microphones, and there are still plenty of the older microphones around. Most high-quality capacitor microphones, even of the older type, attain a signal-to-noise ratio of 72–80 dB. The other factor to consider is the matching of microphones or any other device to a mixer input, as this also can cause noise due to microphone amplifiers working at gain levels that are too high.

THE BALANCED INPUT SYSTEM

As the input system normally used within broadcast work is a balanced system it would be wise to look at what the system is in practice and its advantages.

A balanced system is usually constructed with differential input amplifiers, either balanced electronically, or by using high-quality audio transformers in some equipment. The cables used within a balanced system are twin cables with a separate screen. Both the inner cables are twisted upon each other and covered by a tight braided screen. One cable is labelled +V (hot); the other is labelled –V (cold) plus the ground signal. The design of the differential input amplifiers is such that interference picked up on these wires from outside the equipment is cancelled out by the input circuit. This is because, as both wires are in close proximity, the same interference will be picked up on each wire, and balanced input amplifiers will only amplify the difference between +V (hot) and –V (cold). Any signal on both hot and cold (i.e. noise) will not be amplified. This is known as **common mode rejection** (CMR). Balanced inputs should always have both inputs connected or, if used as an unbalanced input source, the –V connection should be shorted to ground. A typical balanced input circuit is illustrated in Figure 1.5.

Modern audio and musical instruments often have **electronically balanced outputs**; these should not be shorted to ground and should be fed into a balanced input only. Usually there is a warning on such outputs. Generally, transformer-balanced inputs are preferred by the industry, possibly for standardization reasons, and the fact that a transformer offers a greater degree of isolation and rejection of radio frequency interference.

Often **ground-compensated outputs** are supplied on mixers. This is a very effective way to optimize noise immunity. These outputs employ ground-compensating techniques to cancel out effects of variation in ground potentials between the mixer and other equipment resulting in hum. If these types of output are fed to an unbalanced input then the –V (cold) connection must be shorted to ground at the signal's destination, not at the originating mixer end.

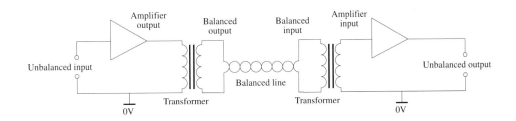

Figure 1.5 Circuit diagram of a typical balanced input system.

Polarity is particularly important in balanced systems. Just as a balanced system is highly effective in cancelling out any unwanted interference, so if two microphones were connected with the phase reversed on one of the microphones, serious degrading of the signal would occur as explained earlier. These sorts of problem are rare in normal domestic systems, with their unbalanced operation, and would only occur because of poor design and phase reversal within the equipment.

Earth loops are difficult to avoid at times, but generally can be eliminated if the earth connection is made at the source end, not both ends. An important piece of equipment to carry within a location kit is a box with an earth-lift switch, so that an earth loop can be cleared at either the transmitting end or the receiving end. It is also useful to have some sort of phase reversal within the unit, and this is normally provided in commercial direct injection boxes.

Balanced and unbalanced systems in the field

Recording audio for broadcast purposes usually entails all the units supplied being balanced, and balanced broadcast practices should always be observed. The 'outside world', however, frequently presents itself in an unbalanced form, technically speaking. It would be advisable in the field to carry the following units for interfacing to the outside world:

- A 600 Ω balanced-to-balanced transformer unit in a mu-metal case if possible, with an earth-lift switch.
- A direct inject box with gain switching from high-level line output to low-level mic input (this is needed if you are short of line level inputs on the mixer) Some mixer units' output sockets only feed outputs at mic level; also, direct feeds from public address systems can be at any level and are often unbalanced sources.
- An assortment of cable adaptors, such as jack to XLR, phono, aircraft NATO and single-pole aircraft jacks to XLR female plugs. Useful also would be 'back to back' converters for XLR plugs and sockets.
- A microphone splitter to allow a single 'front mic' to be split between your output and a public address system, or to feed the same signal to another broadcaster.

Unbalanced microphones

Using unbalanced microphones with professional equipment is usually no problem unless phantom power is being used on the channel input to which the microphone is connected. (Phantom powering is described in Chapter 3.) Unbalancing one leg can short out a phantom power supply and cause damage to the mic and the phantom supply. It is advisable to carry a 'one-to-one' transformer if you wish to get away from the phantom supply or switch away the phantom powering on the individual channel if that is possible.

The usual way to use unbalanced microphones into a balanced input is to short pins 1 and 3 on the XLR input socket, unbalancing the circuit, and to connect the unbalanced microphone's earth cable to these with the 'hot' wire going to pin 2 (Figure 1.6).

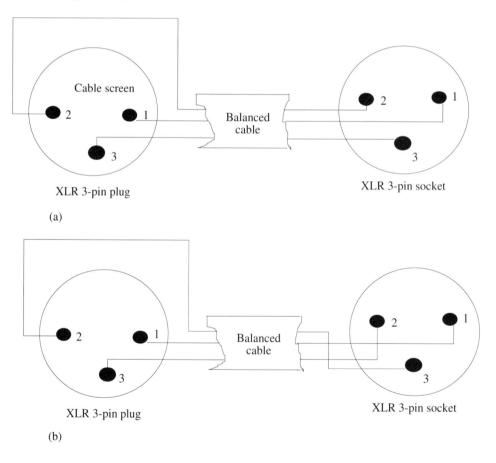

Figure 1.6 Typical connections to XLR plugs and sockets, with (a) correct and (b) incorrect wiring shown.

CHAPTER 2

Measuring and monitoring sound

THE DECIBEL

As the ear is a logarithmic listening device, the chosen unit of measurement for audio measures sound in the same way as the ear. This is the **decibel**. By definition, the decibel is one tenth of a bel. The bel is defined as a scale used to express the ratio of two powers, and so is an expression of power ratios or level changes. The bel is too large a unit to use in measuring audio levels, so all levels are measured as one tenth of the main unit, i.e. the **decibel** or **dB**.

There are many ways of expressing decibels (dBm, dBu and dBV), but all decibels are fundamentally a means of expressing ratios. A ratio is a way of comparing the sizes of two objects (such as signal levels) without referring to their actual size. If an amplifier's output is 100 times bigger than its input, the ratio of output to input would be 100:1. This, of course, says nothing about the *actual* signal level; it could be millivolts or megavolts. You can only express this as 100 times amplification. In the language of decibels you can say this is +40 dB or '40 dB up', compared with the input. You could just say the gain is 100:1 and forget all about decibels.

In the field of audio there is a wide range of signal magnitudes from the lowest noise levels to the highest amplifier outputs, spanning differences in levels of about 1000 million. By using decibels you can simplify these massive ratios, so that, for example, a ratio of 3 160 000:1 is reduced to a simple 130 dB increase. The use of the decibel means that you never have to use more than a three-figure number. Because the numbers are smaller, the chance of error is less, and any mistake is more obvious. Another advantage of dB notation is that, because it is logarithmic, gains and losses in the programme chain can be added and subtracted instead of multiplied and divided.

Decibels in audio are described as positive or negative above a 'zero' reference point. The zero reference level is at 0.775 V r.m.s., all levels being either above or below this reference point. Lower levels than zero are therefore minus x dB and higher levels than zero are plus x dB.

The system of using the references dBm and dBu is more widespread than dBV; they are the standard scales for most professional audio work. From the early days of audio, the reference voltage level was decided to be 0.775 V. This was because it was decided to refer sound signals to 600 Ω termination resistors, and the r.m.s. voltage across 600 Ω needed to dissipate 1 mW of power is 0.775 V. Another reason for choosing 600 Ω was that this was the impedance of standard telephone lines at the time.

Since that time we have progressed, and do not use a fixed load impedance; impedances are higher, and vary from unit to unit. This is where the dBu is useful. Zero dBu equals 0.775 V *whatever* impedance it is measured across; the impedances could be across a range of 4 Ω to 100 kΩ or an open circuit. Zero dBm, however, strictly equals 0.775 V *only* when it is measured across 600 Ω. Today this formality is dispensed with, and dBm is routinely used like dBu: the two are synonymous. When discussing audio signal levels within the studio or on location, it is common to leave out the mention of dBu or dBm as long as you refer to plus or minus. If you say a level is 'plus 4' it will be assumed that you are talking about decibels and a ratio.

1 dB is usually about the smallest change in level that the human ear can detect. The ratio of intensities in a 1 dB change of level is about 1.26:1. The ratio of a 3 dB change is about 2:1: this is worth remembering, because if you double a sound source you double the intensity at the same distance. Therefore, if you have one sound source at 3 dB and you add to it the same sound source at 3 dB you have a level lift of 3 dB. To lift the level again by 3 dB you would have to add four sound sources at the same level, and so on.

In audio work we rarely if ever measure power (only in loudspeaker amplifiers). The meters that we use (VU and PPM) measure voltage. The formula to convert voltage ratios into dB is dB $= 20 \log(V2/V1)$. This gives 6 dB $= 2 \times$ voltage and so on.

The maximum level used by all UK broadcasting companies is +8 dB above zero level. Some Japanese equipment manufacturers set their maximum level as +4 dB, so you would need to line up to that lower level accordingly. Domestic

Table 2.1 Decibel values and the corresponding power ratios

dB Power	Ratios
0	× 1
1	× 1.26
3	× 2
6	× 4
10	× 10
20	× 100
30	× 1000
40	× 10 000

equipment works at a much lower level than broadcast: −10 dB is normal audio output and input level across most home equipment.

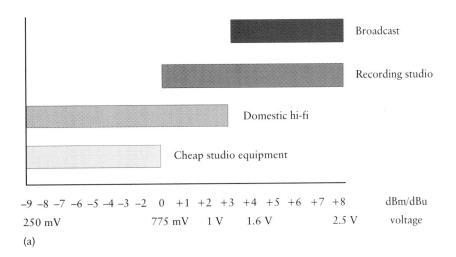

(a)

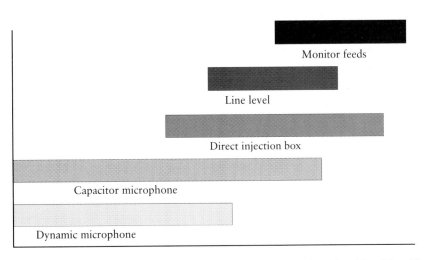

(b)

Figure 2.1 Comparison of (a) typical operating line levels and (b) typical signal levels.

THE DYNAMIC RANGE IN BROADCAST SOUND

The human ear can accept an enormous range of sound volumes. At 1 kHz the threshold of pain is 110 dB above the threshold of hearing; a sound that is only just bearable is a hundred million times as powerful as one that is just audibly detectable (Figure 2.2).

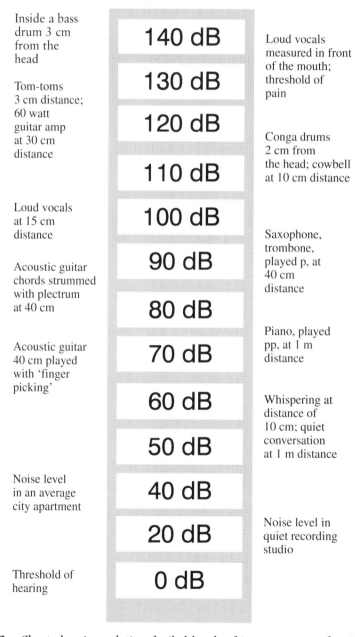

Inside a bass drum 3 cm from the head	**140 dB**
	130 dB — Loud vocals measured in front of the mouth; threshold of pain
Tom-toms 3 cm distance; 60 watt guitar amp at 30 cm distance	**120 dB**
	110 dB — Conga drums 2 cm from the head; cowbell at 10 cm distance
Loud vocals at 15 cm distance	**100 dB**
Acoustic guitar chords strummed with plectrum at 40 cm	**90 dB** — Saxophone, trombone, played p, at 40 cm distance
	80 dB
Acoustic guitar 40 cm played with 'finger picking'	**70 dB** — Piano, played pp, at 1 m distance
	60 dB — Whispering at distance of 10 cm; quiet conversation at 1 m distance
	50 dB
Noise level in an average city apartment	**40 dB**
	20 dB — Noise level in quiet recording studio
Threshold of hearing	**0 dB**

Figure 2.2 Chart showing relative decibel levels of instruments and noises.

Given the immense dynamic range of audio signals, some means of control of dynamics is needed. This is usually done with a form of manual compression applied by the sound engineer by raising and lowering the faders on the sound mixing panel, or by some electronic means.

In general the permitted dynamic range within broadcast television is around 34 dB, which indicates a fair amount of overall level control, if we assume that the loudest incoming sound level may be reaching 120 dB. In a classical concert the dynamic range can be around 60–70 dB.

The signal-to-noise ratio expected within broadcast is around 60 dB, which is far surpassed by modern digital and analogue equipment. However, this must be maintained along the equipment chain, and the operator should be aware of this and recognize any increase in the signal-to-noise area of the audio output. The receiving end of the transmission may well be the home, and in practice the home listener's average maximum listening level is approximately 45 dB above the noise level of a quiet living room. Any sound balancer or mixer should bear this in mind when controlling the audio levels for broadcast transmission.

BBC broadcast practice advises that a sound balancer should keep the dynamic range within a range of 22 dB, allowing quieter passages not to exceed half a minute at one time. Different rules apply for popular music and speech, which are kept within a narrower range. A full list of the suggested PPM ranges for different programme material appears later in this chapter.

A survey of listeners by the BBC suggested that the average listener would like speech following music to be 4 dB down on average, with music following speech to be on average 2 dB up in level. Although this seems to contradict itself it is probably because dedicated music listeners set their volume higher than the average listener in the home environment. It is interesting to note that, in general, men seem to want to listen at higher sound levels than women. Musicians and sound engineers seem to require even higher sound levels, probably because they are looking for greater detail, and are listening for the finer points of fades and mixes.

On location a sound recordist often monitors at a higher level to assess the ratio between background level and the recorded programme material. It is the same in the studio for other technical reasons. Often, in assessing dynamic range, the local visual metering circuits have to be ignored and greater reliance put on the aural balance to judge real loudness levels and relative volume levels.

Currently there is much debate about applying **electronic compression** to broadcast material. Traditionally, classical music has been an area where very little dynamic compression has been applied. With the relaxation of rules, some commercial music stations are applying electronic compression with the aim of 'hitting' the home and mobile environment harder, even on classical music. However, if the same procedure were to be applied to broadcast television, the situation would probably be worse than it is at present: highly compressed commercials already have the viewer/listener reaching for the volume control and continually complaining of varying sound levels.

The broadcast organizations have placed restrictions on the amount of overall electronic compression that can be applied to a programme's audio content. Companies often reduce commercials' peak meter readings on transmission to obtain a more even balance with other programme material, and at times add auto-decompression to highly compressed material. However, this should not deter a sound balancer from using electronic compression within an overall sound balance, to give more prominence to a vocalist's overall sound or to a single instrument within an orchestral balance, or to give more attack on sports commentaries.

Chapter 4 looks at the ways that a sound balancer can control dynamic range and the tools available for doing this. In general, the main decision maker should always be the well-trained experienced ear, aided by suitable visual monitoring circuits.

METERING AND CONTROLLING LEVELS

Across the broadcast and sound recording areas the two main meter types that you are likely to meet are the **VU meter** (volume units) and the BBC-designed **PPM** (peak programme meter).

The VU meter

The VU meter is an American instrument, originally intended to give a measurement of the energy contained in a signal waveform. Most sound balancers and recordists prefer to use the PPM (referring to VU as meaning 'virtually useless'), but this is rarely found on video equipment or audio recorders unless specially requested. The VU meter is typically fitted to commercial and most broadcast equipment by the manufacturer, either a bar graph type or analogue pointer type.

The circuit of the VU meter is usually connected directly across the signal output it is measuring. As it is a passive arrangement it requires no power supply, and can be driven directly from the signal source. The upper scale is marked from –20 VU on the left up to +3 VU on the right, the section beyond 0 VU being marked in red. The lower scale is marked in percentages from 0% to 100%, with the 100% corresponding to 0 VU. Applying a signal of 1.228 V would give a 0 VU reading, which, if compared with our broadcast zero-level reading of 0.775 V r.m.s., would indicate that this is equal to approximately +4 dB on a PPM meter.

The VU meter is also marked in percentages of modulation as well as dBs up to +4 dB level, which is the standard on Betacam and Panasonic video equipment.

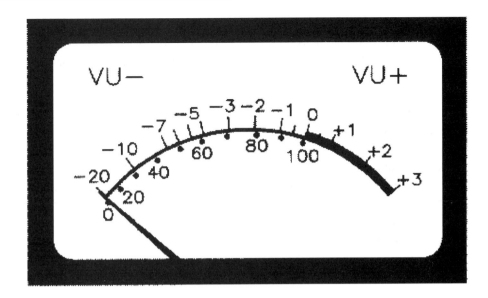

Figure 2.3 A typical VU meter, with percentage modulation scale shown below the dB scale.

The percentage of modulation scale is beneath the meter arc. Some manu-facturers, such as Studer, offer a +8 dB line-up for their VU meters and peak operation similar to PPM meters. Other manufacturers follow a similar pattern.

In practice, it is very difficult to judge levels on the VU meter, as its fast-moving pointer isn't easy to follow, and it is very tiring on the eyes. It is only really useful on line-up tone. The VU meter does not respond in the same way as the ears, and therefore it is difficult to follow.

Most Japanese- and American-manufactured equipment uses VU meters, although it seems to have a certain amount of 'slugging' to make the needles return at a slower rate, giving the impression of a PPM-type meter. A similar 'slugged' meter is supplied on the older SQN 3 mixer unit, and line-up level on this meter is at −8 dB.

VU specifications advise that distortion may occur on speech at levels over the −4 level and at zero level on music recordings. If the VU meter is lined up to −4 on zero level tone and levels are then controlled on a PPM meter to recom-mended broadcast levels the pointer in fact rarely exceeds −7 on the VU meter for speech. This would seem to suggest that mixing directly on the VU meters on video equipment and peaking up to zero would indeed take you into overmodula-tion of the tape. Considering that the video tracks are narrow, and the tape is for-mulated for video, it would seem unwise to overmodulate your recording or overdrive the system.

Most portable mixer units and studio units provide the option to have PPMs or VU meters, and it seems sensible to choose PPMs. Although the music industry has a large number of VU-type meters, it is rare to find these meters within broadcast areas except perhaps on video equipment, as broadcasters wish to keep level control generally standardized to the same type of PPM instrument.

Peak programme meters (PPM)

The PPM is scaled from 1 to 7, with 4 dB of level difference between each segment from 2 to 7. Between the 1 and 2 markings the level difference between segments is 6 dB (Figure 2.4). The movement of the meter and the scaling are logarithmic, and thus follow the action of the ear more closely. In comparison with the VU meter, the PPM is easier to use in judging and anticipating sound levels, and it is the broadcast standard in the UK and some European Broadcasting Union countries.

The PPM has a fast rise time (2.5 ms) and a slow decay time of about 8.7 dB per second, which allows a more precise control of levels and is more easily seen by the operators, with less fatigue on the eyes. The operator is more capable of accessing the average peaks because of this 'semi-hold' facility.

Twin PPMs are available with pointers in line, which allow the operator to watch stereo signals on one meter. Although some control rooms have separate meters for A/B and M/S, there are meters that are switchable between A/B, M/S and +20 dB side signal.

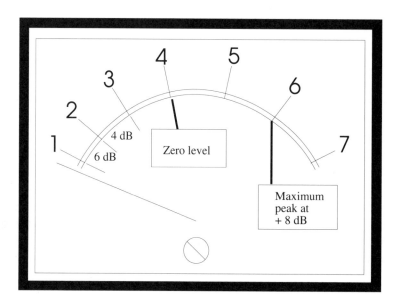

Figure 2.4 The PPM meter, showing reference levels and peak levels.

The stereo PPM

In general, the ears of the sound recordist or sound mixer are the best guide to such things as balance and width in a stereo image. However, it is very useful to have a visual image of this balance, and indeed under headphone operation the only reliable indication that can be obtained will be from meters.

Normal twin PPMs have two coloured pointers: the A (left) signal is red and the B (right) signal is green. Usually the two pointers will weave about each other with just a few dB separation. There will be times when one pointer exceeds the other for a while, when say a section of an orchestra is predominant. However, over time the pointers will generally weave either side by the same amount. If one pointer is consistently higher than the other it may indicate an offset of the stereo image.

M/S meter pointers

M/S (mid and side) and A/B stereo are discussed more fully in Chapter 18 (pp. 163–167). In M/S stereo, the mid signal is recorded separately from the side signal (often referred to as the **difference signal**), which supplies the stereo information. The mid signal could in some ways be termed a mono signal. In the A/B system the two separate signals are A (the left signal) and B (the right signal). These two signals are recorded on tape (or whatever medium is used) and replayed through speakers or headphones. A **matrix** can be used to convert M/S signals to A/B signals.

The following conventions are used in stereo PPM metering circuits. M, which equals A + B, is usually a white pointer, and is equal to the mono signal. S, which equals A − B, is usually a yellow pointer and indicates the side or difference signal. The ratio of the S to the M signal indicates the displacement of the stereo image. This means that if the A and B signal are roughly equal, the ratio of the M and S signals indicates the width of the stereo image, as shown in Figure 2.5.

A signal that is mono will indicate no S (side) signal on the M/S meter (Figure 2.6). A narrow stereo image will indicate as in Figure 2.7, with the pointers wide apart. Normal stereo imaging will indicate both pointers close together, with about 4–8 dB separation (Figure 2.8). If the S signal reads greater than the M signal, this indicates a significant out-of-phase component (Figure 2.9). If the M signal reads zero, this indicates out-of-phase mono (Figure 2.10).

As you can see, great insight can be gained from the readings obtained from an M/S PPM. A total check on phase can be obtained as well as checks on image spread. It is unlikely that the M/S meter will be available on location, as its general uses are in studio and transmission areas.

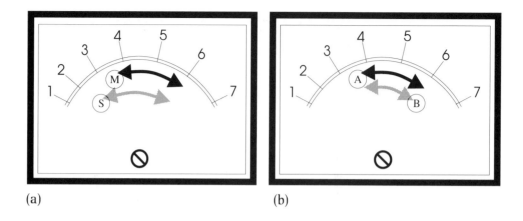

Figure 2.5 Correct readings for stereo on (a) an M/S meter, (b) a twin PPM (A/B).

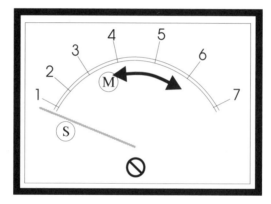

Figure 2.6 M/S meter showing no side signal (S), indicating that the signal is mono.

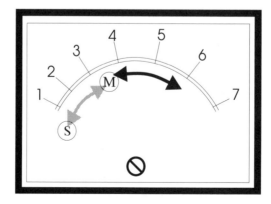

Figure 2.7 M/S meter with pointers wide apart, indicating a narrow stereo image.

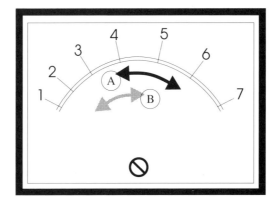

Figure 2.8 Twin PPM (A/B) with pointers 4–8 dB apart, indicating normal stereo operation.

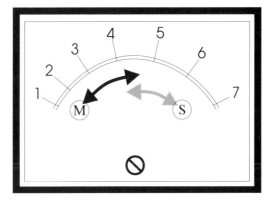

Figure 2.9 M/S meter showing S signal greater than M signal, indicating a significant out-of-phase component.

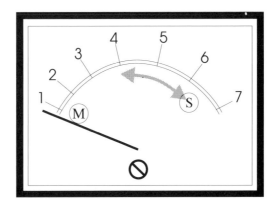

Figure 2.10 M signal reading zero, indicating out-of-phase mono signal.

CONTROLLING SOUND LEVELS AND QUALITY

The tone line-up procedure in the studio and on location

All recordings and transmissions are routed via other areas, and all recordings are routed to other equipment for either direct routeing to a transmitter or recording to another source. To help maintain a constant reference level, standard tones are used by all companies, whether the metering system is the same or not. With VU-metered equipment, account is taken of the scaling of the meter, and levels are adjusted according to broadcast zero level tone.

The main reason for all line-up procedures is to achieve accurate matches of level and interchange between equipment and studio sources. The simple procedure of lining up at PPM 4 can give control rooms, remote transmission areas and transfer bays a positive reference to incoming signal levels, and it helps in finding sound losses within systems as well as setting the standard zero reference level on all equipment in the chain. It ensures that all areas are compatible in level, and that no signal losses or gains affect the signal along the way.

Increasingly, digital signal routeing is being used in studios and facilities. Digital routeing does not normally present a problem with levels, as the signal maintains its level integrity within a digital system: whatever goes in, comes out. Normally these routeings are via **solid-state switching**, which means that computer-controlled electronic switching matrix units are used to route the signals instead of traditional jack panels.

Stereo line-up procedures are dealt with later in the book. Stereo audio signal distribution is much easier to handle in a digital distribution system, as the problem of phase integrity is removed.

For location recordings, tone (mono or stereo) should be placed at the front of all master tapes to aid set-ups in editing or transfer. One other thing worth doing on the first recorded roll of any location recording is to place some spot tone bands from 40 Hz to 15 kHz to help in checking your equipment's frequency response. (This is probably only needed on the very first day of a location shoot.) It is rare to find location equipment at fault, but often line-ups can go adrift in editing. Tone bands at the front of location master tapes can allow a recordist to say 'It was all right when it left me'. They allow investigation into original quality, and can perhaps pinpoint any potential problem area in an edit suite or transfer area – or indeed in the original recording equipment.

As an example, on a recent location shoot in the USA a video unit recorded on Betacam and replayed on location, with all seeming well. The original line-up tone replayed correctly, and the audio sounded fine. On their return to the UK they found that the analogue tracks lacked high-frequency response, the tone replayed wrong and the tracks seemed unusable. On checking the FM tracks, which were recorded in tandem, they were found to be fine. It appeared that the American recorder had analogue head azimuth problems. (Head azimuth is the alignment of the sound recording heads, which should be consistent between all recorder and replay units within a system.) When played back on the location machine, the recorded material sounded fine, with no apparent problems. Played on any other machine, the tracking problem would, of course, be evident.

This shows the need for alignment checks, and also the need to feed the FM tracks on video equipment in tandem with the same programme material as the longitudinal tracks as a safeguard. FM audio tracks are not dependent on a mechanical alignment, which could wander, but are part of the recorded video signal, being recorded beneath it. Remember that the Betacam system does not allow the FM tracks to be recorded unless you are using SP tape in the machine.

The importance of signal-to-noise ratio

Although the introduction of Nicam stereo would seem to benefit only viewers or listeners with Nicam receivers, it has effectively made the complete signal path from a studio to transmitter of near-digital quality. The transmitter output for the normal 625-line mono transmissions is taken from the same feed as the Nicam, with the stereo output summed: the result is a higher-quality audio output to the normal television set than was previously obtained.

This means that any signal-to-noise problems will be more apparent. It is essential to monitor the signal-to-noise ratio throughout the whole transmission and recording system. Levels between equipment should be carefully matched, and high-quality monitor circuits should be used to detect any introduction of noise. Every effort must be made from the very front end of every system to ensure that noise is not introduced. Areas that previously seemed to present no problem, such as microphones, are now seeming noisy, with the better signal-to-noise ratios achieved on current equipment.

The main area outside the original recording where noise can be introduced would now seem to be edit suites, where the audio-monitoring circuits are often masked by equipment noises from the VTR machines during editing. As much material can reach transmission without a final dub or sweetening process, the introduction of noise may go unnoticed. Transfer processes of any kind in the analogue area should be monitored carefully as they are notorious for introducing signal-to-noise problems.

Directors often panic when hearing their rushes on VHS because the audio signal seems to contain noise. This is often due to poor transfer of the audio onto the VHS tape system. All rushes should be assessed from the FM tracks on VHS, and it should be standard practice that all rushes are available on such tracks for production monitoring.

It is a shame that most corporate productions' final format is VHS; often no transfer is made to the FM tracks, which achieve a higher audio quality. Most listeners now have machines that can replay FM tracks. The impact of a higher-quality audio track can make a big difference to a client's appreciation of the overall product. Most audio problems with domestic VHS systems are signal-to-noise problems and built-in limiter circuits crushing the audio signal's dynamic range.

There are indications that clients and viewers are becoming more audio aware. They are now quite used to noiseless backgrounds on their audio systems, with the improvements in quality on domestic audio equipment. We are now seeing domestic equipment with the same audio bandwidth specification as professional equipment. This indicates that the professional sound engineer must be more cautious with regard to signal-to-noise ratios. Before the introduction of modern high-specification equipment, many of the signal-to-noise problems were lost in the system. Today the system is becoming more and more transparent.

RECOMMENDED PPM LEVELS WITHIN BROADCAST TELEVISION

Sound balancers should take care that they present a fairly constant level of sound energy in their balance so that listeners do not have to make constant adjustments to their television or radio receiver volume control. This is of particular importance during the period from the end of one programme to the start of the next, or into an advertisement break in commercial television and radio. Great importance is put on meter levels, but balancers should use their own ears as the main decision makers for smooth level control.

Some companies within the ITV network may apply auto-decompression to commercials that, in their opinion, are over-compressed. Because of the high compression ratios on some commercials, some companies judge their actual audio levels by 'ear' and mark them accordingly, making an aural judgement on loudness rather than a strict meter judgement. Indeed, some companies have used audio expanders, which have the reverse action to compressors, increasing the dynamic range of the original compressed material when transmitted.

Line-up levels and programme levels have been altered recently within the BBC, and to some extent in the ITV network. The general pattern they take is shown in Table 2.2. The peak audio level must not exceed +8 dBu (PPM 6). It is suggested that speech following music must be 4 dB down on the music. Music following speech should be 2 dB up on the speech. Some of the levels listed in Table 2.2 have been changed slightly after complaints from listeners, and compression has been added to some transmissions by the BBC for radio transmissions. Television transmissions follow similar patterns to radio for level control.

Stereo line-up in the ITV network is currently zero level (−8 dB or PPM 4) below peak level fed to both channels in phase. Channel 1 (left) is pulsed for 0.25 s every 3 s to identify the channel as being left. Channel 2 should remain as a steady tone.

The two networks have different views over what to do about the sum of the two stereo signals, or the mono output. When the two signals in stereo are

Table 2.2 Tone line-up zero level (PPM 4, 1000 Hz reference tone).

	Normal peaks	Full range
Talks, news, drama, documentaries, chat shows, quiz shows	5	1–6
Music		
Variety, dance music	4.5	2–6
Brass bands, military	4	2–5
Orchestral concerts	–	1–6
Light music	5.5	2–6
Pop music	5	2–5
Programmes with a high degree of compression	4	2–4
Live 'pop' shows, not containing compression	5	2–5
Commercials		
Highly compressed	4	2–4

combined, the resultant rise is 6 dB if they are coherent, and approximately 3 dB if they are not. This means that a lower line-up level would be required to cope with this summing of signals, which in fact is the case at the BBC. The independent network removes this extra 3 dB at the transmitter; this allows the studio to line up in a normal way but requires the studio sound balancer to take into account a certain amount of extra level in the mono balance, normally by having a separate PPM for the mono output. The Nicam stereo output at the transmitter is fed from a normal A/B stereo signal and the FM mono output is fed to its separate transmitter with a reduction of 3 dB in the level applied.

The PPM is the standard operational measuring instrument for checking audio levels (see p. 30). It is designed and constructed to BS 5428:1981 Part 9, and aligned to ensure that a tone of 1 kHz frequency at a level of 0.775 V r.m.s. results in a meter reading of PPM 4. This is zero level (0 dBu), which is 8 dB below the maximum peak level of PPM 6.

Two versions of dual-movement PPMs have become standard equipment for stereophonic control rooms in the UK: one displays the individual left and right signals; the other displays the sum of the signals (L + R) − 6 dB and the difference of the signals (L − R) − 6 dB. In place of the dual PPMs, it is acceptable to use left and right instruments. In order to ensure that the amount of phase or timing error does not exceed that which could affect the stereophonic image or, worse, impair the compatibility of the monophonic sound, it is recommended that a supplementary instrument is employed to view phase errors. Many instruments are available for this purpose.

CHAPTER 3

Microphone types

All microphones have their own individual pattern or **directional response**. Although the patterns may vary, many other aspects of a microphone's characteristic must be considered before putting it to work for a particular job. Microphones can be compared to loudspeakers. The listener can have a particular preference for the sound of one loudspeaker over another. The same goes for microphones: individual sound balancers have their own preferences. Many microphones can do the same job, and would be equally acceptable to other sound balancers' ears.

Professional microphones generally have XLR connectors of the three-pin type, with the phase correct, as wired from the manufacturer. The impedance of professional microphones is usually low – in the order of 200–600 Ω, with some capacitor microphones exhibiting an even lower impedance. The difference between amateur and professional microphones is usually the impedance, plus the sensitivity, ruggedness, appearance, frequency response, and lack of a professional XLR connector.

DIRECTIONAL RESPONSES OF MICROPHONES

Microphones come in two distinct types: powered, which are known as **capacitor microphones,** and unpowered, which are called **dynamic** microphones. Each type can usually be manufactured to have all the general directional patterns required by a sound engineer, with a few exceptions.

Omnidirectional microphones

The ideal omnidirectional microphone responds equally to sounds coming from all directions (Figures 3.1, 3.2). This type of microphone is known as a **pressure microphone**. Its diaphragm is open to the air at one side only. The pick-up from such a microphone is not the same from the rear: there is a reduction of sensitivity and an uneven frequency response.

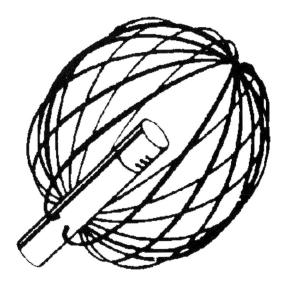

Figure 3.1 Typical 'basket' representation of the polar pattern of an omnidirectional microphone.

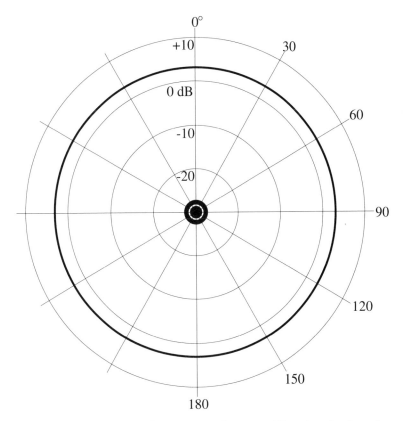

Figure 3.2 Typical theoretical polar pattern of an omnidirectional microphone.

Obviously, with the general all-round pick-up obtainable with the omnidirectional microphone, it cannot be selective in what it picks up, and it is generally not used on location, except on ENG-type interviews (electronic news gathering). Omnidirectional microphones can, of course, be used for gathering general sound effects.

The omnidirectional microphone has an extremely smooth frequency response, and for this reason is often favoured for classical music recordings under controlled conditions, in and out of the studio. The omnidirectional pair of microphones is quite fashionable for stereo classical recordings in a spaced microphone set-up.

Another microphone that is usually omnidirectional is the personal microphone, or neck microphone. This mode of operation uses the advantage of an all-round pick-up to avoid the effect of the person wearing the microphone swinging off the microphone's axis.

Bidirectional microphones

The bidirectional microphone measures the difference in pressure along the path of a sound wave at two different points, and is known as a **pressure gradient** microphone. It is essentially dead to the side of its pattern; the main pattern is a **figure-of-eight** response (Figures 3.3 and 3.4).

Figure 3.3 Typical 'basket' representation of the polar pattern of a bidirectional microphone.

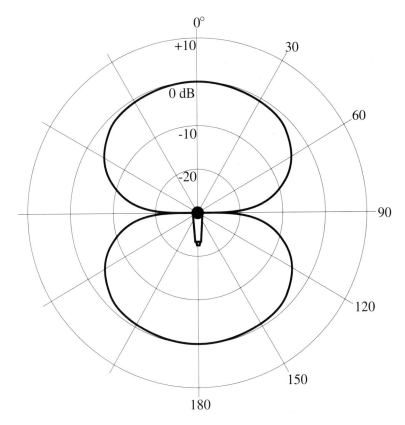

Figure 3.4 Typical theoretical polar pattern of a bidirectional microphone.

The fact that the bidirectional microphone has dead spots off the side of its response is extremely useful to the sound engineer. Two people either side of the microphone facing the capsule can be picked up without the use of a second microphone. In classical recordings it is possible to pick up the direct sound with one side of the microphone while receiving the hall or studio reverberation on the other side. The figure-of-eight polar pattern becomes very useful in the production of a side signal for M/S stereo operation (see p. 165).

When using bidirectional microphones in close proximity to each other, you should take care to ensure that they are both in phase. Most bidirectional microphones have an indication as to which is the front of the microphone. If one microphone is out of phase with respect to the other a cancellation of some of the signal can occur.

The most common type of microphone to have the bidirectional characteristic is the **ribbon microphone**, which is simply a light conductive foil ribbon suspended between a permanent magnet. The output of such microphones is usually very low, and very good microphone amplifiers should be used with such types. One problem found with ribbon microphones is **bass tip-up**, which is an accentuation of the bass frequencies when working close to the microphone.

The same type of characteristic can be obtained with switchable capacitor microphones, where a variable pattern can be obtained. This is obtained electronically, but does not present the low signal output problem experienced with the conventional ribbon microphone.

Double ribbon microphones

This type of microphone uses two ribbons to achieve an extremely directional microphone polar response, which has the capability of reducing ambient sound. The double ribbon microphone can be used for 'tight miking' but with a broad frontal pick-up. It is often recommended for use in acoustic guitar recordings, but could be advantageous when used close to an instrument under very high ambient noise situations, where a closer type of microphone position is required. One advantage of the double ribbon microphone is that it can reduce the bass tip-up that some microphones exhibit at close range.

Cardioid microphones

This type of microphone is often described as a **unidirectional microphone**. It derives its name from its heart-shaped response pattern (Figures 3.5 and 3.6), which shows that it has a dead pick-up area to the rear of the forward pattern, with about half the sensitivity to the side of the microphone. Maximum sensitivity is in the forward direction.

Acoustic or mechanical systems at the rear of the microphone help it to achieve the heart-shaped pattern by introducing a phase error, which creates the pattern. The more expensive capacitor microphones achieve this pattern with a set of switches, which switch and mix between the various transducers to achieve the different polar response patterns.

Most cardioid microphones have a greatly extended bass response when used very close to a sound source. This is known as the **proximity effect**. It can be a disadvantage at times when working close to a microphone, so most manufacturers fit a bass-cut switch to overcome the problem. The usual filter would be a high-pass filter, which reduces the response at around 50–100 Hz by either a fixed amount of 10 dB or a variable amount from around 7 dB to 12 dB. There may also be a variable-frequency filter from 50 Hz up to 150 Hz. These filters may well prove useful when trying to reduce basic room rumble or traffic rumble, but generally this is better done on the mixer unit itself, which can control the low frequencies more precisely.

There can be no doubt that the cardioid is the most popular microphone, as it can help to separate one instrument from another, as well as effectively 'turning its back' to unwanted noises or sounds.

There are two other versions of the cardioid microphone: **hypercardioid** and **supercardioid**. This pattern is rather like the figure of eight, but with less pick-up from the rear, and a frontal pick-up that is much narrower than you would expect from a figure-of-eight microphone. This is often known as a **cottage loaf** response pattern (Figures 3.7 and 3.8).

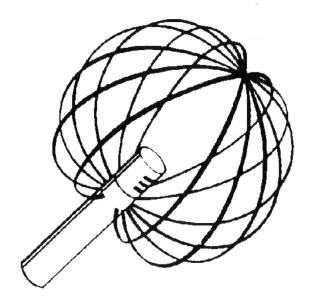

Figure 3.5 Typical 'basket' representation of the polar patters of a carioid microphone.

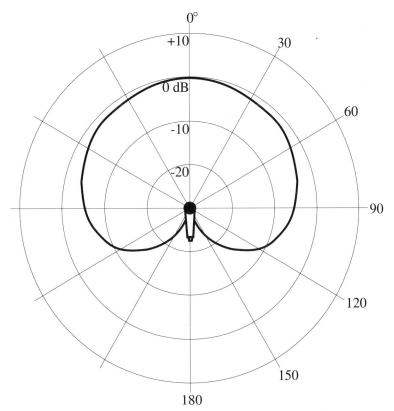

Figure 3.6 Typical theoretical polar pattern of a cardioid microphone.

Figure 3.7 Typical 'basket' representation of the polar pattern of a hypercardioid microphone.

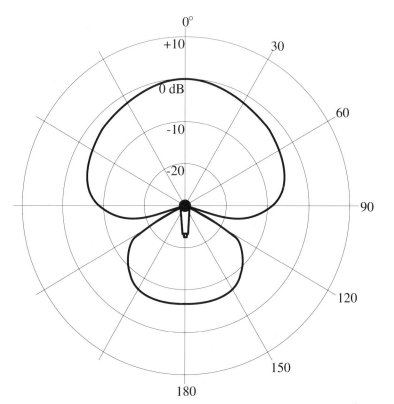

Figure 3.8 Typical theoretical polar pattern of a hypercardioid microphone.

A further extension of the hypercardioid is the **gun microphone** or **rifle mic**. These microphones have even more directional capabilities, and are used generally throughout the industry. They achieve their directional capabilities by a tuned tube rather than by 'back acoustic' mechanical devices. They are described in detail in the next section.

HYPERCARDIOID MICROPHONES

Hypercardioid mics are the generally accepted 'all round' mics within broadcast operations, and are often capable of better quality than close neck mic operation, provided the operator is 'on the ball'. A technique often used on location is to mike the interviewer separately with a radio mic or hard-wired personal mic and cover all other participants with the rifle mic. You should take care in these situations to avoid too much 'spill' in the mix from the rifle mic to the personal mic. In multi-interview set-ups it is as well to identify the main or anchor participants and consider the use of a separate mic or spot mic to allow easy cover of the other participants.

In this industry of ever-reducing crews it is rare to have a dedicated boom operator on location, except perhaps for drama. When using directional microphones, or any microphones on boom poles, great attention must be paid to anti-rumble mounts to avoid acoustic transfer of handling noise on the pole, or mechanical boom, to the microphone head. Most location operators fit their own modifications to commercially produced rumble mounts to improve low-frequency handling characteristics. During boom operations, the microphone is further away from the sound source than under hand-held stick or personal microphone operation, so that the operator has to use higher gain settings on the sound mixing unit.

Great care must be taken with changing background situations, as the highly directional properties of rifle mics could have the microphone 'looking' at heavy traffic or other distracting noises, where only a 30 degree pan could 'look' at a much quieter background. Taking a 50/50 position between these two situations is the most sensible arrangement.

Foam or basket **windshields** are devices used to reduce the effects of high wind or high levels of human breath on the microphone capsule. For use by singers and performers they are simple foam devices to avoid **popping** caused by close proximity to the capsule. For outdoor use under extreme high wind conditions, a more elaborate device can be used, consisting of a basket with a fluffy fur outer cover. Often a simple foam windshield can be placed over a microphone used on a boom or fishpole indoors to reduce any 'swishing' noises caused by fast microphone swings or repositioning.

Remember the following points when using highly directional microphones:

- Keep the windshield on the microphone while working on outside locations, but use the supplementary shield only when essential, as it reduces the high-frequency content of the sound. Under high wind conditions try to shield the microphone from the offending wind.

- Equalize the microphone by only the minimal amount needed for the situation, as equalization can be better applied later in the studio or dub.
- Any movements between participants in a two-way or larger interview situation should be gradual, rather than fast, as changing backgrounds would be more apparent. It is always worth considering a microphone on the interviewer as a separate item to avoid wide 'splits' between participants. The separate mic can also be fed on a separate track on the video recorder and mixed with the boom microphone at the later edit stage.
- Remember that the traditional place overhead is most likely to point you towards some distant offending noise. You should consider whether 'underneath' the shot is not a better position, as it is pointing the microphone skywards where there is less likelihood of any offending background, excepting of course next to an airport!
- It is always better to edge towards your subject of interest rather than swing the microphone violently. This gentle 'ease' of sound is easier to deal with in a dub or edit following the location recording.

It is worth considering what part the sound you supply will be playing in relation to the pictures. It is possible to bring out the interest points within the picture and enhance their impact. It would be sad if, by your lack of attention, a person in the foreground was adding picture impact while you were concentrating on background action.

However, with modern zoom lenses on the camera it is not easy for the operator of the boom or rifle mic to see the actual shot size, and often impossible to see a monitor, or indeed to do the two things at the same time (unless the operator is working a studio boom, where a video monitor is usually available with transmission output or a selected preview picture). On location, this means that the recordist must know the cameraperson's mode of operation, which is not easy at present, with the trend to fragmentation of crews and the departure from the fixed-team format of crewing. The location video monitor is often supplied for the sole purpose of production viewing, and is often placed in an unsuitable position for a boom operator to view easily.

PRESSURE ZONE MICROPHONES

The conventional microphone is usually hindered by interference from sound coming from sources other than the direct source: walls, floors or ceilings closest to the microphone. This causes interference because it reaches the microphone capsule at different times. The resulting effect is a reduction of some frequencies and a reinforcement of others. The design of a pressure zone microphone (PZM) is such that it creates what is called a **pressure zone**. It has a capsule mounted a short distance from the primary mounting plate. When sound waves hit this plate, a pressure zone is created in the space between the microphone capsule and the boundary, in which zone the direct and indirect sound waves are coherently in phase and therefore reinforce each other. The capsule detects the differences in pressure in the pressure zone, rather than the moving sound waves, and so is unaffected by the distance between the sound source and the microphone, as long as the source is within the hemisphere pattern of the primary boundary plate. The principle is very similar to the old 'stage mouse' design, in which a wedge of foam was used in front of a microphone to point it at the stage.

The PZM principle is quite effective for covering stage shows, as well as being used in a similar way fixed inside the roof of cars to pick up interior sound or dialogue. Other applications are for the miking of the piano or choirs or, indeed, round-table discussions. Excellent results have been achieved on choir recordings in studio productions, but the boundary plates have had to be very large. For TV work, the design and camera departments need to be involved in positioning, to avoid any objections – from an artistic point of view – when the plates are in camera shot. One good use for a PZM would be on a lectern, although you need to ensure that speakers do not place their notes on the microphone. As PZMs can handle high-pressure outputs of up to 135 dB, they can be used on drum kits and other high-output instruments.

The actual elements used as the capsule in a PZM vary from manufacturer to manufacturer. They can be either the dynamic or capacitor type, and are often the cheaper electret capacitor. Using the usual boundary plate a reduction of bass response would be heard. To obtain the maximum bass response a hard flat surface of up to 8 ft square would be required. Various new shapes have emerged for the boundary plate to help in the frequency response. You will need to experiment to find out which type gives you the best results. An attenuation of approximately 20–25 dB can be achieved at the rear of the microphone by placing a piece of carpet or other acoustic material at the rear of the boundary plate behind the capsule. This material should not extend beyond the edge of the plate.

PERSONAL MICROPHONES

Personal microphones are also known as **neck microphones** and in the USA as lavalier microphones, named after the pendants worn by the mistress of Louis XIV.

The common type of pattern used for these microphones is omnidirectional, although there are a few types that use a cardioid capsule. The omnidirectional pattern is usually chosen to avoid the person wearing the microphone from swinging off the microphone axis. The usual type of capsule is an **electret**, which is a form of capacitor microphone with a permanently polarized capsule (see p. 52). These capsules are easy to power from a phantom power supply, from internal batteries, or (in the case of radio mic operation) from the radio mic's internal transmitter battery.

Normally the position of a neck microphone under the chin would cause some reduction in the high-frequency response at around 3–8 kHz. Some manufacturers take account of this by limiting the bass response. One manufacturer used to provide a slidable collar around the top rim of their dynamic neck microphone to improve the response at these frequencies. It is possible to apply a similar collar to current microphones to achieve the same effect.

The very small size of current personal microphones makes them ideal for interviews and for radio mic operation, as they are inconspicuous in picture.

Placing and hiding personal microphones

Many sound engineers have their own little tricks for hiding personal microphones when this is required for artistic reasons. The main problem when hiding them beneath clothing is the rubbing of clothing against the microphone. Synthetic materials cause the worst problems. One simple technique is to use a small bag of chamois leather with a facing of acoustically transparent material and the microphone capsule let into a piece of acoustic foam, taped to the inside of the shirt or blouse. This forms a fairly effective barrier against clothing rustle. Another extremely effective method is to place the microphone in the artiste's hair, and run the cable down the neck. Microphone cables can be run round the back of the collar of a jacket, with the microphone placed underneath the collar. Many more variants can be used, depending on the ingenuity of the operator.

It is important to caution the wearer against interfering with the audio output by bumping the microphone; you should remind them that they are wearing such a microphone and that it is 'live'. People being interviewed are often very nervous, but even if they are not, they usually want to get away from location or the studio as soon as possible. Always warn the interviewee about the cable attached to their person, and keep an eye on the interviewee's movements as a safety precaution. This does not, of course, apply to radio mic operation, although with radio microphone operations it is good practice and a matter of courtesy to warn the interviewee when the microphone is live, and to disable the transmitter when the interviewee requires privacy.

Take great care with the routeing of cables on personal microphones so that they do not show in vision and look untidy. With radio mic operation it is not advisable to coil cables from personal microphones close to the transmitter aerial, as problems can be caused. This will be outlined in the radio microphone section of this book.

ARTISTIC AND PHYSICAL RESTRICTIONS ON MICROPHONE PLACEMENT

There are a number of restrictions placed on the sound department in the television studio: restrictions that do not exist for sound departments working in the radio studio. During a radio broadcast the sound mixer can usually place the microphones in precisely the right position for optimum pick-up, but for TV work this luxury doesn't always apply. A compromise is quite often needed between finding the right location for the sound mixer to achieve perfect sound and for the director and camera operators to get the pictures they want.

Recent advances in technology have resulted in microphones that are smaller and slimmer, and hence less intrusive than in the past. They are produced in a range of colours that can enhance the television pictures; it is now possible for artistes to use microphones that can complement their costume. Microphones used on an orchestra or band are now less obvious to the viewer, and are more readily accepted by the director and camera operator.

SPECIAL-PURPOSE MICROPHONES

This section concentrates on close-speaking microphones, but there are other types of special-purpose mic, such as underwater microphones, contact microphones and other audio transducers. Contact microphones and transducers, for example, are fitted to instruments like guitars and the output sent to the sound mixer as a 'direct feed'. These feeds are usually taken via a **direct inject box** at either line level or microphone level, with the unit having the capability of a balanced output.

Some microphones have been designed for close talking and are supplied fitted to headsets, but they are usually just a variant of the microphones already discussed. They can have either a corrected frequency response suited to close speaking, or a restricted bass response to lower the background noise and avoid the 'popping' effect caused by the capsule's being close to the mouth. When using this type of microphone it is advisable to place it to the side of the mouth rather than directly in front, to avoid popping.

Conventional microphones used close to the mouth do not normally give the sound mixer enough separation from background levels, but they can be an emergency alternative when no specialist types are available. Small Sony or other manufacturers' personal microphones can be employed as close-speaking microphones, thanks to their ability to handle high signal levels and their small physical size when in camera shot.

One microphone specially designed to be noise-cancelling is the **lip ribbon** microphone. This can almost completely eliminate background levels, and is used for commentaries on outside broadcasts and other events. It is a pressure gradient microphone, and so has the bass tip-up effect, so that by reducing the bass response the background level is also reduced, leaving the voice with a level response. The microphone has a guard that presses against the lip, leaving the ribbon element a fixed distance from the mouth. With the built-in low-frequency correction, and the close distance that the microphone is placed from the mouth, the overall effect is a dramatic reduction of background noise. Frequency correction is applied at around 6.5–7 kHz, with the response 'tailed off' above this to help reject noise at the higher frequencies.

The lip ribbon microphone is perfectly adequate when used against sports event backgrounds and similar noisy environments, but under quieter circumstances the quality leaves a lot to be desired, and could perhaps be improved by using a double ribbon microphone placed close to the commentator, if he or she is not in camera shot. The lip ribbon cannot be used in shot as it is so ugly, and obscures the commentator's mouth. Only in extreme cases will you see this microphone in picture.

DYNAMIC MICROPHONES

From the early days of radio and broadcasting, dynamic microphones have played a major role in producing high-quality sound.

The construction of a dynamic microphone is quite simple. It is similar to a loudspeaker, but is much lighter and more delicate, as it has to respond to much lower pressure levels and be light enough to react to higher frequencies without offering any real mechanical resistance.

In general, the microphone will have a cone with a coil at its end, which is suspended within a permanent magnet. Movement of the coil within the magnetic field causes an electrical current that corresponds to the sound wave, moving the coil by pressure. The very low output from the coil can then be fed into a microphone amplifier, where it is lifted in level to produce a line-level signal that we can hear. The directional pattern of the microphone is usually altered by mechanical or acoustical means from the rear of the microphone.

The range covered by dynamic microphones is generally the same as that of their capacitor counterparts, though they usually have a lower sensitivity and are therefore more susceptible to outside electrical or inductive interference. They are much more robust, and can stand heavy handling in the studio and on location. The dynamic mic has a much better capability to withstand high amplitudes of sound level and generally has a smooth response. It is the fairly universal choice where hand microphones are concerned, and is often used in miking the bass drum and on brass sections of brass bands and modern dance bands, where it performs very well.

It is not unusual to see a dynamic microphone as part of a classical music recording rig. Indeed, on a recent large live broadcast from Salisbury Cathedral the spare mics for the whole concert were a dynamic pair. So, if all else had failed, the good old-fashioned robust dynamic microphone that required no power supply would have saved the day!

CAPACITOR MICROPHONES

Many microphones used in the broadcast and recording field are capacitor microphones. These microphones are usually of particularly high quality, and can easily be used on location, except where it is not possible to windshield them adequately for the extremes of climate they may meet under location conditions. In general, capacitor microphones are more fragile than their moving coil counterparts and should be treated with greater care. They do, however, present the sound engineer with the finest frequency response available.

Often a location recordist is loath to use some of the higher-quality microphones. Usually they are not easily available from stock; perhaps he or she has not had experience of the specific types on location, and is not confident in the microphones' ability to do the job. The main problem on location work is protection of the microphones from damage and (sometimes) from the elements experienced on location, such as humidity and high wind. Windshielding for capacitor microphones is getting better, with the introduction of Rycote windbags and supplementary covers for extreme wind conditions. These can be very effective under even the worst wind conditions.

The normal capacitor microphone requires a **polarizing voltage** applied from an external source. The microphone has a thin flexible diaphragm close to the surface of a rigid backplate, and hence acting as the plates of a capacitor. For the microphone to work, a polarizing voltage is applied between the diaphragm and the backplate. As the diaphragm moves, a variable capacitance is created in sympathy with the sound waves, producing changes in the voltage across the plates. These changes are very small, and require amplification.

Switchable-characteristic capacitor microphones have two diaphragms, one either side of the backplate. By varying the voltages to the plates the directional pattern of the microphone can be changed. Polarizing both diaphragms produces an omnidirectional pattern; polarizing the first diaphragm only, and not the second, produces a cardioid pattern. The figure-of-eight pattern is achieved by polarizing the second diaphragm in the opposite direction. Many other combinations of directional patterns can be obtained by intermediate combinations of the polarizing voltages.

Most professional units are capable of being phantom powered externally (see next section), as well being powered from a radio microphone transmitter directly without an auxiliary power source.

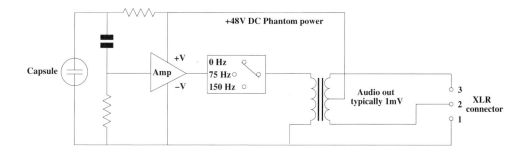

Figure 3.9   Typical capacitor microphone block circuit diagram.

Most small personal microphones within the Sony, Sanken, Sennheiser and Beyer ranges are, in fact, capacitor microphones, but are the **electret** type. Electret capacitor microphones have a permanent electrostatic charge applied to their diaphragm when manufactured. As the diaphragm is permanently polarized, the only power required on these microphones is to power the head amplifier. The electret microphone usually has an internal battery supplying the power for the amplifier.

As electret microphones age, they gradually use their permanent charge and become electrically noisy. Signal-to-noise ratios are, in any case, worse on electret microphones than on normal high-quality capacitor microphones. A problem experienced when operating under very humid conditions is a temporary break-down of the insulation across the capsule, which in practice results in 'crackling', or extremely noisy performance of the microphone. This can also happen with the higher-priced capacitor microphones, so you need to be careful which mic you use. You should also take care when using a personal microphone close to the body, as perspiration can cause similar effects as humidity.

The theory of capacitor and other microphones is well covered in other publications; see the list of further reading in Appendix A.

Phantom powering

The voltage needed to power capacitor and electret microphones can be incorporated into the cable from the microphone. This is called **phantom powering**. It can be achieved at three standard voltages: 12 V, 24 V and 48 V. The operating current from the source (mixer or external battery unit) is fed through two high-tolerance feed resistors dividing the voltage equally. (The feed resistors vary according to the voltage available.) It is carried via the two conductors in a balanced mic cable. Inside the microphone unit the two currents are combined to power the microphone amplifier circuits (and polarize the diaphragm if required), and are returned through the cable shield or screen to source. Direct current through microphone transformers creates equal but opposite fields, thus cancelling magnetization effects. There is no voltage difference between the two conductors to the microphone (both carry the same voltage): hence the term 'phantom', as, in audio terms, it is not there.

An electromagnetic or moving-coil microphone that has an earth-free output can be connected to a phantom power supply without any ill effect. However, if an unbalanced microphone is connected when phantom power is switched on it can seriously damage both the microphone and the phantom power source. No switching is required to operate dynamic microphones on a phantom power system provided all microphones are of the balanced type.

Most modern studio mixer desks and portable location mixing units have the capability of powering capacitor microphones. The SQN, Filmtech, TLA and Audio Developments portable mixer units cover all the types of microphone phantom

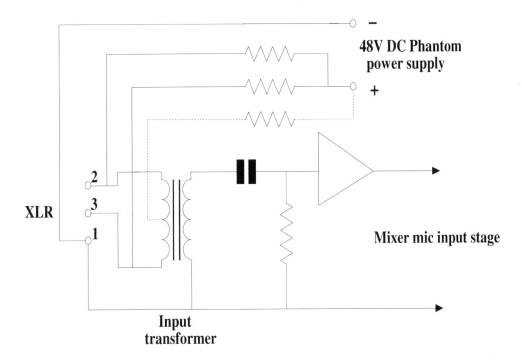

Figure 3.10   Typical circuit diagram of a capacitor microphone phantom power source.

powering you should require in the field. If a supply is not available from the mixer unit, you will need to use a separate external unit.

T-powering

T-powering is also known as A/B powering. The letter T is an abbreviation of **tonander**, which was used on early microphones by European manufacturers (and is still used on Sennheiser mics). Usually the serial numbers on Sennheiser types end with the letter 'T'.

The operating voltage between leads A and B is 12 V ± 1 V. Both feed resistors have a value of 180 Ω, and have to be matched within 2 Ω. The supply current flows through one resistor into the microphone and returns through another resistor. Any supply voltage is kept away from the mixer input by blocking capacitors.

Only T-powered microphones should be used with T-powering circuits. The result of using normal phantom mics would be a 'one legged' sound: thin and lacking in bass. The voltage difference between the two conductors in T-powering can force a current into the coil of a dynamic microphone and might result in distortion or damage, so great care must be taken not to use dynamic mics on 'powered-up' T-power channels.

Most portable mixer units and studio units have the facility for supplying T-power to microphones, but it is essential to select the correct type of powering. External battery-powered units are available for use with equipment that does not have its own self-contained power supply for T-powering.

CHOOSING THE RIGHT MICROPHONE

Physical features

If the microphone is to appear in shot, then both its size and appearance are very important. Directors and camera operators don't like to see a large, unsightly microphone spoiling their pictures, so size is obviously a prime consideration. The actual looks of the microphone are also important when it is to be used in vision. It should, if possible, be complementary to the shot and not cause distraction. Many modern microphones are finished in colours, which helps with regard to their appearance in the picture.

You have to consider the mechanical robustness of microphones when using them outdoors, as well as their performance under humid conditions. There is also the problem of wind noise on the microphone capsule unless a suitable wind-shield and/or basket are fitted. In general, the sensitivity to noise is an important factor, as it can often cause unnecessary interference on the original sound; where possible, anti-vibration mounts should be used. Of course this is not always possible, and the anti-vibration devices are mounted on the base of the microphone stands.

Rugged construction is also a requirement in situations where the microphone is likely to be used as a hand mic, or may be subjected to rough conditions and handling (perhaps on outside broadcast and location use). For use as a hand-held microphone, it should be free from handling noise, and sufficiently screened so that it is immune to pick-up from any nearby electrical radiation (hum, clicks etc.)

Audio quality

The frequency response of the microphone is of the utmost importance. It should adequately cover the frequency range that you require for the instruments or whatever audio you wish to record, and the audio must be accurately reproduced without coloration or distortion. Generally, a microphone that covers the frequency response of the instrument you wish to record should not pick up 'spill' from other instruments unnecessarily. Figure 3.11 charts the frequency ranges of various instruments, for comparison with microphone frequency responses.

The impedance of a microphone should be as near as possible a match to the input to which it feeds, to obtain maximum signal transfer. The input to which

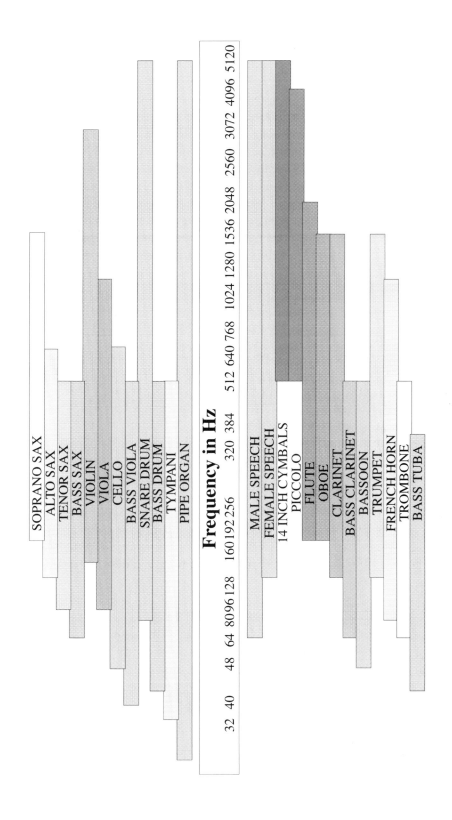

Figure 3.11 Approximate frequency ranges of various musical instruments.

you connect the microphone should also be of a suitable sensitivity range, and the input channel sensitivities should be adjusted accordingly.

Sensitivity

The overall sensitivity of a microphone should be considered. The sensitivity of a microphone determines how large a signal it produces for a given sound volume. A microphone with too high a sensitivity would be unsuitable for recording high-output music or noises. Equally, a low-sensitivity mic would be unsuitable for recording low-level signals (in this case it is likely that noise would be introduced). When using a high-sensitivity mic, distortion or overload may well be introduced. For example, a microphone may receive signal levels of 65 dB or more when placed at the 'business end' of some brass instruments.

As it is normal for all mixing to take place at line levels, the shortfall between the dynamic microphone's low output level and line level is made up by the microphone amplifier in the mixer unit. In general, a sensitivity of approximately −55 dB is typical for dynamic microphones. This means that you must have this amount of amplification available in your microphone amplifier, plus a little extra gain available to lift lower-level input signals. Although most amplifiers can compensate for even the least sensitive mics, excessive amplification will add spurious hiss and hum to the signal. Capacitor microphones have a higher output, as they have their own internal amplifiers lifting the overall output. Some capacitor mics have switched attenuators to reduce the possibility of input overload on the microphone channel.

Any microphone will usually have to work closer to quiet sounds than louder ones, but low-sensitivity mics must be positioned that much closer. However, they are less likely to be overloaded by loud sounds so, in certain applications (on drum kits for example), they may be preferred to more sensitive types. Any microphone chosen for use on a sound boom needs to be highly sensitive, otherwise it will need to work too close to the sound source, perhaps causing shadow problems.

Directionality

The directional properties of a microphone (shown by its polar diagram) give an indication of its sensitivity pattern in space. Sometimes you will need an omnidirectional mic that picks up everything equally well in all directions, and at other times you may require a very directional mic, which is able to pick out a particular sound while ignoring other sounds nearby. This latter type of microphone is very popular with sound recordists, and is normally part of a location sound kit.

CHAPTER 4

The audio mixing console

THE BASIC STUDIO ANALOGUE MIXING CONSOLE

The large size of studio consoles, and the fact that they are powered from mains supplies, restricts their use in the field. However, it is not unusual to use a mains-powered studio unit in the field for music recordings and large discussion programmes. The studio console is more complex than the portable location model, and has more flexible controls and facilities, but I shall deal only with the basic user controls in this section.

Usually **channel inputs** are the same as on the higher-quality portable units, with some differences in the type of input attenuation controls. Most mixers have signal attenuators, which are continuously variable on some units and switchable in steps on others. Variable input control is preferable to switchable control. The operator will usually have preset input level, and will only need to increase or reduce this if there is some unexpected problem. Variable control provides a smoother change of level in such an emergency.

Switching between line and microphone levels is usual at the front of most studio units. The input level control normally works for both line and microphone inputs, although some manufacturers provide separate controls for the individual inputs. Other manufacturers supply a further switch to allow two inputs to the same channel. It is now common on studio mixing consoles that channels are dual for stereo, with one fader for both channels and a balance control between the two channels. The ability to switch the input on a stereo channel to either of the stereo inputs independently will allow mono operation. A choice can be made between supplying a mono input to both channels or either side of a stereo input to both channels.

Phase reverse switches are placed at the top of the panel. These can be used to correct phase errors in microphones or their cabling, or to set one channel in the opposite phase, as would be required to set the desk up for mid–side (M/S) stereo operation (see p. 166).

Equalization controls follow the input level and select controls. They usually cover the whole audio range, with extra controls around the presence area of the

audio range between approximately 250 Hz and 8 kHz, but these vary from manufacturer to manufacturer. Usually two controls are supplied in the presence
range, covering approximately 120 Hz to 2 kHz and 400 Hz to 7 kHz. These controls can be parametric or simple slope or cut controls.

The reason for the concentration of controls in the mid area of the audio
range is the need to add presence to the human voice and, at times, on individual
instruments to give them prominence in the audio mix. This is often not available
from the microphone itself, as the main attribute of a microphone should be its
smooth response to all frequencies. An exception to this is vocal microphones
such as the Shure SM58, which is designed to give presence to the human voice
and vocals. Another microphone that is distinctly designed for one purpose is the
lip ribbon microphone, which is designed for close speaking and maximum noise
rejection under high background conditions, and has a specially contoured frequency response (see p. 49).

The other equalization controls are for the low end of the frequency spectrum, usually 30 Hz to 600 Hz, and the high end of the spectrum, 700 Hz to 15
kHz. The low-frequency controls can reduce rumble and any low-frequency
boominess, and the high-frequency controls can accentuate the top end of the frequency range, or reduce it (for example, to reduce hiss and noise, which usually
occur at the high end of the spectrum). It is not unusual to find a switchable
fixed bass attenuator at around 100 Hz, to remove extreme room rumble, hum,
and low ends of male vocals. Usually the fixed control is a high-pass type, with
reductions at the specified frequency in the order of 12 dB per octave.

Insert points are usually available prior to the equalization controls for the
insertion of 'outboard' equipment such as limiters, compressors and other effects
units. This allows the equalization to remove any hiss or hum problems that
these may generate after they are inserted. It is not unusual to insert a compressor at this point, as you may need to add more 'punch' to an individual vocal or
instrument, rather than apply an overall compression to the final mix (see p. 63).

The term **outboard equipment** refers to any equipment that does not form
part of the main mixer unit, but is generally in a studio environment. The main
outboard facilities are usually effects units, such as reverberation units, graphic
equalizers, some audio limiters and compressors, and any recording device. All
such units should interface fully to the main mixer unit and be capable of doing
this with regard to level and impedance. It is essential that these units have a
good signal-to-noise ratio and that they are correctly aligned. Any problem of
noise within these units will be passed on into your main recording.

Auxiliary sends will be available to feed to special effects such as reverberation, to mix-minus feeds, to foldback, or to public address feeds. Extra gain controls are usually supplied on studio desks, and on some portable desks, to control
the overall feed of these auxiliary outputs. This may be required to avoid PA
'howlround', or to reduce levels on the equipment that the auxiliary outputs are
feeding. The latest mixer desks feed auxiliaries at up to +8 dBm and beyond that

signal level, and usually have a balanced output. These auxiliary outputs can be selected prefader or postfader. It is usual for feeds to be **postfader**, as they will be controlled by the amount of level you are actually using, and only feed the ancillary equipment when you actually lift your fader. It is usual to feed foldback from postfade auxiliaries, or to feed extra PA 'fill' systems or 'down the line' mix-minus feeds, on occasions.

Often, other broadcasters or PA systems may need to feed independently from your output to an audience, or to mix your output with their own feeds to gain a different mix. They would then need a 'clean feed', which is not controlled by your fader; you would need to provide a constant standard output, leaving external level control to whoever is operating the system. In this case, you would provide the signal from the **prefader** auxiliaries. This does not stop you from reducing your output level via your prefade output level control, if you have trouble with howlround or coloration on the mixed audio. There may be a requirement to listen to your incoming sound on a separate monitor speaker prior to 'taking' the source: this would, of course, be taken from a prefader facility. Sometimes a commentator or presenter may need to talk to the director, the sound operator or even another commentator; again, this could be achieved via a prefader signal being fed to all interested participants.

It is unusual to find these facilities on any truly portable mixer, but they are beginning to be required on current operations, particularly on live injects. Some of the latest portable mixers, such as the Filmtech LSP4 and the Soundcraft LM20, now have prefade listen facilities (see below).

Pan controls will be available to enable you to place the output of one channel in an appropriate position in the stereo sound field. These controls may double as a balance control on stereo mixers with dual channel stereo facilities within the one mixer input module, which makes controlling a stereo channel easier and avoids the 'weaving' effect on the stereo image.

Each channel will usually have a **peak-level** LED, which will indicate the onset of overload on that channel, to warn of incoming overload problems or potential problems. Often it can suggest overload within a particular frequency range, which can be very useful. It is not unusual for this indicator to double as an indicator for prefade listen selection.

The **prefade listen** control takes a feed of the channel output to either the control room loudspeaker, small separate monitor speaker or headphones, enabling the operator to monitor the channel on its own for separation, distortion, quality or, indeed, its actual operation while using the channel, or prior to using the channel. Often on live productions the sound mixer can talk to a remote source on talkback and monitor the return on prefade listen. This system is much used in sound radio, as it saves a separate audio return line for talkback.

The outputs of all the separate channels are now fed to the **main output** modules via **groups**, which have their own separate fader controls, and often metering circuits that monitor the individual groups. Usually each channel can be selected to a **group fader** and also the main stereo mix bus or a separate mono mix, all of which can have their own dedicated outputs. This facilitates submixes, which could be for orchestras or any group that you may need to add intact to the overall mixed output in stereo or mono. The use of groups allows you to control the sound level of this particular group independently from another group; this can then be fed into the overall sound mix or mixes. For instance, a singer may be on a separate group from an orchestra, or a small jazz group may be placed against a larger orchestra.

After passing through the group faders, the submixes are then applied to the main faders of the mixer desk. It is usual to have **insert points** at this stage, prior to the main faders, so that units such as compressors and limiters can be inserted to control overmodulation in the submix output. As the insert points are also usually prior to the meter circuits and audio loudspeaker monitor circuits, the effect of the inserted items can be monitored both visually and aurally.

Effects returns for reverberation and other units will be supplied in the output module. These will have their own separate level controls, sometimes with some form of slope control for equalization, allowing the sound mixer to correct the audio quality of the return signal. Effects returns on modern mixer desks can accommodate a wide range of input levels, and now allow for semi-professional (i.e. domestic) levels below the standard broadcast zero level; such equipment is now commonplace, even in broadcast environments.

After the main mixer are the **audio distribution amplifiers**, which in custom-built applications have permanent send and return feeds to all installed outboard equipment. All equipment that is capable of recording will have its input circuits fed with the mixer outputs, in the same way that all outboard equipment will have its replay channels returned either to a permanent fader on the mixer, to an audio jackfield, or to an electronic switching matrix.

The main **PPM monitor circuits** are usually on the main output after the audio distribution amplifiers, as are the main control room monitor loudspeakers. The main loudspeaker system and the PPM monitoring system are usually switchable between many outputs, including monitor returns from outboard equipment such as tape recorders and video recorders. Many custom-built studio systems have permanent PPM monitoring at the crucial points, which need not be switched. It is not unusual to have visual monitoring with separate metering of all outgoing sources, such as auxiliary feeds. This gives an instant reference of a signal leaving the mixer desk. The audio monitoring reference is usually a switchable loudspeaker monitor circuit.

Audio jackfields are usually supplied in the control room with all mixer input and output connections made available, and permanent linking across the rear of the individual jacks to allow permanent feeds to the mixer desk. However, the wiring is such on jackfields that any input or output can be broken away from its source and fed to another source, making the system very flexible. Permanent links, or **normalling**, save the jackfield from having a large number of flexible

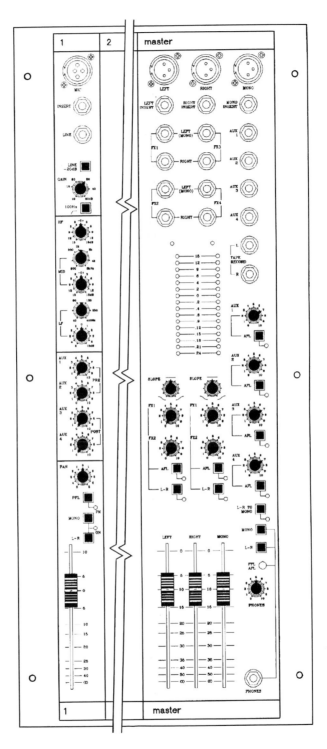

Figure 4.1   Typical small mixer desk with broadcast capability.

cords plugged into the sockets. Outboard equipment is also routed to the jackfield so that it can be connected to whatever input or output source is required. The audio jackfield is rapidly being superseded by the **electronic switching matrix**, which provides similarly flexible facilities, with connections being made from a computer keyboard or simple pushbuttons.

Separate jackfields are usual for feeding **talkback** to and from the studio. This is kept distinctly separate from the normal audio feeds, to avoid breakthrough onto the audio output. Again, electronic matrix systems are taking over from these jackfields. Talkback within the audio studio is fairly normal. The sound mixer has a basic talkback output facility to send via distribution amplifiers to any external source, and can patch in any incoming source to his own talkback system for monitoring or control purposes. The ability to send talkback into programme is usual for music recording sessions, as well as the requirement to send talkback down a telephone line via a telephone hybrid unit.

Lines from external studios or to transmission areas and remote recording areas are usually on another jackfield, which has its own individual set of lines to the mixer jackfield, often to facilitate their use by a separate operator when a programme has intensive use of incoming lines. It is now common to have a separate **lines area**, which supplies external sound sources to assigned faders or to assigned tie lines. A superb example of such an area is the European Broadcasting Union Switching Centre in Brussels.

IMPEDANCE AND SOURCE MATCHING

When a source has many different components, which have both reactance and resistance, the combined effect is known as **impedance**. If you were to measure a loudspeaker of say $15\,\Omega$ with a meter, the reading would be probably about 5 or $6\,\Omega$. The remainder of the impedance consists of the reactance to a.c. due to the inductance present in the coil.

All sources of voltage – microphones, amplifiers, and batteries – have an output impedance, caused by a combination of reactance and their internal resistance. None of these sources will deliver its maximum power unless the input source and the circuit are correctly matched. If sources are mismatched, power losses will occur. It is important to pay attention to impedance matching for many reasons, but the main reason is to ensure that you can transmit your signal accurately without losses in level.

Earlier broadcast equipment used $600\,\Omega$ matching between devices. This created the situation of double terminations where two sources were fed into the same input or fed from the same output, thus causing power losses. Some current equipment does have $600\,\Omega$ input impedance but has termination switches to avoid double termination signal losses. In any case, these losses can often be taken up by the following circuit, provided it has the additional signal gain available.

Normally, headphone monitoring directly across programme lines can be achieved by using high-impedance headphones or a high-impedance monitor amplifier; this avoids signal reduction while monitoring, as a high impedance normally causes little or no signal loss on the monitored circuit.

Current practice is to feed at much lower impedances; the accepting equipment has a high-impedance input, of up to 10 kΩ. If the equipment accepting the signal has a high-impedance input, placing other equipment across the input source causes less signal drop. Most broadcast microphones are of the low-impedance type and suffer far less from interference. Again, most broadcast mixers and outboard equipment send their output at a low impedance.

It is common to have much more accurate impedance matching at microphone level, so that inputs are typically about five times the output impedance of the microphone, which would be 200–600 Ω. If the mixer or recorder input is too high (say above 10 kΩ) then signal transfer is reduced because of the increased mismatch; as more gain will have to be added, the noise is increased, as the mixer's amplifiers are having to be used at higher gain settings. The result is a reduction in the signal-to-noise ratio.

LIMITERS AND COMPRESSORS

Programme levels are normally controlled manually, but on occasions electronic devices called **limiters** and **compressors** are applied. The gain of these devices is controlled by a d.c. voltage obtained from the actual signal level input to the device. This voltage is fed back to an earlier stage of the limiter or compressor and controls the overall gain of the unit.

These types of effects unit contain the following adjustments:

- attack time – the time taken to reduce the gain, usually 0.1–200 ms;
- release time – the time taken to restore the gain, usually 50 ms to 3 s;
- threshold – the signal level at which limiting or compression occurs;
- input and output set up levels for system gain matching.

Limiting

A limiter does not affect the signal going through it until that signal reaches a particular preset threshold. Above this threshold point, the limiter prevents the signal becoming any 'stronger' by providing as much gain reduction as is needed to keep the signal from exceeding the threshold. Then the limiter 'goes back to sleep' and leaves the signal alone until it again exceeds the threshold level.

This limited signal has a much higher average level than the original. This is why limited signals can 'punch through' at you. Commercials frequently use limiting to obtain a higher-than-average signal level. TV and radio stations use limiters for the same effect to obtain a high dynamic range, which helps them to cope with the broadcast systems limited dynamic range.

In general, limiters have two types of response. The **soft knee** response attacks the signal gently, then clamps it at the threshold. The limiting action becomes progressively greater past a certain point until it eventually flattens out and clamps the signal fully. This tends to produce a smooth limiting sound, which helps to even out the dynamic range of an instrument or voice. The **hard knee** response goes from no limiting to full limiting at the threshold point. When the limiter reaches the preset threshold level, the sound level output will not increase, despite changes in the input level. The soft knee limiter is more suitable for general applications; the hard knee is used to eliminate clipping on amplifiers or speakers.

It is essential to set the speed of a limiter's response in line with the material you are recording. If the limiter tries to follow every nuance of music it will become very 'choppy'. It is often better to set the release over a longer period to avoid the noticeable rises of signal level. Clamping a signal too rapidly can greatly reduce transients, producing a rather dull sound. The attack control determines how long it takes for the limiter's clamping action to begin.

On location, limiters fitted in most portable mixers and Betacam equipment do not have sophisticated external controls on attack and threshold, and so are not user-adjustable in real terms; they come in at a preset level, which is usually maximum peak or slightly earlier.

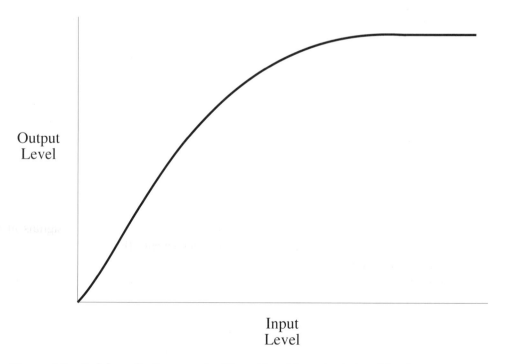

Figure 4.2 Soft-knee limiter: graph of input level to output signal level.

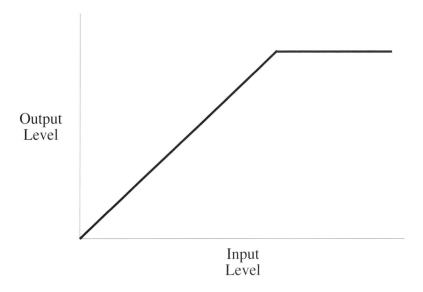

Figure 4.3 Hard-knee limiter: graph of input level to output signal level.

The automatic level controls on Betacam and other video equipment controls are very crude; they tend to bring up the background by making a lot of signal level available and then limiting this level at the peak end. This tends to make backgrounds 'pump'; even speech at times seems to 'pump'. In many ways the use of automatic limiters or gain control in Betacam equipment or any camcorder equipment should be avoided. This does not apply to the limiters in SQN and other portable mixers, as they come in at maximum peak or just before, but care should be taken not to mix 'into the limiters', as this can cause undue lifts in background levels and hence create a sound like the Betacam limiter.

Compression

A compressor is similar to a limiter, but rather than clamp all signals at a constant threshold, the output changes at a lesser rate than the input. For example, with a 4:1 compression ratio (set on the ratio control), a 4 dB input level produces a 1 dB output level change. Increases of 8 dB of level would produce a 2 dB output level change, and so on.

Compressors generally cause the background level to be higher, but produce a limited dynamic range of the overall signal, which effectively sounds louder to the ear. As the main aim while recording on location is to supply a recording with the best signal-to-noise ratio and lowest background levels, making editing easier, the use of limiters and compressors is not advised on such material. A wrongly set-up limiter or compressor can often give background pumping while it is working, pulling down the peaks or lifting the lower volume levels.

All those TV commercials that cause you to go and turn down your speaker are due to high compression being applied to a signal while the programme following has very little compression. Some broadcasting companies apply auto-decompression to commercials, or peak commercials at a lower level to the main programme to obtain a better dynamic balance for the listener. Often the level is determined by the ear of the VTR operator or transfer operator preparing the material for the eventual transmission as an overall commercial break.

Most limiter and compressor units contain a side-chain circuit, which can be used for 'de-essing' (removing sibilance from a voice). Usually an external graphic equalizer is placed in this chain and adjusted to give a high signal gain at the offending frequency; this signal then controls the compressor/limiter circuit and reduces the signal in this selected area. In a similar way, another audio signal can be used, such as a voice-over or presenter: this signal then reduces the overall signal going through the unit and performs signal 'ducking' to accommodate the control voice.

Noise gates

Imagine that you are listening to an audio signal that has a relatively noisy background beneath it. As long as the audio signal is present its level will generally be higher than the noise, causing a masking effect. When the audio signal is absent you are left with the noisy background. If you lower the volume control after the audio signal has ceased, you eliminate the background noise; when the audio signal resumes, you lift the volume control and effectively eliminate the noisy background once more.

The noise gate performs a similar function, but automatically. It compares the incoming signal with a preset threshold. If the signal exceeds the threshold, the gate acts like the volume control and lets the signal through. If the signal is below the preset threshold, the gate acts like a fully closed volume control and does not allow any signal through. So if you set the threshold just above the residual noise level, the gate will be closed whenever there is hiss, giving a quieter signal.

There are other uses for a noise gate system, such as automatic control of microphones on instruments or even voices, although levels must be set very accurately, as must noise gate attack and decay times. It would, for instance, be possible to gate a voice-over microphone into programme and leave the fader open, although any coughs or loud movements might open the gate and prove an embarrassment to the sound balancer.

A great deal of automation can be obtained with noise gates, but they need to be used with great care.

INTERFACING DOMESTIC EQUIPMENT AND PROFESSIONAL EQUIPMENT

Many pieces of domestic and semi-professional equipment find their way into the broadcast studio. Equipment such as domestic DAT and cassette machines, and some effects processors, are used for transfer of original domestic material, and are also used for supplying check copies to clients. This equipment requires some form of interface to match the differing audio levels within the domestic and semi-professional fields.

Most of the problems in interfacing professional equipment and domestic equipment revolve around two things:

- Domestic equipment's working levels are generally at –10 dB, whereas professional levels are generally at +4 or +8 dB maximum.
- Semi-professional and domestic equipment is usually unbalanced on its inputs and outputs.

There are many ways of modifying equipment to interface it, either permanently in the studio or semi-permanently in the studio and on location. Modifying equipment in a permanent way usually requires external or internal units that attenuate the input level from broadcast levels to domestic levels and include a balanced input at the front of this attenuator. The output side of the units would include a small amplifier, which would increase the domestic equipment level up to the +8 dB levels required for broadcast use and include a balanced output. These units are generally called **pro-interfaces**, and currently cost around £300.

In the field, the usual occasion when you need to interface to domestic levels is when taking direct feeds from domestic equipment. Often minimal time is allowed to make such connections. One major problem with taking feeds from external sources is **hum loops**. These can be caused by separate earthing systems, which cause different potentials on equipment and result in hum on the incoming signal. Most problems occur when the feed to the newly connected equipment is being supplied from public address systems or 'in house' systems: this can even include inserts supplied from broadcast environments.

Most mobile mixing equipment, and now larger equipment, has enough gain on its input channels to cope with lower levels, so simply placing a 'one to one' balanced transformer between the mixer unit you are operating and the external equipment will isolate you from the other equipment. This transformer arrangement should be of high quality, as the use of a poor transformer can result in significant losses of low-frequency response.

The active type of **direct inject box** usually has a better overall frequency response than the transformer arrangement. The unbalanced input can be shorted to earth on one leg of the input, creating an unbalanced input source, while the output to your equipment will remain balanced.

The inclusion of an **earth lift** switch in the direct inject box will enable you to isolate your equipment from any hum loop, unless of course the hum you receive is within the actual equipment that is sending your feed. There is little that you can do about such a situation unless the equipment itself has a hum loop problem and that loop can be cleared. Direct inject boxes are currently available at below £100, which serve the purposes of the unit described above; they are of the active variety, and require battery powering.

One advantage of including a commercial unit is that they usually contain some gain lift or reduction, allowing you to either reduce or increase the input level. The commercial unit's output level is at microphone signal level and is balanced, giving you the advantage of being able to run long balanced lines back to the inject point, and hence avoiding the possibility of electrical or inductive interference. These units should be placed as close as possible to the units that are sending the signal to you, keeping the unbalanced feed from the equipment as short as possible, and hence avoiding any induced signals between the unit and your interface. The more expensive units often include a high-frequency filter; this should be used with care.

It is a good idea to keep a selection of adaptor leads from domestic-style plugs to the professional XLR plugs; it can save you a great deal of time.

When taking external feeds, it is worth considering having some sort of emergency feed of your own, by covering the situation with your own rifle mic or other microphones. There is often a requirement to add your own 'feel' to a direct feed, which quite often sounds a little too 'tight' for broadcast purposes, and perhaps does not concentrate on areas of the sound field or picture field on which your director's camera or cameras are focused. Spot mics can be added to either 'loosen' this feed and allow you to identify certain items or add audience atmosphere and applause, which would rarely be included in music or stage public address feed.

Feeding to other broadcasters usually requires you to feed your signal at +8 dB levels and balanced. Most portable mixer units allow two output feeds, and if the feed is mono you could, on a stereo mixer unit, feed at least three other parties. Without the facility of many output feeds on your own mixer unit, audio distribution facilities would be required. The ability to feed reference tone in mono or stereo to other broadcasters and sources requiring feeds should be an essential part of your equipment. This ensures correct alignment of your recorded audio throughout the system.

At present, much semi-professional and domestic equipment is appearing with balanced outputs, at +4 dB maximum output and input levels, with switching to reduce the levels to −10 dB levels. These switchable levels are appearing on some professional equipment as well. These units are generally of Japanese manufacture and present no problem in the normal broadcast chain, as the level matching can be taken up within the system's gain controls.

With the advent of RDAT and the new formats of DCC (cassette-based digital) and minidisk (floppy disk digital), modern domestic equipment is perfectly adequate for professional recording in some areas. Indeed, the frequency response of some of this equipment far exceeds that of professional analogue equipment of five years ago, and is certainly better than the analogue tracks on video equipment. The only differences are the rather less professional input sockets and perhaps lower input and output levels. And from a mechanical standpoint, domestic equipment generally falls short on what we would require professionally; it is often flimsy in construction, with small, poorly placed operational controls and poor protection from the elements.

Most Japanese professional equipment works at +4 dB levels, which is not too far from broadcast levels to cause any worries about level matching, provided you have no confusion as to what zero level on a VU meter and zero level in broadcast terms mean. Broadcast zero level is 8 dB below maximum level. Maximum broadcast level is +8 dB above zero level. Zero level line-up for broadcast is PPM 4 and the maximum level is PPM 6. VU zero level, as marked on the meter under a +4 dB lined-up system such as Betacam, is in fact equivalent to PPM 5 in the broadcast set-up. As broadcast peak programme level is 8 dB higher than 'line-up level', these correspond to 6 and 4 respectively on the PPM meter. To keep programme signal levels within range on the VU meter the operator would line up broadcast zero level at −4 dB VU: this allows a full 8 dB above this point to maximum signal level on the VU meter. This would then relate to the broadcast level maximum of PPM 6 (0.775 V r.m.s).

USE OF EQUALIZATION

The equalizer or equalization controls are an effective way to contour your sound, and shape the overall quality of a sound system. Remember that all equalization is, in fact, a form of distortion, so you should use it with care.

The main forms of equalization that you will meet are banded, and cover specific areas of the audio frequency range, with comprehensive controls on the more expensive equipment and much simpler devices on the portable equipment, which will be dealt with in later sections.

The equalization controls usually are switchable into a circuit as a complete set of controls on each channel, which allows comparison of the signal with the equalization switched in and out of circuit. This is normally known as **A/B comparison**. It allows you to judge the effect of equalization applied to an incoming signal. Often only an extreme bass cut control or high-frequency filter has a separate switch or button; all the other controls are switched out of circuit by one main button or switch.

When applying equalization, be careful not to fall into the trap of applying progressive equalization that gets sharper as you go along. There is always a temptation to equalize just a little bit more as you proceed down a programme, and thus end up with an over-corrected product.

General areas of equalization

The main types of equalizer that you will meet are high-pass filters and low-pass filters. The **high-pass filter**, as its name implies, allows the high frequencies to pass through while restricting the low frequencies. It reduces frequencies at a pre-determined frequency around 100–200 Hz, with either a sloping or a gradual cut-off. High-pass filters are useful in reducing mains hum, rumble and low-frequency wind noise on audio material. The **low-pass filter** allows the low frequencies to pass through while reducing the higher frequencies. It is used to restrict frequency response on low-range material on a wide-range system, usually to restrict noise and distortion in the upper frequency range from around 3 to 12 kHz. Again, these filters can have a sharp cut-off or a sloping cut-off. These controls are similar to the controls on domestic hi-fi systems.

Parametric equalizers provide variable control across specific frequency ranges, which allows you to choose a particular spot frequency at which to correct or adjust the frequency response. This is backed up by a second control, which will boost or cut at this particular frequency, usually by up to 15 dB in each direction. Controls can be selective as to where they apply the particular boost or cut by being sweep controls, which select a particular area of the frequency range, or by only applying correction at one point, in the way that a **graphic equalizer** has a number of sliders or faders to apply boost or cut at fixed points up the audio spectrum. The rotary control can fix a particular point in the equalizer's audio range and apply the boost or cut at that point.

Starting at the bass end of the spectrum, you would expect to find a basic **rumble filter** at about 100 Hz, which would be effective in reducing close microphone problems and studio ventilation or traffic rumble. This would be followed by variable bass controls, which would deal with frequencies up to about 800 Hz.

Moving up to the mid-range controls, you enter the area where the human ear is most sensitive and has its natural resonances: usually between 900 Hz and 7 kHz. Controls for all frequencies are generally similar, but you are likely to find this range covered by two or more controls, as this is possibly the most useful area of equalization for broadcasting.

You can add more punch to the human voice by boosting or cutting the frequency response in the mid areas. You can add 'body' by boosting the lower frequencies at around 200-400 Hz, add clarity above 3 kHz, or make the voice sound 'hot' around 8 or 10 kHz. At the other end of the scale you can minimize problems of nasal quality by reducing the response at around 1 kHz, reduce 'popping' by correcting at about 80 Hz and remove 'scratchiness' at around 2 kHz. It is as well to tend towards a 'thin' sound when mixing or blending a voice with other voices.

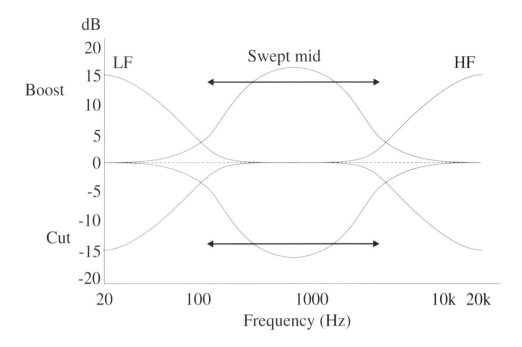

Figure 4.4 Graph of typical response curves for mixer unit equalizers.

The higher frequency range from around 8 kHz to 20 kHz would be more involved in 'hiss' reduction, and is where we would put 'edge' into the audio range. For sounds lacking top-edge bite, boosting these frequencies would be appropriate, but there is always a danger of introducing hiss. Often acoustic howlround between adjacent tracks on multitrack recordings has to be prevented by a steep cut-off around the 11–14 kHz region. You are more likely to find a steep cut filter available for this purpose that is switchable into circuit.

Table 4.1 gives some indication of where to boost and cut the frequency range for the human voice and some common instruments. These are the general areas for improvement, and where you are likely to meet problems, but they are not absolute. Make comparisons, and experiment in these areas in choosing your own 'favourite' combination of equalization.

In assessing the amount of correction to apply, you must take into account the audience to whom your material is addressed. A live transmission will be to a general audience, with widely varying monitoring environments and equipment. Obviously, a happy medium must be met. The difficulty comes where higher-quality systems exist, such as Nicam stereo television receivers, but where most people are still listening on lower-quality circuits supplied from the transmitter's FM mono output. You should make constant checks in the studio on any available lower-quality monitor circuits, which can give you a home-quality check when applying equalization. With the near-perfect monitor circuits in the studio

Table 4.1 Use of equalization

Instrument	Cutting	Boosting	Comments
Human voice	Tinny at 2 kHz Nasal at 1 kHz Popping p's below 80 Hz	Hot at 8–12 khz Clarity < 3 kHz Body 200–400 Hz	Tend towards thin when blending many vocals
Piano	Tinny at 1–2 kHz Boomy at 320 Hz	Presence at 5 kHz Bass at 125 kHz	Not too much bass when mixing with rhythm section
Electric guitar	Muddy below 80 Hz	Clarity at 3.2 kHz Bass at 125 kHz	
Acoustic guitar	Tinny at 2–3.2 kHz Boomy at 200 Hz	Sparkle above 5 kHz Full at 125 Hz	
Electric bass	Tinny at 1 kHz Boomy at 125 Hz	Growl at 620 Hz Bass below 80 Hz	Sounds vary greatly with strings used
String bass	Hollow at 620 Hz Boomy at 200 Hz	Slap at 3.2–5 kHz Bass below 125 Hz	
Snare drum	Annoying at 1 kHz	Crisp above 2 kHz Full at 125 Hz Deept at 80 Hz	Try adjusting tightness of snare wires
Bass drum	Floppy at 620 Hz Boomy below 80 Hz	Slap at 3.2–5 kHz Bass at 80–200 Hz	Usuall record with drum head off. Put blanked inside drum resting against head
Tom-toms	Boomy at 320 Hz	Slap at 3.2–5 kHz Bass at 80–200 Hz	Tuning head tension is very important
Cymbals, bells, and tambourines	Annoying at 1 kHz	Sparkle above 5 kHz	Record at conservative levels
Horns and strings	Scratchy at 3.2 kHz Honky at 1 kHz Muddy below 125 Hz	Hot at 8–12 kHz Clarity above 2 kHz Lush at 320–400 Hz	

it is easy to assume that the home listener will hear the same as yourself: they rarely do.

If a production is going onwards for a final dub or sweetening process, do not overcorrect the frequency response; the dubbing mixer should be given as much of the original frequency range to work with as possible. Otherwise, in extreme cases, the dubbing mixer might have to reduce his overall quality to match your insert.

The whole question of equalization is a matter of taste; no two people will necessarily agree on what sounds good. If directors are present at recording sessions their opinions should be sought, as it would be a disaster if a programme was completed, but not to the taste of the production department, and a full understanding of the audio requirements was not discussed with the production team.

Digital equalization

Many new equalization units are available for the studio, which can be programmed alongside timecode to apply equalization automatically as a programme proceeds along a dub or edit stage. Some are outboard units; some are built into the mixer unit itself alongside automatic fader control. Often the whole system is operated by the programme's timecode, or by preset positions set manually within the timecode.

Naturally, these units are very quiet, with high signal-to-noise ratios. They often include **spectrum analysers**, which give a visual display of the audio to be equalized. A simple example would be to obtain a visual readout of a telephone-quality voice on the spectrum analyser, note the areas of boost and cut on the frequency range, and then apply this in reverse to a piece of normally recorded voice to achieve a telephone effect. This frequency pattern could then be stored in a preset register and retrieved at a later date to use when this effect is next required.

Other uses for the digital equalizer would be to set up your own personal equalization preferences over a range of voices, say, or to deal with regular problems, and store these within presets to use whenever needed. This type of unit could save a great deal of time if used for live programming or dubbing purposes: the unit could be permanently in circuit and the preset equalization settings switched instantly into circuit when required.

Digital equalizers can make the dubbing operation much easier, allowing you more time to concentrate on level matching, while the programmed unit takes care of the equalization at preset points down the code. Alongside the ability to programme equalization, some units can also programme level changes, as well as mixes between level and equalization modification. Again, a little time spent going down the programme presetting these changes can make the overall production a speedier operation all round. Most of the facilities found in the separate outboard units of course are now appearing in the new digital mixers as well as some of the hard disk editing systems.

THE AUDIO JACKFIELD

The audio jackfield is an integral part of all studio set-ups, as it is the hub from which everything leaves the studio and where everything arrives. Although it is now being rapidly replaced by electronic switching units, the audio jackfield will be with us for a long time to come.

Standards vary between different organizations, but they follow a fairly simple pattern. Normally you would expect to have all inputs on the same rows, above all the outputs in rows in a similar way. Outboard equipment would be in similar groups as well as outgoing lines to other remote areas. So, for example, you might have a permanent arrangement where the output of a tape machine is above a high-level audio mixer input. In some studio situations the inputs have a permanent feed from the equipment across the back of the jack socket. By pushing a patch cord into a particular jack, you will have on the end of that jack whatever item is marked on the jackfield, and you can disconnect whatever was originally fed by the 'inner connections' to an input, or remove an output source from its previous input. By this simple method you can over-patch faulty equipment or rearrange the fader grouping on a mixer desk.

It is usual to place blanking plugs in any jack sockets that are used as a permanent arrangement, to avoid disasters with over-patching. Strips of jacks are likely to be available with the facility to parallel certain outputs or inputs in an emergency; these are particularly useful as a temporary measure when you are short of audio distribution amplifiers. Permanent distribution from the mixer to other areas might have the outgoing lines beneath the distribution amplifiers' outputs, with permanent wiring (normalling) on the rear of the jack sockets.

All studio jackfields are balanced, so all the jack plugs would be three-pole, either Post Office style jacks, or bantam jacks, which are smaller in size. It would be unusual to find standard domestic stereo jacks within sound areas but they are often used in outside facilities. Indeed, even XLR plugs and sockets are often seen as distribution boxes within outside facilities.

In some facilities, dismantling a jackfield can be an eye-opener. Often the outside looks fine, with stereo balanced jacks, but inside you may find single-pole units, or double-pole units wired unbalanced at the rear of the socket. These are often the areas where serious level losses occur, and mismatches and phase errors are introduced.

DISTRIBUTING THE AUDIO SIGNALS

The **audio distribution amplifier** is the normal analogue way of distributing audio signals, and has been for many years. This amplifier has a balanced input, usually at zero level, with internal controls for some slight adjustments of input and output levels. It can be produced in a stereo version, with two sets of inputs, and the outputs leaving the unit in pairs. The unit can have up to ten or more outputs, all matching the inputs with unity gain through the system.

Until the introduction of stereo to television, most signals were distributed by using the audio distribution amplifier. Stereo has presented its own problems, by requiring all studios to distribute two signals instead of one. This has sometimes necessitated a massive rewiring operation to supply extra lines. In extreme cases, badly designed or faulty distribution amplifiers could cause some phase errors, altering the stereo image.

Digital distribution has been introduced, in which the analogue audio output of the studio is converted to a digital signal via an analogue-to-digital converter. The resulting signal is either allowed to proceed in the digital domain to its remote source, or is converted in a local transmission area through a digital-to-analogue converter for retransmission in the analogue mode.

The advantages of digital transmission are its freedom from phase errors for stereo, and the fact that two signals can be distributed at the same time as one single digital signal with no loss of level or frequency response. Greater distances can be covered without losses, and the amplification of such signals is within the digital domain, again creating no loss in quality or signal integrity. All audio signals are sent and received at standard zero level, with the maximum peaks being +8 dB. However, greater care must be taken when feeding to digital circuits, as they do not like peaks over the normal maximum, and tend to go into a 'crunch' situation of complete loss of audio. This perhaps is the reason for the introduction of an **absolute maximum** of +8 dB in broadcasting.

With the introduction of Nicam stereo, certainly under the BBC system, audio information can be sent digital all the way, leaving a studio digital and arriving at a transmitter still digital. This has been achieved by the use of digital **sound in syncs**, where the audio signal in digital form is integrated within the video signal and distributed at the same time. The only problem with this is that a loss of picture or syncs will create a loss of audio: the time-worn announcement 'We apologize for your loss of vision; we shall continue in sound only' will become redundant. The complete programme audio is lost with the picture, and to some extent, the picture sync losses.

There are some discrepancies between the BBC and ITV networks on transfer bit rates, which you have to watch out for if you are attempting a pure digital transfer. Independent producers rarely distribute directly to the network down landlines; they usually deliver their product on tape.

Mix-minus feeding to remote input sources

When a remote source outside the studio requires a feed of the studio sound output, and the remote source is itself an input to the studio, you use a **mix-minus output feed** from the mixer desk. As the name of the feed implies, it is the studio mix *minus* the incoming feed from the remote source. It is perhaps easier to remember if you see the 'minus' as the signal that is coming into the studio. If you were to feed the incoming signal out and back into itself you would have an acoustic feedback or howlround.

Studio control rooms usually have an auxiliary output available that feeds all selected outputs that the remote source may wish to hear, to help them to participate in the programme. But the incoming source is deselected on this auxiliary feed from the accepting studio. Normal monitoring of this outgoing feed can be either visual or on a loudspeaker for checking purposes. It is sent down a separate line to the remote source or to an earpiece to the participant; on occasions where many participants are contributing, the remote source may use a loudspeaker foldback system for this purpose. However, this can often cause howlround problems back in the studio on the programme, if not correctly controlled on location. With satellite inserts a problem occurs with the time delay incurred in the up-and-down link, which can both cause delays and be much more noticeable if loudspeaker units are used at the remote end.

Mix-minus feeds are always sent at zero level, and are usually distributed by the master control area of the studio, and connected and tested by that area at the time of establishing the lines to the remote source.

Checking audio levels

Whenever a studio or remote source are to feed each other, an audio level check must be established. It is common on some live transmissions only to check levels as far as the master control area of the studio, with that area checking onwards to the remote source. You would be expected to feed zero level tone to the area checking your output. This would be stereo EBU tone or GLITS tone if the output was in stereo; if not, to avoid confusion on a mono transmission a steady tone of 1 kHz would be sent. Practices can differ, and often a tone of 800 Hz can be sent to identify your source as being a different one.

Sometimes on very large network productions you may require a continuous tape loop or digital voice identification to identify your location or studio, followed by a tone ident; this can be extremely useful for a remote sound mixer or the master control area, to confirm that they have the correct source selected for transmission.

With respect to incoming sources to a studio, you would be expected to check any incoming source for level and, where possible, listen to the actual material you are about to receive. Often, tone can come from a source other than the material being used for the replay. If possible, the tone must come from the actual recorded tape used as the insert into the programme. It is always advisable to ask the remote source to momentarily break the tone sent to you, as there is always a possibility that you have been listening to another source. Similarly, it is good practice to break your own output when sending tone from your own studio or remote area.

DIGITAL MIXING CONSOLES

The introduction of digital mixing consoles has revolutionized the sound mixing world. The main advantages of digital mixing are the extremely quiet operation, the high signal-to-noise ratio, and the high levels of automation that can be achieved.

In essence, the digital console offers the same facilities as an analogue console, but the level of saved preset configurations that can be achieved is endless. With an analogue console you have first to check on the condition of the console before you use it: you have to ensure that all controls, such as equalization, are in their normal positions. You must check that your routeings are all back to normal. In a digital set-up all reset conditions can be achieved when you switch the desk on. Your own desk set-up can be saved to floppy disk or the system's own hard disk, and re-established in the time that it takes a disk to load. So, for example, a whole orchestra set-up can be re-created with a simple computer set-up. Routeings for particular programmes can be set up for communications and signal feeds by re-creating a previous set-up from floppy disk.

Put all these facilities alongside a timecode signal in, say, a dubbing area or editing area, and you can have any operation timed to happen where you want it to, including motorized faders, automatic equalization and other tasks. If, of course, you combine a hard disk recording and editing system you have a fully re-creatable situation, as long as you save all the system settings on a separate disk alongside their timecode references.

It is possible to complete one section of a programme in one centre and, provided another centre has the same equipment set-up, or some way of converting the information, to finish the production elsewhere by programming the information from the floppy disk or datastream into the new equipment on the new location, or in the new facility. Sometimes this can be achieved down telephone lines. **Edit decision lists** (EDL) are often sent down phone lines and used in conforming audio to the edit lists at remote sound-dubbing centres. Systems are being developed that will allow the whole audio file to be transmitted at high speed down lines or by satellite. ISDN circuits can be used to send raw audio down telephone-style lines.

New techniques need to be learned. It is probably not as easy to sit down at a digital console and know its inner workings as it is with its analogue counterpart. Obviously, you have to get familiar with the new way of working. However, the basic techniques are the same; only the set-ups are different. There will also need to be a change towards more digital mixing. The equipment may include internal hard disk recording and editing systems. Perhaps the main disadvantage is when there is an equipment breakdown: the analogue mixer could perhaps still struggle along, and it would be easier to find the faults, or perhaps over-patch the problem. An operator in the digital system is more likely to say or think 'Is it me?', knowing that computer systems are prone to 'hang-ups'. With current digital equipment this is now less likely to happen; the software has gone through much field testing to remove the 'bugs'.

The latest digital mixer units can accept pure digital inputs and can output in digital form to a remote source. With this ability, and with a digital distribution network within a studio complex, it is possible to avoid all the signal degradation that conversions to analogue can cause. The total digital route to the transmitter is now a reality. All that is required now is a digital input socket to the listener – but perhaps even then the listener would still not agree with the sound balance!

CHAPTER 5

Balancing audio levels in the studio

MONOPHONIC PRODUCTIONS

At present most viewers listen to their television programmes in mono and at poor quality levels. The obvious maximum signal level restrictions apply in broadcasting on mono productions, and are as stipulated by the particular broadcasting organization that is employing you at the time. It is important to keep dynamic ranges correct, as well as to maintain the overall tonal quality, smooth balance and transition between sounds and inserts. In a mono production, separation is most important. The aim is clear and unhindered music, and dialogue clear of any signal-to-noise, or interference such as annoying background noises or unexpected changes in background levels.

Human beings have two ears and a brain, aided also by sight, and we can make more of a sound we hear than a simple monophonic soundtrack can. In mono, you are giving the listeners only one part of a complicated process, although they do at least have the picture to help them understand what they are hearing and hence separate the intended signal better. This of course assumes that they are seeing the correct picture; if not, the result will be confusion, unless this is a deliberate dramatic effect that you are trying to create.

For example, consider a simple shot of countryside taken alongside a motorway. The camera has its back to the motorway and the interviewee has his back to the countryside. All the viewer and listener can see is beautiful countryside, but they hear the roar of motorway traffic. This is a confusing situation from the viewing point of view; combined with the audio, it is not a normal one for a listener to perceive. There are various ways to resolve the problem. We could show the motorway in the picture, which would satisfy the viewer and give a reason for the previously unseen interference. We could move somewhere else, away from the motorway, and record the audio. Or we could just mention the motorway in the interview. All these things will satisfy the listener in some way and help to make things seem more realistic.

With a monophonic output to a home listening in mono we have other things to contend with. The home will generally have a high level of background noise, and the listener cannot concentrate the directional ability of the ears in the way we do in stereo, to effectively ignore or reject the background noises. A mono signal does not provide the extra information that is contained within the stereo signal that enables the ears to do this.

The way you can achieve penetration into the home environment is by providing a constant level of audio, with some added presence in the human hearing frequencies. However, there is a potential conflict here, as we are under strict orders from a technical point of view to transmit a full and even frequency response. As a sound balancer, you are allowed a certain amount of leeway in equalizing your audio to give an even response by applying frequency correction. Often it is of little or no use to have extended low frequencies, as this will probably rattle the loudspeakers in all the television sets in the area should the frequencies actually reach the listener, which is possible now with the near-digital route to the home television set.

You should observe these important points:

- Wherever possible, the audio should match the picture.
- The dynamic range should be such that it does not have the listener reaching for the volume control.
- The audio should have clarity and enough presence to have impact in the average home.

Of course, by sticking to all these rules or suggestions, you will inevitably upset the audiophiles in your audience; sadly, you will never please everyone, often not even yourself.

DRAMA

The production of drama in the studio presents its own problems. The main point is that, with drama, you are creating an illusion. To an extent all television is an illusion, but drama must create a 'feel' and have a particular style as far as sound is concerned. The studio operation has to be a larger operation, which needs to be well planned (drama planning is covered later in the book; see p. 147).

To achieve a successful result in drama you must have the correct audio perspectives in the sound that you pick up, both on the studio floor and on location. You must, of course, have the highest speech quality that you can obtain, and you must create an atmosphere with suitable background sound effects to create the feel of the times or situation.

The drama sound on the floor is normally achieved by using mobile booms. It is usual to have two booms with operators, plus one or two assistants to 'track' or move the boom to its predetermined location on the floor. The number of booms required and the number of operators needed to crew the operation will have been decided at the planning meetings. Problems such as projections within the sets, and areas where a movable boom could not reach in practice, would be covered by a fixed slung or hidden microphone or, on occasions, hidden radio microphones. A portable fishpole operated by the sound assistant can be used for supplementary cover of difficult areas that are not accessible by a mobile tracking boom.

It is rare nowadays for drama to be transmitted live, and also rare for sound effects to be run into the actual programme while it is being recorded. Effects and music are normally added to the production at the edit or dub stage.

Often a drama production is made on a 'rehearse and record' basis, where each scene – or even just a section of a scene – is rehearsed and then recorded. At times, this allows a more minimal crew to be used. It is also not unusual to have just a single camera operation, where a studio drama is shot by an extremely small crew, similar in size to a location crew. This method seems extremely wasteful, and gives little advantage if done in a studio, except perhaps the benefit of working under controlled conditions.

Creating a drama in stereo is more difficult, as you may not know exactly how the end product will be cut, which presents problems with stereo perspectives. It would be perfectly possible to record a drama in normal A/B stereo, but this is rarely attempted because of the massive changes in the audio perspective it could create. However, to do a drama in M/S stereo is a practical proposition, as one element in the microphone or microphones used in this system picks up the mono signal, while the other element in the microphone picks up the difference signal, which provides the stereo information. The overall perspective can be smoothed out later in dubbing or editing by varying the side signal, or even by forgetting the whole thing as a M/S production, and adding a stereo atmosphere to the separate mono signal.

The BBC record drama in M/S stereo, and assume that all drama is stereo. The results are excellent, but the BBC have well-controlled technical facilities, and have given directions to staff as to how they expect a production to be achieved from a technical point of view. Independent television does not have an overall plan for drama production, and it is left to the individual companies to work as they see fit. This makes it difficult for freelance operators to approach stereo drama in a uniform way, even if they wish to. Chapter 17 provides a general run-down of how the BBC and the ITV companies would normally handle stereo on location. However, the situation is constantly changing, and what is a rule one month may not be the next.

MUSIC

Music productions present their own difficulties. The art of mixing music is really outside the scope of this book, as it merits a book on its own. However, music inserts and programmes are items that all sound balancers will meet in the course of their careers; some people are better music balancers than others. A knowledge of music is desirable when editing the material; if the sound person doing the editing does not read music, it can be like having roads with no maps. But this should not preclude anyone from mixing music, as a good ear and an enthusiasm for music can produce excellent results. Often, too technical a knowledge of music can make a sound balancer over-critical of a performance that is actually perfectly acceptable. Many sound engineers have experienced situations where an artiste spots one imperfection that no one else has heard.

Planning of music productions is essential to obtain the correct microphone complement and orchestra layout. Microphone choice is often a matter of personal preference, but of course, even with microphones of different makes, there are 'horses for courses'. It would be foolish to recommend individual microphones here, as all sound balancers have their own ideas. In Chapter 6, the section on suggested microphone positioning (pp. 90–92) offers some general suggestions by microphone manufacturer AKG on the placing of microphones and the choice within their particular range of microphones. Most major manufacturers have similar ranges, and a selection of manufacturers is listed in Appendix C; it is not an exhaustive list, as there are many small manufacturers that also produce excellent microphones.

Microphone choice can often be governed by the looks of the mic, and you should bear this in mind if the mic is in vision. When the recording is out of vision you can obviously use what you wish. The production may not permit, or the director may not want even to see, microphones in shot; this often restricts choice and compromises the sound balance. This is an occasion where you need to use great cunning to hide microphones.

As a general rule, as sound balancer you will decide whether to do a multi-microphone balance or rely on a simple stereo pair set-up, with some reinforcement from other microphones. The multi-microphone balance allows finer control of the audio quality should any particular instrument need to be forward to match the picture. It is always a bone of contention with sound balancers whether to bring an instrument forward if it is in close-up or to leave the overall general balance intact; the current trend is to bring the instrument forward in the overall mix.

In considering the overall sound mix you have to take into account the shots that the director intends to take. It would be totally wrong to make the sound mix one that matches shots from the back of the concert hall, when the shots to follow may well be close shots of sections of the orchestra. The best compromise is a generally pleasing balance that is fairly close. In stereo, the added complication of camera shots from behind an orchestra or band can completely reverse the viewed image of the orchestra. You must of course maintain the overall stereo image of the orchestra by deciding your fixed layout from 'front of house' and keeping that relationship at all times.

If the production is recorded and further dubbing is required, it would seem unwise not to multitrack the recording, so that subtle changes can be made to the recording at a later stage. This, of course, would not be the situation on a live transmission. The separate recording should, wherever possible, be referenced to the programme's recorded or edited timecode for future synchronization within the dub. Obviously, session notes and layouts should be recorded on the audio session log sheets, as well as details of microphone types and positions if you feel it is necessary. A written record of microphone positions and types is useful if re-takes are required; it will save time in re-rigging a location, or can help a different sound balancer to match the original recordings.

The rigging of music sessions should be well controlled, with the sound balancer giving the floor operators details of the programme requirements and of where the microphones are to be routed to the wall boxes. However, this can often be left to the floor operators to decide, and a suitable patching list could be supplied from the floor operators. This will enable you to repatch to your own desk layout. When you are rigging the session, take care that cables do not obstruct movements on the floor, nor present a safety hazard to others using the studio floor. Take care where audio cables cross mains cables, to avoid electrical interference. Take account of any cables that are actually within camera shots, and take measures to hide them or disguise them – with the help of the design department if necessary.

Some form of **music playback system** may need to be supplied, either in the form of large foldback loudspeakers, or as individual headphone feeds to musicians. The musical director will require an overall output feed as well as a talk-back feed from the sound control room and director's gallery. You will quite often be required to supply members of the rhythm section in modern bands with a feed of overall balance, individual instruments or vocals to enable them to hear clearly and aid their close musical integration.

The audience public address feed can often be a separate item controlled from the floor, or one that is controlled from the sound control room. However, the studio sound balancer would wish to have the overall control should they require to reduce the level for feedback reasons, and to control the 'spill' of these feeds onto the overall sound balance.

It is now not unusual for an independent company to rig a pop band and control the public address system, and send to the control room only the outputs of the individual microphones at either microphone level or line level. Equally, some outside broadcasts employ a mobile unit to rig and record on multitrack or digital tape, with the outside broadcast unit receiving its overall feed from the mobile recording unit, while within the outside broadcast unit the sound balancer concentrates on the links and communications with network or the mobile video-tape recording unit. Certainly, major stage productions are handled this way, as well as some opera productions.

NEWS AND CURRENT AFFAIRS

By its very nature, news and current affairs programming is usually live. The incoming material is usually of a lower audio quality, and often requires much closer attention than any material in other programme areas. The time constraints of news programming usually dictate that inadequate time is allowed for checks on quality. The urgency applied by journalists, who are usually not interested in the quality, only the transmission of the news item, presents its own problems.

As sound mixer, you will often hear the actual product only when you are 'on the air', and so you will have little or no chance of doing anything to assist the quality, except perhaps a quick application of gentle equalization. Where material is edited locally, some amount of equalization can be applied, and most news and current affairs areas have a small dubbing area for distinct problem items, or have a general policy of dubbing the majority of material. With current cutbacks in staffing, these areas are decreasing, and the dubbing mixer's role is being absorbed within the video editor's area. Usually the edit suite has limited facilities for frequency correction, and is not equipped with the ideal audio monitoring system. This results in limited attention being paid to the audio side of things; pictures and transmission time constraints always come first in the list of priorities.

The fact that the responsibility for sound quality has transferred to the editor is not all bad, as some companies use the video editor as the dubbing mixer. Now that the individual editors have experienced the 'other end' of the situation, it has prompted them to pay more attention to the editing of audio tracks, with an overall smooth audio output in sight. In general, editors are trying to avoid the 'bumps' in level that are common on edits, having experienced the problems when dubbing programmes themselves.

One regular requirement in news and current affairs programmes is the recorded or live phone call or 'phone-in'. This requires the use of a **telephone hybrid unit** that basically interfaces the studio with a telephone line, and allows a two-way or one-way operation down the phone line from the studio. The hybrid unit has a certain amount of automatic level control within its circuitry, as well as a frequency response that is tailored for maximum quality from the telephone circuit. It is usual to feed these units with a mix-minus feed and also to have the ability in the control room to feed their own local talkback down the line for cueing purposes. It may well be a requirement that the studio live talkback has to be fed down the hybrid unit with a switch made to programme or studio output at the required time, or perhaps a mixture of both.

Often, when time is scarce and planning is impossible, a reporter may use his or her own mobile phone and be cued directly from that phone. Another possible way of obtaining a cue is from a small portable television receiver and an earpiece, with the television receiver tuned to the local transmitter output. However, this type of facility would be useless if the insert was to a company outside the originating company's area, and the programme was not being transmitted live.

With its own internal cancellation of signals, a properly set up hybrid unit can produce good results back in the studio, or at least as good as the phone line allows. The introduction of ISDN (digital signals down phone lines) circuits can dramatically improve audio quality, allowing digital quality on inserts, but the system is rarely used in television news broadcasting.

Overall, news and current affairs is a hectic operation, with many jobs now being multiskilled. It is too early to see how successful this will be; only time will tell. Certainly, some reduction in audio quality has been observed, as peer training as such has disappeared. Experience, sadly, is something that is normally passed down over the years.

CHAPTER 6

The studio floor

WALL BOX FACILITIES

All studios have facilities around the floor area and sometimes on the lighting grid for interconnecting audio lines to the sound control room. Naturally, they vary from organization to organization, but the basic facilities will include balanced lines to the control room, dedicated talkback lines, often dedicated foldback lines, video feeds and often mains and phantom powering for microphones, although it is common for microphone powering to come down the microphone lines from the remote mixer desk.

Wall boxes are situated in convenient places for general operational work. The usual audience area may have its own dedicated wall boxes, with perhaps feeds available for public address loudspeakers and audience microphone returns to the sound control room. It is fairly common to have available stage box extensions from a wall box to allow a multiway cable to extend from the wall box to, say, an area where a large number of microphones may be needed. Areas usually requiring such extensions would be the rostrum area or whatever area is chosen for an orchestra, or other large groups of people needing many different facilities.

Care, of course, should be taken with all cables leaving wall boxes, both from a safety point of view and to ensure that they are not likely to be disconnected by careless placement. Careful marking of cables at the remote end should ensure quick checking under any fault conditions; although it is obviously sensible to mark the remote end with what microphone or facility the cable actually feeds, it is also sensible to mark the same cable with its wall box destination.

It is usual to have a safety zone marked on the studio floor, conforming to fire regulations. This should not be obstructed; any cables crossing the zone should have a suitable sloping protection bridging the cables to meet with current safety rules.

RIGGING THE STUDIO

The sound supervisor or sound mixer gives the floor crew their requirements, having attended planning meetings, and leaves the rigging of microphones and facilities to the floor crew, headed by the senior member on the floor. Television companies normally issue staff and freelance operators with their safety regulations required on the premises.

Cables should be laid out in a safe manner, and care should be taken not to place them where obvious camera movements are to take place. If microphones are rigged overhead these should have some form of safety cord attached, and particular rules apply over studio and audience areas, as they do on location audience rigs.

Any sound that is fed to the studio floor that is not generally generated or created within the studio, but which is required to be heard in the studio, is called **foldback**. This sound will be fed from the audio mixer unit in the sound control room via an auxiliary circuit and amplified to be played out through loudspeakers on the studio floor. The normal foldback facilities should be rigged and tested by the floor crew, playing out some form of signal from the control room. Additional loudspeakers should be placed where they are known to be needed; however, this may only prove necessary as the rehearsal goes on. If loudspeaker foldback is fitted to the trackable boom, then this should be checked; this is not a facility used by all companies. Often it is felt better to localize foldback audio to a very tight area to reduce the effect of coloration of the studio audio.

Talkback facilities should be checked with the sound balancer in the control room, and additional facilities rigged where required for presenters and musical directors or other operators. It is usually the responsibility of sound engineers on the floor to check that everyone has adequate talkback coverage.

Once the general facilities are checked, the rigged microphones should be checked up to the sound balancer in the control room, and any requested attenuation at the floor end made to the microphones with their built-in controls. Obviously, radio talkback is better for anyone doing the check, as it is often difficult to receive and give instructions secondhand; radio talkback allows the operator mobility.

During the microphone checks all radio microphone equipment is checked and new batteries are placed in transmitters where required. It is good practice to place a piece of camera tape on the transmitter annotated with the battery replacement date; it is even better practice to start the day with new batteries. New batteries cost a lot less than an expensive retake of a scene, or perhaps a total sound failure on a live transmission! During the radio mic system checks it is as well to check that the receiving aerials have not been damaged or moved, and that they are suitably positioned for the transmitter's working area, although it is likely that the optimum position has already been found for the studio. A general walk with a live transmitter around the expected working area is advisable, to confirm a strong transmission from the radio mic units.

PROVIDING PLAYBACK OF AUDIO

Audio playback to the audience and the floor is important on all productions and has to be checked regularly. It is fairly obvious when an artiste cannot hear the foldback, as they usually make this fact known to all concerned. This does not, however, apply to audiences, as they do not know what to expect, and in any case would probably never complain until after the event.

Many floor cues are triggered from an audio effect, or happen at the same time, so adequate coverage should be given and checks made with the participants that the sound level is adequate for their use. However, the sound balancer will wish to keep such foldback to a minimum for their own reasons; a compromise, therefore, should be reached. Artistes should be asked whether they are happy with the levels of foldback as a matter of courtesy, as it makes them feel more involved and part of the action.

If the programme has a participating audience, the audience area should be checked during rehearsals for public address facilities and general levels, although these levels will need to be increased when the area is full, as the sheer mass of the audience absorbs the signal to a great extent. If the audience public address is being handled by a separate operator, he or she should be asked if all the feeds are satisfactory, and the result conveyed to the sound balancer. It never hurts to keep everyone happy and fully informed.

BOOM OPERATION IN THE STUDIO

It is difficult to cover the role of the boom operator fully, as so much of the job is learned by experience, but basically he or she must be able to place the microphone to gain maximum signal from the source while obtaining the maximum rejection of unwanted signals. Obviously the boom operator has to maintain an even perspective that is relevant to the shot or angle being used, and also give the best sound pick-up possible with respect to the shot size. Many splits of dialogue will have to be handled, and this necessitates keeping a close eye on the script to anticipate any splits or repositioning of actors. Good boom operators know camera angles by experience. An experienced operator will find a similar pattern to the size of shots that will be cut together within a production.

The actual boom positions will have already been decided at planning meetings and rehearsals, and also whether two booms are required within a particular set. Often it will be necessary to have boom changeovers within a scene, where for either lighting problems or problems of space, a two-boom operation may be necessary anyway. The boom operator will have a copy of the script, and decisions may be made jointly between the senior boom operator and the sound balancer or just by the senior boom operator alone.

Any lighting problems with shadows will be sorted out between the boom operators and the lighting director, with the boom operators advising the sound balancer of any areas where they may be required to give more headroom than normal, owing to camera angles or lighting constraints. Least of the problems experienced by a boom operator are shadows caused by the boom itself on the background, the floor or even the artiste. The efficient boom operator must have a knowledge of basic lighting techniques, and sometimes good negotiating skills are useful, to clear any problems with the lighting director.

When achieving boom changeovers during drama productions, the two boom operators have to choose exactly the right moment to make the change, and themselves take precautions not to cause any problems for the sound balancer, who often has no visual reference of the boom positions – only an audio or script cue as to when the changeover will take place.

To assist the boom operator it is normal to have a video monitor on the boom, to enable the operator to judge the headroom available above the shot for working the microphone, bearing in mind that the monitor will display a slightly wider angle than the one that will be transmitted.

MICROPHONE POSITIONING

In this section we are not going to cover the best position for any particular microphone or group of microphones, as this can only come from experience. Often, picture restrictions mean that you cannot obtain the best position anyway. Certainly it would usually be required that microphones are out of camera shot, but this is not always possible. With the reduction of crewing levels, the use of boom microphones has reduced. It is becoming normal to see more microphones in shot than ever before, and this has increased the need to rig these microphones tidily. Minimum crewing has also made it essential to rig spare microphones on live transmissions. If spares are rigged and no sound personnel are available to fetch them, then the sound mixer must tell the floor manager where they are, and which possible emergencies they are intended to cover.

The use of more 'in vision' microphones has, in many ways, made life more difficult for the sound mixer. With the extra numbers of microphones comes the extra problem of coloration from one microphone to another. Care must be taken in the positioning of all the microphones to avoid 'spill' between microphones. When positioning microphones, and cardioid microphones in particular, ensure that they back off to the sources you do not want to hear or reject. So, for instance, any audience microphones should be 'looking' for the audience and isolating the studio floor, giving you maximum separation.

Careful placing of dynamic mics is important when they are close to television monitors, as induction from such sources is more likely with a dynamic microphone. It is also fairly obvious that cabling to microphones should try to steer clear of running alongside power cables or across television monitors. Although most balanced line systems can cope with these problems, sometimes the problem is too great to overcome, and a simple rerouteing of a cable can clear a fault.

Figures 6.1–6.3 provide suggestions for microphone positioning for a variety of instruments, as well as suggested microphones types. These are taken from one manufacturer's publication, and are reprinted with their permission. Of course, other manufacturers' microphones could be used.

Figure 6.1 Typical microphone types and positioning for speech and musical instruments. (Courtesy AKG)

Figure 6.2 Typical microphone types and positioning for musical instruments. (Courtesy AKG)

Figure 6.3 Typical microphone types and positioning for percussion instruments. (Courtesy AKG)

CHAPTER 7

Stereo operations in the studio

Stereo is a relatively recent innovation in the television studio, particularly for the ITV network. In many ways the BBC pioneered the system in this country, being responsible for inventing the Nicam stereo system and the stereo 'sound in syncs' system currently used in the UK. They had a policy of making all programmes in stereo at an early stage, and used the period when programmes were not being transmitted nationally in stereo for training and familiarization. This has helped to iron out many problems. All major BBC studios have the equipment in place to deal fully with all aspects of stereo production and post-production, and all sound balancers are used to transmitting and recording in stereo.

ITV does not have an overall programming policy for stereo except for Channel 4, who usually request stereo. The situation is improving, but companies still exist who do not even have a stereo mixer desk in their main studio, and rely upon outside broadcast units for their stereo facilities. Under the circumstances, when planning recordings or stereo transmissions within the ITV network, it is always wise to first check that you have the necessary backup facilities in post-production and that, indeed, it is the company's policy to do such programmes in stereo.

The actual recording of the production and the live transmission are little changed by the introduction of stereo, and only become difficult when edited if suitable stereo track-laying facilities are not available. Fortunately, these facilities are fast becoming available; some are cheaper than others, and can be equally as efficient.

TECHNICAL REQUIREMENTS FOR STEREO

Technically speaking, it is relatively simple to record in stereo. It is easy to see why production personnel with a non-technical background might assume that it is just a matter of using two mics or two channels. Outwardly the equipment looks exactly the same as the equipment used on a mono operation. However, the actual recording is probably the simplest part of the process. It is in post-production that the complications arise, and these are often not considered first in the initial planning or shooting of a production. If a company has to hire in extra equipment for stereo, or only has limited equipment, the audio handling in stereo could prove labour-intensive and time-consuming, possibly adding extra cost to a production's budget. If post-production in stereo is not considered at an early stage, even higher costs can be added. However, if the proper equipment is available in the video edit areas to handle tracks in stereo pairs with full synchronization to the picture, there should not be any significant time restraints on the editing time of a production.

Before making the decision to do a production in stereo, it is important to check that the decision you have made can be followed through with suitable backup facilities. There have been horror stories of outside facilities saying they could deal with a stereo production, only to call the location sound recordist months after the event and ask 'What's this M/S stereo bit then?'. It is often difficult to predict what will happen to a programme at the edit stage, and whether the powers of observation of the editor and director at times will go as far as noticing a movement of a stereo image in the monitored audio tracks.

In situations where two systems run side by side, with one area making its programmes in stereo and the other not, transmission problems can occur if VTR operators wrongly transmit a mono programme as stereo, with the lower track offset, or even a rough earlier copy of the dubbed programme on the top track. This is a case for careful marking of material and some form of coding on transmission tape boxes. Companies need to have strict rules about track layouts on master tapes for mono transmissions. Tapes can easily pass through the system thanks to poorly marked boxes and be a disaster on air. A recent programme was transmitted for about half an hour before the director, sitting at home, realized that an undubbed copy was being used, and that there should have been large amounts of commentary on the production. The viewers had not noticed; nor had the transmission controller.

Very few restrictions apply for stereo transmissions, except perhaps those mentioned in the previous sections, and the limited facilities available in some studios. Some of the earlier analogue audio equipment caused phase errors on transmission. Many of the mechanical errors of the old analogue replay systems have been eliminated by the introduction of digital audio tracks on the videotape recorders used for transmission and within the edit suites, and also by the use of digital audio followers and hard disk systems in the dubbing and editing areas of studios.

The use of extreme left and right placing of dialogue in stereo can cause a significant drop in the centre of the image when summed for the transmission mono output. The way the stereo image is summed for the mono output varies slightly from one broadcasting organization to another.

There are no other real problems across the transmission system, and full audio bandwidth transmissions can be achieved.

CONSERVATION OF THE POLARITY OF AUDIO SIGNALS

The European Broadcasting Union recommendations (R50 1989) on audio phase are as follows.

An audio signal is deemed to be positive when it results from an increase in the acoustic pressure on the microphone diaphragm and thus in the displacement of the diaphragm towards the rear. In the case of an XLR connector, which is probably the most widely used type, a positive signal anywhere throughout the chain should produce an instantaneous positive voltage on pin 2 with respect to pin 3.

An instantaneous positive audio signal applied to the input terminals of any magnetic tape recorder should magnetize the tape in the same direction as that of the motion of the tape. Furthermore, the magnetic recorder should be designed such that the polarity of the audio signals is conserved from the input connectors to the recording head and from the reproducing head to the output connectors.

It is also important to ensure that when in the standby position (i.e. when the output is being fed from the input possibly through some or all the signal processing stages) the polarity is conserved throughout, including the monitoring loudspeaker. In fact, all loudspeaker monitoring points throughout the whole chain should be wired in such a way that the instantaneous presence of a positive audio signal on pin 2 of the XLR plug with respect to pin 3 should cause an increase in the acoustic pressure at the normal listening position; this should apply to all frequencies within the audio bandwidth.

It is convenient to simulate the presence of an instantaneous positive audio signal at the playback head by temporarily mounting a closed $100\,\Omega$ wire loop adjacent to the gap, such that an asymmetric audio signal generator (1 kHz) will produce a current that travels in a vertical direction from the bottom to the top of the head. The direction of the magnetic flux with this arrangement will be in the direction of the tape or film travel. Compliance of the playback channel with this convention can be verified most simply by playing back a standard test tape, recorded with a significantly asymmetric test signal. When the playback channel is known to comply, the recording channel can be verified by means of the application of a similar test signal to the recorded input.

The EBU document is concerned with programmes produced on either magnetic tape or film or both. In the case of film, if there is a sudden exposure of the photosensor to light, this should also produce a positive pulse on the audio signal terminal pin 2 with respect to pin 3. In the case of FM recording, a positive-going audio signal applied to the input of an FM recorder should bring about an increase in the instantaneous FM carrier frequency, and this should remain positive-going at the output of the demodulator.

The final link in the broadcaster's chain is the dual-channel sound-in-syncs equipment; a positive-going change in the amplitude of the audio signal should be represented by a positive number, and a positive audio signal should correspond to an increase in the numerical value of the equivalent digital signal.

CHOICE OF PROGRAMME MATERIAL FOR STEREO

There was an initial tendency at the start of stereo to make as many programmes as possible in stereo. Since that time it has been realized that some programmes do not seem to benefit from this enhancement, except perhaps for the music at the start and end of the production.

Programmes that *do* benefit from stereo include:

- drama production;
- music productions, including light entertainment;
- sports programmes;
- some documentaries (but mostly from the effects tracks).

Local programming, with its fast turnround, seems to have little chance of turning to stereo, because of its immediacy and the limited editing time. In most documentary situations little is gained from recording interviews in stereo, as decisions in editing sessions are often taken that can reverse the stereo image given in the sound track, and negate all that went before in presenting a good stereo image.

Drama productions, when shot in stereo on location, often end up with effects reversed on the edit when cutaways from the opposite direction to the fixed stereo image are inserted in the main editing session. This has always been a problem in feature film shooting, and led to the almost universal shooting in mono by film companies for dialogue, restricting the use of stereo A/B recordings (on quarter inch tape or DAT) to effects.

It is easy to place a stereo microphone in a suitable position to cover the camera angle and get a good stereo image, but any intruding noise or sound from a fixed position would of course reverse direction on the reverse angle, leaving the dialogue positions perfectly correct but the effects wrongly oriented, with traffic moving in the opposite direction or clocks swapping sides! This problem can, of course, be countered by reversing the left–right orientation of the microphone, which is an easy matter on microphones of the Neumann RSM191 type. This has a simple switching matrix to obtain image reversal in both mid–side (M/S) and left–right (A/B) operation by the operation of a switch on the external unit.

Although all the indications are that only certain programmes will benefit from the stereo effect, this should not stop production personnel or sound balancers and recordists tackling other programme material in stereo. However, this will often mean spending longer in sound post-production and, usually, some sort of dubbing or sweetening process.

BOOM OPERATION FOR STEREO

The basic operation is the same for the boom operator in stereo as it is in mono, but there are now extra considerations with respect to the stereo image. During a boom changeover, great care has to be taken to maintain a stable stereo image.

When one boom or two booms are deployed, the operator and supervisor must decide on a suitable **image orientation point** (IOP). This is the point within the set where the image will centre. All moves are taken with this point in mind, and it must be replaced on boom changeovers. This can be a difficult operation, as frequently one camera may present a reverse stereo angle followed by a quick return to the original angle, requiring the operators to assume some precise positioning.

Under the M/S stereo system, which is the one most commonly used in studio drama productions, much can be achieved after the event by altering the side signal on the dub process; however, when the need for a boom changeover occurs, the two operators must make sure they are in a similar IOP. One problem with the M/S combined microphone configuration, which the operator must be careful to avoid, is the susceptibility of the figure-of-eight capsule to wind noise caused by rapid movement of the microphone.

When using mono spot microphones to pick up difficult dialogue areas, the sound balancer will pan these mics according to the stereo image. The overall stereo image can be maintained by the M/S boom microphone or A/B boom microphone. The 'mono feel' of these microphones can be somewhat reduced by feeding reverberation onto the mono channel, with the phase reversed, and then feeding this reverb signal back into the A/B mixed output.

The operator should always keep the mono mic portion of an M/S mic in mind when picking up dialogue. In mono operation, boom swings and fast racks with dialogue are fine, but in stereo this can cause a disturbance of the stereo image, and so should be avoided. The style of operating should be one that allows the operator to cover the dialogue from a fairly constant angle without having to make wild movements to follow single artistes.

Prior to any operations the actual microphone fitted should be checked for correct stereo orientation and phase. It is all too easy to place a stereo microphone in a boom cradle with the left and right elements incorrectly placed. This could cause great image confusion if two booms were employed.

CHAPTER 8

Editing techniques for audio

QUARTER INCH EDITING

You will probably be required at some time to edit quarter inch tapes, but with the introduction of hard disk editing, quarter inch editing is now becoming a thing of the past within broadcast circles.

The standard method of editing quarter inch tape is fairly well known. The basic principle is to mark the tape with a Chinagraph wax pencil at the 'out' point of the section you wish to join, and then mark an 'in' point to which these two pieces will join. Cut the tape at an angle of 45 degrees, and join it with special quarter inch jointing tape.

When cutting the tape it is essential to use non-magnetic scissors or an Ever Ready type razor blade. A cutting tool that was magnetized would cause clicks on the edit point. It is essential to use a jointing block to align the tape. Semi-automatic jointing blocks are available, which can also apply the jointing tape as part of their action. Take care that the jointing tape does not project beyond the edge of the magnetic tape, as this could create an irregular path in the motion of the tape, causing it to lift from the heads at the joint and making the edit audible.

DIGITAL HARD DISK EDITING

Many new systems are coming into operation for hard disk editing, and prices are dropping quite fast. The early arrivals of systems by AMS Audiofile, Synclavier, Digital Audio Research and other manufacturers helped to revolutionize the editing of audio sound tracks with video. These have been followed by systems that work from a standard PC, and can be obtained at much lower prices.

Hard disk editing systems are usually capable of retaining the original recording in its entirety, so that it can be recalled and used again; any edits made within the system leave this master track intact. This system is called **non-destructive editing**.

In hard disk editing the normal amount of disk space required for a full band-width stereo recording is around 10 megabytes per minute of running time. This means that to maintain 30 min of stereo audio you require 300 megabytes of disk space. To edit this material, you need the same amount of space again to retain the original material. If more tracks are required, this increases the storage requirements, so that a system that uses a PC or Macintosh type of computer needs to have many external hard disk drives to cope with the full storage requirement.

Basic editing on PC hard disk systems is done in a Windows program environment, with tracks displayed on screen, either as blocks representing tracks or as waveform graphical displays. Generally, a 'cut and paste' system is used, whereby the operator can remove and insert sections visually. Monitoring is supplied within the system, to perform rehearsals of the edit or listen to the completed edit. As these systems are usually non-destructive, the original recording remains intact, barring any possible system crashes.

Most audio hard disk editing systems can display time against the actual sound waveforms; some provide sound time stretching and compression functions. These time compression systems do not alter the actual pitch of the audio and so can be extremely useful to a sound engineer or production department: for example, in making commercials to an accurate time.

It is normal to be able to 'stream' the data from any of the hard disk editing systems to tape storage on other media such as Hi-8 or other tape streaming devices, thereby freeing the system's hard disk of the programme material. Material can be fed into the systems in digital or analogue form. The obvious advantage of digital inputs is that no change to the original material is made. The output to the tape streamer is also digital, which again does not change the original material. Tape streamers normally output at more than real time. Outputs are also available to normal digital sources like DAT in real time to copy an edit to a master tape.

USING THE AUDIOFILE SYSTEM

Video dubbing with timecode

Since the early days of film production, all sound post-production – usually called **dubbing** – was carried out using film transports, with the sound on sprocketed tape locked to a film projector. However, the invention of the videocassette machine and timecode allowed the picture to be accurately locked to a multitrack tape recorder. This paved the way for a newer method of dubbing, and many dubbing theatres changed to the new method of operation.

These multitrack machines had been in use very successfully for many years in music recording studios: George Martin used a four-track machine to mix one of the Beatles' records in the early 1960s. One of the first sound post-production

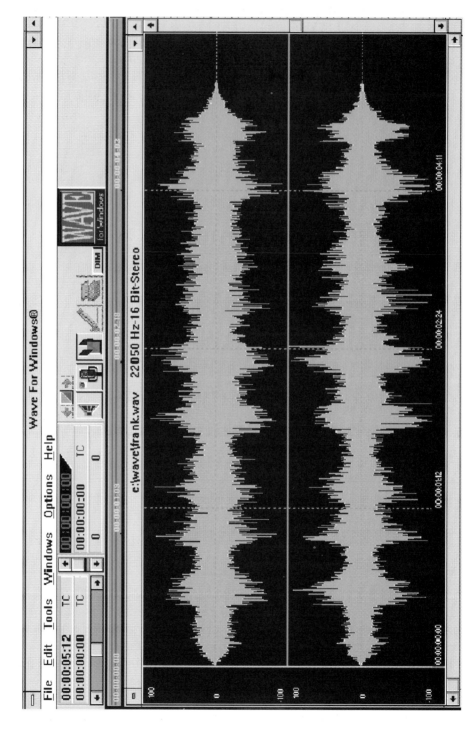

Figure 8.1 A screen grab from a typical low-cost PC hard disk digital audio editing system.

studios to use multitrack for dubbing was the eight-track SYPHER suite at the BBC's Television Centre. It wasn't long before the eight tracks became 16 and then 24, and using timecode to synchronize video to audio, the dubbing mixer had a large number of tracks at his disposal for track laying and mixing. However, unlike film dubbing systems, where the picture and sound tracks maintained sync by use of the sprockets during high-speed wind or rewind operation, when a video machine was rewound at high speed it took some time for the multitrack machine transporting large, heavy reels of tape to synchronize, thus slowing down the dubbing process. All the while, video machines like the Sony Beta and U-Matic were getting more sophisticated and faster in operation, but in general the sound technology didn't make dramatic changes to the speed of the dubbing operation.

Music recording studios were investing in the new generation of digital multitrack machines, but as these cost upwards of £250 000 each, very few sound dubbing studios took the plunge into digital dubbing technology. In the mid-1980s, Advanced Music Systems (AMS), a company in Burnley who had a reputation for the development and manufacture of digital reverberation devices, responded to a request from the internationally known singer and musician Peter Gabriel to build a digital sampler that would produce audio samples at full bandwidth. The amount of audio that could be sampled was very short, but the single-channel device that they developed was used by Peter Gabriel with great success on a number of his tracks.

Around that time, an ITV company making a new quiz programme asked AMS to make a sound sampling unit that would capture, store and play back music stings and sound effects in non-volatile form. This idea was developed into a computer-based system – and Audiofile was born. Complete sound cues could be recorded, edited if necessary, titled, catalogued and assembled into playback order ready for instant play-in.

The introduction of Audiofile

The introduction of the eight-track Audiofile, based on the same technology, into the post-production suite represented a major step forward. It gave the dubbing mixer many more options than had been available in the past. Suddenly he was freed from the constraints of the multitrack machine and synchronizer system, which, regardless of how good a system it might be, was still the slowest part of the post-production operation. Now the audio would synchronize with the picture immediately the video rewound and a timecode could be read.

However, more importantly from the mixer's point of view, the audio recorded into the new system was in digital form and could be manipulated instantly: no more 'track bouncing', with the subsequent loss of an audio generation, which would have been the case with an analogue system. Gone also was the need to edit a quarter inch tape, which would have been necessary prior to recording it on the multitrack. Now the tape could be recorded, and very quickly edited, within Audiofile.

Operating Audiofile

Operationally, after a short instruction course, the Audiofile system is very user-friendly. All the individual items of audio to be used for a particular programme are recorded into Audiofile, stored on the hard disk as 'cues' complete with any existing timecode information, and placed in a cues library. They can then be edited, expanded or compressed into an exact length, duplicated, titled and put into an 'events' or playback list. Editing accuracy used to be measured in milliseconds (thousandths of a second) but the modern systems enable the operator to achieve an accuracy measured either in microseconds (millionths of a second) or in 'bits'.

From the events list the cues are arranged in programme order, and any cue that has a timecode reference (an edited master track from VTR, for instance) will immediately go to its place in the list. Non-timecode cues can then be placed on the list at whatever point they are required, and each event can be assigned a track for playout. Unlike conventional analogue recorders, tracks can be changed instantly, and events can be 'slipped', edited, have audio levels adjusted up or down and can also be expanded or compressed to an exact length. Fades can be added to the front or end and cross-fades made between any of the tracks. All editing is non-destructive, and this means that cues edited to a particular length can be used again and again in different forms. This is particularly useful when perhaps only a short sample of the audio exists, allowing it to be copied and repeated many times without any generation loss or signal degradation.

Many pages of information can be displayed on the green screen; as the events list is being played out, all the tracks, highlighted where audio is present, move across the screen towards a cursor that represents the playback heads, giving the sound mixer an indication of when the signals will arrive at the faders on the sound console. As the programme is being played back and mixed, it can be recorded back into Audiofile and stored there on the hard disk or optical disk until it can be laid back to the master videotape.

An optional part of the Audiofile system is the LOGIC mixer, a digital mixing console that can be fully integrated into the programme, and which is used to input information such as cross-mixes, equalization, fades, and all the other features that one would require in a mixing console.

Should it be necessary to keep a copy of the programme, then all information associated with each cue as well as all other events can be backed up to DAT or other digital storage media for later use.

As mentioned above, the major advantage of using such a system is the elimination of mechanical tape transport devices such as the conventional multitrack machine. However, it is still possible to use these to provide additional tracks by locking the Audiofile to them with timecode.

OPTICAL DISK EDITING SYSTEMS

The optical disk offers more memory space on board a digital editing system, which allows the operator to have more tracks of longer lengths. Some systems have removable optical disks, so that a programme can be stored outside the basic system. There is less possibility of damage to the optical disk than to a magnetic disk when stored. However, they are currently rather expensive, and so are used only in the higher-grade systems like Synclavier and Audiofile. In the future we are likely to see optical disks being used for video recording on location, with digital audio tracks included within the recording system.

CHAPTER 9

Dubbing

DUBBING A VIDEO PROGRAMME

Once the original sound tracks have been edited along with the pictures, the moment arrives for 'audio sweetening' or 'dubbing'. It is rare that a production can be transmitted or distributed without some form of audio processing. There are inevitably some sound 'bumps' within the course of an edited programme, and voice-overs, effects and music may need to be added to add interest and atmosphere.

News operations do not always dub items; instead they use the practice of merging two tracks as a composite, with the commentary on one track and interviews or effects on the other. This is allowable, considering the time restraints under which they work. Some independent television companies *do* dub their news and magazine output; although the operation is very fast, the improvements gained are quite high. This sort of 'quick' system allows freer use of their reporting staff, and indeed editing staff. Voice-over recordings are often recorded within the dubbing area immediately after the rushes have reached the studio, thus allowing the reporter to proceed to the next assignment.

The basic procedures for dubbing are listed below, assuming that the end dubbing source may well be multitrack analogue tape or a digital system such as Audiofile (see p. 102). The obvious advantage of the digital-based system is that there will be no change in the original recorded quality, except for deliberate alterations. The digital system also provides faster synchronization to timecode, as it has no mechanical interfaces.

In **normal edit and dub procedures**, track 1 is used for laying voice-overs and interviews, and track 2 is used for laying effects and music. Stereo has presented its own unique problems in news edit suites, as usually only two tracks are available, and the tracks will have to be laid in stages. However, for news operations 'straight cut' tracks are usually the normal procedure. AFM Betacam tracks are really of little use in the edit procedure, as they require a 're-laid' video signal simultaneously applied. The AFM tracks are, however, of better quality than the analogue tracks and can be a good original source or standby track.

Voice-overs not recorded on location are often recorded in edit suites on lip ribbon or close-speaking microphones, or in dubbing areas with voice-over booths. Some companies have a central voice-over booth to feed edit suites. The main advantage of recording voice-overs in separate booths prior to editing is that it allows the editor to proceed with more items and also have an overall idea of the item or programme's verbal content, enabling him or her to select the appropriate pictures to accompany the soundtrack. However, this is not a practical proposition for long documentaries.

Lift off involves copying the two edited audio tracks from Betacam, or whatever format is used, to the master recording on either multitrack, Audiofile or similar digital-based system, with the timecode transferred onto a separate track on the record source machine at the same time. At the end of the completed dubbing session these will be replaced 'in sync' on the original master tape with the new enhanced tracks locked to the original timecode.

Treatments are now applied. The usable parts of the original two sync sound tracks are selected and combined while each part of a scene is controlled or processed (level, equalization, hiss, etc.). Background levels are smoothed, with new or additional sound effects from an 'in house' library or from location wildtracks supplied. The object of this operation is to provide an uninterrupted continuous smooth track, with no unintentional sudden changes that would otherwise distract the listener. Where necessary, additional or missing spot effects are added to enhance the realism of the scenes. It may be that effects are added to give particular impact that was not present at the time of recording.

Music track can be laid to additional tracks on the multitrack or Audiofile, and at roughly the right levels and equalization in stereo and mono. Most dubbing theatres have available a commercial music library, and some have the facilities to bring in 'outside' composers to create music as required.

From the voice-over studio the commentary is laid down in sync with the picture, 'rocking and rolling' as required. (Rocking and rolling is a method of moving pictures and sound across a fixed point to find the start and end of a particular sequence.) If the commentary has already been recorded on the master or on a separate quarter inch tape it is still useful to have it on a separate track. On many occasions an edit is performed with a 'guide track' voice-over for the edit and the new original recorded track fitted in the dub.

At this point in the dub there will probably be four premixed tracks, or eight if in stereo. Tracks for stereo will of course be on a single fader, which will avoid any level differences between tracks on the fades. Without this facility, stereo may suffer from 'wandering image'.

The sets of tracks will be:

1. Sync from the original master;
2. additional sound effects;
3. music;
4. commentary.

The four tracks are now **mixed down** to produce the final mix.

In **layback**, the new mix is recorded in one continuous pass onto the original master tape back at its original sync points. At the same time, VHS copies can be made for clients or interested production personnel. Note that the original master tape is only used twice. On the original lift off a picture copy is usually taken with **burnt-in timecode** (BITC) to U-matic format videotape, or whatever format the dubbing theatre uses for its picture transport. This ensures that the picture original is unlikely to suffer any damage from constant rocking and rolling in the dub procedure.

In broadcast operations where fast dubbing is required, such as local magazine programmes, it is likely that the original is used for the dub and transported many times across the heads. In some companies this operation often requires a pass to another machine of the same format, with a generation degrade of pictures, the dub being done **on the fly**. ('On the fly' implies that the operator switches the record machine from playback mode into record mode while the tape is running and inserts new sound at this point). The 'in' and 'out' points for such record inserts can also be preselected on the timecode; these are usually called **punch-in** points. It is not uncommon for dubbing mixers working on current affairs programmes to have to run in music and effects on the fly because of time constraints.

Broadcasting companies will often have edit-capable machines such as the Sony BVW75 for SP tape and BVW40 for standard Betacam available within dubbing areas, but you are unlikely to find these outside broadcasting, except in very sophisticated dubbing suites. These machines have the capability, without an edit controller, of being programmed for very accurate audio punch-ins; the output of the machine is capable of monitoring the actual edit. This facility makes it possible for the dubbing mixer to monitor the actual dub in real time.

DUBBING A FILM PRODUCTION

Traditionally, film dubbing is the process of mixing down magnetic film sound-tracks containing dialogue, music and sound effects into a final mix that is artistically and technically satisfactory. These tracks are prepared by the dubbing editor from various sources: location dialogue, post-sync dialogue, location-recorded sound effects and atmospheres, post-sync effects, music from scored music sessions, CD and disk. The timing and lengths of these tracks are recorded on a dubbing chart compiled by the assistant editor as a guide to the dubbing mixer. These charts can be timed in minutes and seconds, 35 mm feet or 16 mm feet. (See Appendix H for a sample dubbing chart.)

The film dubbing sequence

The dubbing sequence usually involves a series of premixes. The dialogue tracks are reduced from several tracks to one dialogue mix. Similarly, the effects and music can be reduced to an effects mix and a music mix. This mix is often referred to as an **M&E** (music and effects) composite track, and is useful when making multi-language productions, the new dialogue track being added to the original M&E tracks. In practice, however, there are usually extra tracks such as post-sync footsteps (foleys) and moves, which are added to the music, dialogue and effects mixes in the final master mix of the film. These processes are performed by the dubbing mixer under the supervision of the director, with input from the film editor and dubbing editor. This would seem an organized and simple system; however, sometimes it is not so straightforward.

The director's responsibility in the dubbing process

Dubbing takes place near the end of the film production. Directors adopt various attitudes to dubbing. Some believe that their work is virtually over, and take little interest; in fact some do not even attend. The dub is really the director's responsibility, and he or she should previously have decided what sort of soundtrack the film should have. The editor and dubbing editor will know the film and its soundtracks very well, which is essential if the director does not attend. They will assist the director in any decisions that have to be made with regard to the balance of music, dialogue and effects, as will the dubbing mixer, who is, after all, the specialist.

There can sometimes be a strained atmosphere in a dubbing theatre if there are personality clashes between a producer, director and executive producer: for example, over decisions on sound balance. These conflicts lead to 'dubbing by committee', which extends the dubbing time and is often detrimental to the end product.

Problems in balances for dubbing mixers

One of the major problems that a dubbing mixer has is persuading the director not to play the music too loud. The director knows the dialogue by heart, and does not realize that the music could be drowning it. Another problem in the dubbing theatre is that the repetitive process of 'rocking and rolling', continually going over the same small section of the film, can give a fragmented impression of the film and can be very frustrating to those not involved in the mechanics of the operation. The dubbing mixer must take pains to explain what is happening to those with no experience of the system.

These production problems, along with the technical considerations of level control, distortion, operating the various types of equipment etc., present a challenging but rewarding task for a dubbing mixer.

CHAPTER 10

The roles and responsibilities of the sound supervisor

When first assigned to a particular programme, the sound supervisor may know only the title of the production or series, who the producer is, and the date of a planning meeting. Every production, no matter how simple, must be discussed in detail by all the departments involved to explain what type of programme it is and to outline any special requirements that the producer or director may have.

Prior to this first meeting the producer, writer, director, designer and researcher will have had preliminary discussions and ideas, which they will present to the technical and production staff: camera and lighting supervisors, production assistant and others representing stage, props, wardrobe, make-up, electrical department and studio managers. In addition, someone from the facilities department may be there to allocate suitable studios and crews to service the production. By the end of the planning meeting, many of the problems that might occur will have been aired and discussed, and no one should be in any doubt about what the requirements are for their particular involvement in the production.

With this information, and armed with a studio plan from the designer showing the proposed set layout, the sound supervisor will decide how many sound crew are necessary to staff the production. The size of the crew will obviously be determined by the number of sound facilities that are required; for example, will microphone booms be needed and, if so, will they be static or moving? If the latter, it may be necessary to have a boom tracker for each boom. During the time leading up to the first rehearsal the sound supervisor will brief the crew on which microphones to use and, if necessary, will discuss music requirements with the musical director. Microphones and special equipment that are not available in house must be hired. If the production is an outside broadcast, then a survey of the site will be essential in order to anticipate any sound problems prior to the recording date.

It will be the sound supervisor's responsibility, with selected members of the sound crew, to attend any **walk-through** or **technical rehearsals** that may have been organized prior to the recording or transmission of the production. This is where the floor plans will probably be finalized. The actors or artistes will walk through their moves scene by scene, to allow the technical staff to spot any potential problems that may be developing, and for the sound supervisor to decide if two booms are needed, for example, or whether slung or concealed mics would be preferable.

After the studio has been set and lit, the sound crew can begin the **sound rig**. For safety reasons this is always done when the set is in place and all the lights are rigged and in position. Upstairs in the sound gallery the supervisor will be patching the channels on the sound console and checking the tape and grams sources.

When the rig is completed the **camera rehearsal**, sometimes called the **stagger-through**, can take place. This involves blocking out each camera shot in turn and rehearsing it perhaps several times with frequent stops to sort out problems as they occur. This can be a time-consuming business but is very important not only to the camera crew but also to the sound crew, as it gives them a chance to work out boom positions and also to sort out with the lighting crew any shadow problems that may exist. The sound supervisor meanwhile will have assembled all the music and sound effects that have been ordered, and all sound sources will be patched via an audio jackfield to channels on the sound-mixing console. As the rehearsal proceeds, scripts will be marked up and any changes from the original noted.

Hopefully, most sound problems should be sorted out by the end of the camera rehearsal, but if an orchestra or band and vocalists are involved then the sound mixer will need a band-call. This will be organized to happen when the rest of the crew have left the studio, leaving the sound crew, the director and the production assistant, one of whose jobs it will be to time each number as the musicians play through some or all of the music, giving the sound mixer a chance to set a sound balance and vocal levels and to adjust mic placements, public address levels etc.

The next stage in the production schedule will be the **dress rehearsal**. It is here that the sound supervisor will get the first opportunity to get proper voice levels from the artistes, and to set other levels such as equalization, studio foldback and reverberation.

On the day of the **recording** or **transmission** the supervisor will make sure that any last-minute problems, perhaps due to script changes or cuts, are sorted out. At this stage the only unknown factor will be the laughter and applause levels from the audience, if one is present, and these are usually obtained during the audience 'warm-up', which immediately precedes going 'on air', and so into what will hopefully be a smooth, trouble-free recording or live transmission.

CHAPTER 11

Radio microphones

Radio microphones are often seen as the 'saviour' on location, but they present their own unique problems. It is inevitable that a director will see radio mics as the 'first solution' to any wide-shot material.

Radio mic systems do not have a high r.f. output as far as transmitter power is concerned, and are regulated as such. Even though operators within the television networks would observe sensible rules, there seems no chance that any higher-power unit will become available.

The main rules to observe in the use of radio mics are:

1. Ensure that batteries on the transmitter are up to full power; the r.f. output is dependent on battery condition.

2. Ensure that receiver batteries are OK; but this is not as important as the transmitter's batteries.

3. Make sure that all aerials are the correct types for their respective transmitter and receiver and make good electrical connection. Check that the frequencies of transmitter and receiver match each other.

4. Receiver aerials should be as close to the 'action' transmitters as possible to obtain maximum r.f. transfer. If necessary, fit an extension to the aerial lead to get the aerial closer to the action.

5. Diversity systems can be a big advantage as they 'sniff' the signal between two aerial systems and feed the receiver with the stronger signal, depending on transmitter position.

A very useful device is an aerial amplifier tuned to your frequency band with four receiver outputs, allowing single aerial operation across all the receivers. Suitable units are available from Camtech Electronics, Audio Engineering Ltd and other specialist manufacturers. These units have in-built r.f. gain, which helps signal pick-up.

The current situation on **licensing** of radio microphones for studio and location used is outlined in Appendix G.

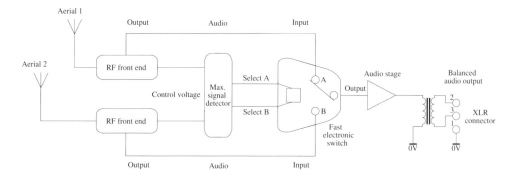

Figure 11.1 Diagram of a typical diversity radio mic system.

SETTING UP RADIO MICROPHONES BEFORE USE

1. Ensure that all battery supplies are up to full power.
2. Check that limiter settings on units are set up correctly if needed.
3. Ensure that aerials on transmitter and receiver are in the optimum positions. Make sure that the transmitter aerial is not touching the artiste's body, which can absorb a great deal of the transmitted power. Check that there are no large metal structures between you and the transmitter.
4. Wherever possible, ensure that the transmitter frequencies are at least 400 kHz apart. When three transmitters or more are in operation, watch out for intermodulation frequencies.
5. It is often possible to 'split the difference' between the recordist and the artistes, and gain maximum signal strength, by using a long cable or extension aerial cable. This gives some added range to the system, owing to the closer proximity of the aerial to the receiver. However, with the emergence of radio timecode systems and the use of RDAT machines, with and without timecode, similar techniques, like moving closer to the action, can be employed as are used in the film industry.

COMMON PROBLEMS WITH RADIO MICROPHONE SYSTEMS

*   It takes longer to rig the extra equipment, such as aerial amplifiers, that is required.
*   The recordist has to carry extra equipment, and crewing levels are being reduced.
*   The extra sound sources used invariably cause more things to go wrong, and may necessitate larger and more bulky mixing equipment to cope with the extra channels.

- The new radio mic regulations have caused a substantial reduction in transmitter power, if using the deregulated channels, causing some problems, in addition to the difficult licensing situation with its tightly controlled frequency regulation.

SUITABLE PERSONAL MICROPHONE HEADS

On most of the popular broadcast radio mic transmitters it is possible to fit different personal mic heads or hand mics. The earlier units only supplied Sony ECM50 personal microphones as their primary head. At present, many heads can be fitted to Micron and Sennheiser and most other systems, provided a suitable cable with the correct connections is made up to suit.

Windshielding of personal mics is a big problem for outside work, because most windshields supplied are inadequate. Recordists usually devise their own 'fiendish' auxiliary windshields from foam and chamois. It is essential to form some sort of barrier to keep the microphone head from rubbing against clothing. Another problem is the reduction of high-frequency response by the clothing itself. A small sleeve fitted around the head of the microphone, extending beyond the microphone rim, can increase high-frequency response, and can be adjusted to yield the appropriate increase of HF.

Microphone types

- **Sony ECM50/55**: Slightly large in modern terms, but generally a good all-round performer. Not easy to hide.
- **Sony ECM77**: Easy to hide because of its small size, and often liked because of its high quality. It would appear to be better for wind noise, but this may be due to its less sensitive response to low frequencies.
- **Tram Neck Mic**: This microphone has a particularly high amount of presence, and in the author's experience is very suitable for hiding beneath clothing. It is very good for picking up 'two way' conversations under 'crash' recording situations as it has an adaptor plate, which makes it work very much like a PZM microphone.
- **Sanken COS11**: The Sanken is a relative newcomer on the scene, has a wide frequency response, and is the smallest of all personal microphones available. The unit is hardly noticeable, even 'in shot' on clothing. Sanken has recently introduced a flesh-coloured microphone, with the case made of ceramic material, which is said to reduce clothing rustle. Also available is a PZM adaptor, made of rubber, which is very useful for planting in obscure positions for a 'set in' microphone.
- **Sennheiser MKE-2/3**: This microphone is supplied as standard with the Sennheiser radio mic transmitter units, and seems to be a reasonably good

mic under studio conditions, but is not easy to windshield effectively for outside locations. A 'drilled out' ECM77 windshield is quite effective as an auxiliary windshield. A 'flesh-coloured' version is available, which is more difficult to see in shot.

Any criticism expressed of the microphones mentioned is, of course, only the opinion of the author. Many other suitable heads exist that can be used by a sound engineer, and which may be just as suitable for the particular use to which they are put.

RADIO MICS IN THE STUDIO

It is difficult to envisage a studio programme nowadays that will not require the use of at least one radio mic. In the past, radio mics were viewed with suspicion as likely to give more problems than they might solve, and it was not unusual for a sound supervisor to use a cabled personal mic on a presenter or artiste rather than risk unexplainable problems like noise or 'birdies', which often occurred without warning and for no obvious reason. However, with the advent of the **diversity system** many of the problems were eliminated. This system provides two receivers for each channel; each receiver is constantly monitoring the incoming signal from the transmitter and switching the output to the receiver providing the best signal. In the studio, for a big production, it is not unusual to have a large number of channels of diversity. As mentioned elsewhere, by using the smaller range of personal mics, it is possible for the sound supervisor to provide good quality pick-up in virtually any situation.

The diversity receivers can be mains powered, thus avoiding the problems with regular battery replacement that can occur on location, where no mains supply is available, but of course it will still be necessary to replace the batteries in the transmitters immediately prior to use and for a member of the sound crew to regularly check and monitor the incoming signals to the receivers. The incoming signal strengths are displayed on the receivers, usually as LED indications, and careful monitoring of these can give adequate warning of any possible problems.

Careful siting of the aerials is another extremely important consideration prior to a studio production. They must be placed in the optimum position to obtain unrestricted pick-up, but of course remain out of picture. A lot of metal hardware such as camera cranes and microphone booms is moving around, which may give problems, and of course the shape and construction of the set must also be taken into consideration: lots of metal might mean lots of problems with the radio mic signals.

CHAPTER 12

Location recording

THE ART OF LOCATION SOUND RECORDING

Sound recording is an art, but too often it is treated as a simple requisite to accompany the picture on screen, and not given the respect and importance it deserves. Look at the range of TV programming. Drama, music programmes, and documentaries that include drama content: they are all created illusions. The sound added to the pictures can create whatever atmosphere the director wishes to convey to the viewer. The simple addition of sound effects or music can create different moods. Often these effects can create a feeling in the listener that is quite the opposite to the displayed picture, perhaps enhancing suspense before the event. Simple production sets can be used, with sound effects and music adding the suggestion of the set's location. By simply adding seaside effects the listener could think that the whole action was by the seaside. Swap these effects to airport effects, and the listener will assume that they are within an airport.

So audio has its role to play in accompanying visual illusions, and the sound recordist has an equal role in supplementing this illusion. For example, it would be entirely wrong on drama material to present sound quality recorded in a room or hall next to a motorway over shots that are intended to represent an 18th century drawing room. On location, the visual setting might be perfect 18th century, but there are high levels of 20th century background noise. However, with careful shooting (and traffic control) you can obtain perfectly acceptable audio for the period portrayed by the pictures.

We have become used to high-quality drama audio produced by choosing ideal locations and controlling extraneous noise by good unit management. Alas, modern streamlining of crews and shortened shooting times have reduced the chances of achieving such a high-quality product. Post-sync is still common on film productions, and is preplanned as part of the budget, but it is rarely included as a budgeted item in current television productions.

The cameraperson and sound recordist working alongside the production team can help to create an overall image, with good audio tracks supplementing the location pictures. But there is no sound effect library that can supply a track that will exactly match the atmosphere at the moment the original sound was recorded. Indeed, in recent discussions on the future of audio in TV and films, senior dubbing mixers and editors have complained that the tighter shooting conditions in film and television have caused a lack of suitable wildtracks, atmosphere tracks and buzz tracks. To have to swamp out dialogue in a dub with an inappropriate stock atmosphere can cause serious disruption to an otherwise 'clean' base soundtrack.

Two events from my own casebook will serve to describe the type of input that a recordist can have, and also how it is possible to make the wrong decisions with the best of intentions.

On a drama documentary production it was decided at the preplanning stage that the drama portions would be shot as drama and the documentary portions shot as traditional documentary inserts. The recordist's decision was to follow the same pattern, and use personal mics for the documentary portions and boom-operated open microphones for the drama portions. On viewing the completed programme, it was clear that this was the wrong decision. It seriously disrupted the overall flow of the programme: the changes in location from period to modern times were quite acceptable pictorially, but the corresponding changes on the audio tracks were all too obvious. It would have been far better to record the audio in the drama style, giving smooth transitions between sections. This is a good example of how illusions can be spoilt by bad planning and decisions.

The second case concerns a social documentary production, which required a large amount of secret filming. In the preplanning stages it was decided to use radio microphones with extremely large high-gain aerials, allowing the camera to 'stand off' from the subjects. During filming on Day 1 this proved to be the right decision. The 'dodgy subjects' in the programme were duly 'miked up' with their radio transmitters. Within 10 minutes they had forgotten that they were 'wired for sound', and one of them uttered the immortal words, 'We had better be careful with this lot; they may rumble us'. Until then, the producer and researcher were not sure if the subjects were genuine or not, but from that moment on it was clear that they were. During the course of the shooting of the documentary, participants in the programme were used as portable microphones by putting themselves into the required situations with them; the subjects were the only sound source.

The second case shows how recordists can add their art to enhance a programme in a dramatic way. The first case could perhaps have upset only the professional sound engineer and the recordist, but in fact it helped to stop the smooth flow of the programme. It is difficult to reverse your techniques on a production once you are well into shooting. A basic principle of good location recording is to obtain a smooth audio track, to supply the cleanest track possible to the dubbing suite, where the illusion can start to be created almost like a plain cake with no decoration. The dubbing process enhances this location track; the dubbing suite can add all the niceties, and from a clean base track create almost any 'feel' that they wish.

Choice of microphones can add to the artistic feel of the audio tracks. The 'open' type of microphone gives a more natural feel than the closer sound of the personal microphone. In choosing the right microphone for the job at hand, many of the decisions are based on experience and personal choice. No two sound recordists will make exactly the same choices given the same situation, but in general terms the use of personal microphones is more prevalent in documentary material and news and current affairs programming, as wider picture angles can be obtained. Modern location shooting speeds do not allow a recordist time to experiment with different types of microphone; this often causes the recordist to go for a safe, and even standard choice of microphone coverage.

Some of the extremely high-quality studio microphones cannot easily be used on location because of their very good low-frequency response and hence susceptibility to wind noise and rumble. Although a lot of this interference can be reduced by low-frequency equalization, this will not help if the high frequencies are modulated by low-frequency disturbances at the time of the recording. The Sennheiser and other ranges of microphones have frequency responses that are ideally suitable for location work, and have set a standard for drama quality. However, setting a standard to a particular microphone can make other perfectly acceptable microphones of even higher quality seem unacceptable after long periods of time. For example, recordists often have doubts when first using a new stereo rifle mic, as it often seems to be lacking in 'presence' compared with a microphone used for mono.

Many dubbing mixers, like recordists, tend to 'play safe', judging quality by their previously set standards, which is understandable. They will often correct the audio track to the audio quality of the Sennheiser or other type of microphone previously used. In effect, they are taking the previous microphone as their standard, and correcting all other sound to that standard. This could easily be a retrograde step, as it does not allow for the improving quality of the more modern microphones. Great changes have occurred on the distribution side of broadcast sound with the introduction of the near-digital quality of the Nicam system. People often forget that as quality has improved all the way to the transmitter, so improvement of the mono FM track at the transmitter will also benefit the normal TV listeners' received audio quality.

Audio quality is a personal choice. Often two directors will disagree on audio quality, as would two recordists. The main aim of the recordist is to supply the highest-quality sound under the prevailing conditions, with the assumption that what will follow will inevitably be a loss of quality in some form. (This would not be the case with a suitable all-digital audio chain.) BBC training always made sound engineers aware that they must go for the highest quality under all conditions, and there seems no doubt that this should be uppermost in all recordist's minds, bearing in mind the location limitations, and the possibility of degrading the signal if it is not handled totally within a digital environment.

Equalization on location should be restricted to the minimum, and only used across the low-frequency areas. EQ can be much more easily applied in the dubbing or sweetening areas after the audio is recorded, provided the location recordist has left enough of the original broad band of audio for the post-production dubbing mixer to equalize.

Monitoring audio on location on headphones presents a few problems. High-quality headsets of the 'open ear' type are not often used because of the risk of acoustic spill from the sides of the headset onto the location audio. The location requirement is for the 'closed ear' type, which will allow the recordist to judge background levels correctly.

Much criticism can be made of monitoring on headphones for stereo. Because it is almost impossible to have any time-of-arrival difference on headphones they are unreliable for judging a stereo image. Often, monitoring music on 'closed ear' headsets results in the recordist mixing with far too 'tight' a balance, and generally not giving a good representation of the stereo width. Stereo image is better judged on loudspeakers. However, it is rare that the location recordist can have a separate room to monitor in this fashion. As well as the problems that there may be due to long cable runs back to the camera recorders, there may also be problems in getting a reverse confidence return (a monitoring signal of the actual recorded sound) from the source recording the material.

Headphone monitoring is generally all right for speech, although in 'high background' locations it can be difficult to judge separation between background and dialogue, particularly when using headphones of the 'open ear' type. Headphone monitoring can also make the recordist too critical of background noise and extraneous noise, which may not be as obvious when replayed via loudspeaker monitor circuits.

MICROPHONES SUITABLE FOR GENERAL LOCATION WORK

The standard broadcast kit

The standard broadcast standard kit for general location work is set up as follows:

- Sennheiser 816 or 416 rifle microphone, or similar by alternative manufacturer;
- two or three personal microphones, usually Tram or Sony ECM55/77;
- one or two radio mics, Sennheiser, Audio Ltd or, more commonly, Micron types;
- hand mics, usually Electrovoice RE50, Beyer M58, or AKG D130.

Two most useful microphones for extreme background situations (on board aircraft or within noisy factories) are the Beyer M160 and the Electrovoice DS35. A less directional microphone, such as the AKG D130 or Beyer equivalent, is a more practical proposition in the hands of an inexperienced interviewer, as you are likely to have fewer 'off mics' than with the highly directional type of microphone. The addition to the above kit of a stereo microphone, such as a Neumann RSM191 or a suitable figure-of-eight microphone, 'piggybacked' with the rifle microphone, could facilitate stereo operation (see below).

You can make your location kit up from whatever manufacturer of microphones you favour. The above list is not definitive; many other combinations can be made and prove successful on location, as the list of suitable microphones is continually growing.

Using stereo rifle mics on location

It is advantageous to have a small range of stereo rifle mics for location use. The choice of rifle mic element should be one that has enough 'reach' for the job but does not have too much pull from the distance, as this can cause a confused stereo image. The Neumann RSM191 seems to be the most popular, thanks to its one-piece construction. All the microphone elements are housed in one case together with the matrix box that allows variable microphone pick-up patterns. The RSM191 has the capability to work in M/S or A/B stereo. The microphone has an adjustable side signal, which effectively alters the pick-up angle: the forward pick-up angle decreases with more side signal. This can be confusing, as some studios require as much side signal as possible. However, if the studio has the facility to remix or reduce this signal, no problems will occur, as the required width can be obtained by altering the level of the side signal.

As the side-signal microphone is basically of a figure-of-eight type, some problems can occur with low-frequency signals, such as wind noise while working on outside locations, so suitable windshields should be used. Some extra built-in reduction of the low-frequency component of the side signal is applied within the RSM191. There is some criticism of the Neumann RSM191 from film industry dubbing mixers, who say that it upsets their Dolby surround systems with phasing effects. Some BBC dubbing mixers have also expressed doubt about the stability of the stereo image, but none has cited any problems with mono image stability.

Many recordists prefer to use their usual rifle mic for the centre component, with a suitable figure-of-eight microphone mounted above in a 'piggyback' mode for the side signal, for operating in M/S stereo. Sennheiser has produced a microphone with very low noise level for the figure-of-eight microphone; however, windshields are still important, and the system is not as convenient to use as the all-in-one microphone. Generally, this configuration is a little tight for the usual windshields used for, say, the Sennheiser 416 type of microphone, which is pretty standard across the industry as the rifle mic element. An external matrix would be required for A/B stereo operation. These matrix units are now available either as separate units or built into the front end of the new range of portable mixers.

Balance of the stereo channels must be accurate as far as any microphone pairs are concerned, and must be accurately set up by the recordist to avoid an unbalanced stereo image. The overall stereo level control should be of the ganged type on each individual stereo pair to avoid image weave. When considering the position of any dialogue or interview material, remember that any spread towards the outer limits of this dialogue will decrease the central mono image and reduce mono compatibility when the A/B legs of the stereo are summed for mono transmission.

SUITABLE PORTABLE CONSOLES FOR LOCATION WORK

The unit should have the lowest noise level possible for broadcast purposes. Size and portability are also very important. One aspect that is often forgotten is battery power: with 12-hour days now common, it is essential to have long battery duration. Most sound recordists tend to use auxiliary battery supplies, which gives them longer potential working time while keeping overall costs down. The front end of the portable mixer must be sufficiently flexible for you to accept the extremely variable levels of sound that you are likely to meet in everyday use. Now that the quality of semi-professional equipment is so good, it is useful to be able to accept line levels at –14 dBm.

Line or **high-level signals** usually range from –14 dBm, which is domestic line level, to +8 dBm and higher (professional levels). **Low-level signals** from microphones and guitar pick-ups are generally much lower than this: in the region of –70 to –14 dBm. Signals as low as this require good-quality high-gain amplifiers, with good signal-to-noise capabilities. It is possible, particularly with guitars, that you can obtain an amplified output from the head amplifier after the guitar. Capacitor microphones generally output levels much higher than the –70 dBm levels, somewhere in the region of –20 dBm; they can output up to 0 dBm if placed close to, say, a guitar amplifier or similar high-level sound source. It is important to take great care with screening of leads carrying low-level signals, as they are more susceptible to interference from outside electrical sources. This does not, however, apply to the higher output line level signals usually met on location.

It is important to be able to switch between these levels at the mixer channel input, and that the switches are convenient. This is perhaps the main variation

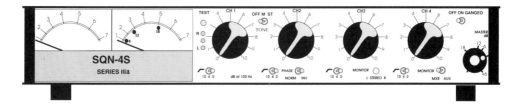

Figure 12.1 The front panel of the SQN-4S Series IIIa portable mixer, showing the operational controls.

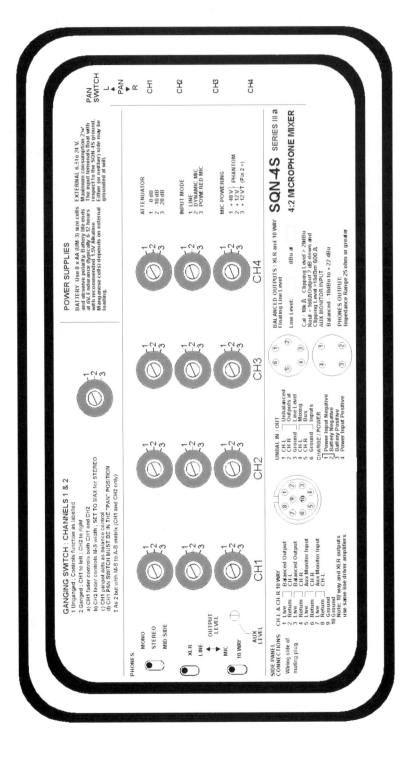

Figure 12.2 The baseplate of the SQN-4S Series IIIa portable mixer, showing the preset level controls, microphone powering, headphone monitoring and output level controls.

in portable mixer units: the faders are always on the top panel, but this is not always true of the operational adjustments and input switching. Portable studio style mixer units, of course, have all controls on the top panel, as do the larger studio desks. Phantom powering for all types of capacitor microphone is required, and balanced line inputs are essential.

Stereo operation is essential, with at least two pairs of outputs switchable between microphone-level and line-level output. The output must be balanced; it is a simple operation to unbalance a balanced output, but not so easy to balance an unbalanced output. Four outputs from the mixer will be required to cope with the four digital tracks on the new location digital video equipment. At the time of writing the only truly portable UK-designed location mixer with four outputs is produced by Filmtech, but SQN will have a version of their mixer with four outputs available in 1995.

Very few portable units have **slider-type faders**, but SQN currently have one available as a modification to all the 4-S series models. Filmtech have available within their new mixer unit a socket on the rear to accommodate an external slider fader unit. Sliders are easier to handle when the fader count is high, particularly in music balancing, as more channels can be handled with one hand.

Portable mixer units like the SQN-3 and 4-S provide **bass attenuation** on each channel, which is switchable and operates around 100 Hz, giving two cuts of −4 dB and −10 dB. These attenuators are provided primarily to cut room boominess and wind noise on microphones, but there is no real substitute for a good efficient windshield on a microphone.

Most portable mixers currently on sale are equipped with **PPMs**, although they can be ordered to your own requirements, either V/U or PPM. PPM metering gives the best results, as it reflects the ear's response more closely and is easier to follow. PPM types differ, so most manufacturers will supply the type applicable to the country concerned.

Provisions are made within the SQN and other portable mixers for monitoring stereo and mono, with the capability of monitoring an M/S stereo recording, as a switchable matrix is available within all the current models. A useful facility in portable mixer units is an auxiliary return feed that can be fed from the headphone monitor socket from the Betacam system or, indeed, any system that you may be feeding with your sound mix.

Currently available from SQN is a lead that takes a feed from the playback adaptor socket on the side of some Sony cameras; this lead does not suffer from timecode breakthrough on the output when monitoring. It also allows monitoring of stereo, as the Sony camcorder headphone socket is a mono feed. Another advantage is that it frees the headphone socket for the cameraperson to monitor the audio, and the monitor feed will not be subject to changes resulting from adjustments of the camera headphone level. The auxiliary feed at the mixer end is normally adjustable for a wide variety of levels, either balanced or unbalanced.

A **monitor return** is always seen as an essential item while recording in the field, as so many connections are temporary, and require constant monitoring to avoid accidental disconnection during recording. This 'return' monitor feed gives the recordist the ability to monitor his outgoing audio and check for level drops or even total signal losses on the remote recording device by the flick of a switch. Special multicore leads are available containing return and output feeds, enabling the recordist to eliminate a heap of tangled cables.

The current range of portable mixers includes a **phase check** for stereo operation. This is effected by merging the two outputs on the monitor circuit, to give the recordist a check on the phasing of the overall stereo mix, in the event of any cabling or other phase errors.

SQN was the first manufacturer to produce a broadcast-quality mixer back in 1980. This was the SQN-3, originally available in two versions. The Type C was dedicated to the Nagra SNN tape recorder, and gave it more facilities than the larger quarter inch Nagra machines could offer (the tiny recorder being mounted on the mixer). The Type M was designed to feed any recorder by cable, and this latter version remains in production to this day. Despite its name the SQN-3 has always featured four inputs, but only three microphone channels able to power all professional microphones. It is interesting that the people responsible for the design and production of these units were themselves film sound recordists, so a model was produced that exactly fitted the bill for location film work in the original concept. Much of this knowledge has now been used by other manufacturers to cover recording alongside video.

The stereo SQN-4S followed in 1984 as a logical development for stereo recordings, and the growing requirement for flexibility with video. In the UK at least it has acquired the status of 'industry standard', just as the SQN-3 did. The name SQN came from the Latin *sine qua non*, which means 'indispensable', and seems very apt.

LOCATION RECORDING PREPARATION

Before setting out for location, it is essential for the sound recordist to determine the following information.

1. Does the sound kit that is to be used have all the necessary equipment (including spare batteries)? A thorough check of the kit at this stage can save embarrassment later when actually on location.
2. Will the recording(s) be made inside or outside? This information will determine the choice of microphones and ancillary equipment that may be needed, such as desk mics and stands, which may not be part of the normal complement of gear in the kit.
3. Will the participants be seated, standing or perhaps even walking? If walking, then there could be a requirement for radio mics, and as these

may not be part of the standard equipment contained in the location kit, they may need to be hired before leaving for location.

4. Will it be necessary to record wildtracks or Amos tracks for use later in editing or post-production? It is often much better (and more realistic) for the editor or post-production sound mixer to use tracks actually recorded on location rather than use effects (FX) from a CD or tape library.

Having as much information as possible before the event should help to ensure a smooth, trouble-free operation, which could save time and perhaps budget. Preferably, the recordist should be able to reconnoitre the location beforehand, so that any additional equipment that may be needed, and which is not available from stock, may be hired. A director will choose a location for light, for its decor, and for attractive backgrounds that will enhance the pictures. This may not suit the sound recordist, whose ideal location would be one that had good acoustics (not too lively), and was free from traffic noises or other unwanted sounds that might give sound problems on the day, such as loud air conditioning, or frequent aircraft passing overhead. In practise a 'recce' is not always possible. In this case the recordist should try to anticipate what the requirements may be, by using any information gathered and perhaps any local knowledge of the location.

MIXING SOUND ON LOCATION

When mixing sound it is the recordist's role to maintain an equal balance between all participants in an interview, and a good overall pleasing balance on music. These levels should be kept within a good dynamic range, up to the maximum limits of the system's headroom, always keeping a good signal-to-noise ratio in mind.

Keeping the audio well up towards the system maximum helps to avoid the introduction of hiss or noise, although a certain amount of system noise is introduced by any mixer, except perhaps a digital mixer. The requirement for broadcast and, to a certain extent, all recordings is to ride the levels manually and keep a reasonable dynamic range: not so wide as to cause the listener to reach for the volume control. Broadcast level control was covered in Chapter 2: see p. 26.

Choice of the correct microphone is vital. Remember that there will be some spill between microphones, which will add reverberation and external noise to the mixed tracks, so the fewer mics required on a given location the better. Once you have chosen a microphone, place it in the optimum position to gain the best signal-to-noise ratio. *Any* offending background noise or interference is noise as far as recording an audio signal is concerned, and the source of sound being recorded is the signal.

You should always consider the use of other microphones to supplement the main microphones. This might entail an extra microphone in position at a fixed spot, or the use of other microphones to loosen the perspective of the camera shot. These techniques are particularly important when you are using radio microphones, because of their closeness to the source of sound, and because you may be having to use them for a shot that is too wide to use conventional techniques. If a shot is very wide but the actual sound is very close the resulting effect can be very peculiar: hence the need for an extra microphone to add perspective to the audio.

Ensure that you are not overloading prior to entering the mixer unit, as you will be unable to remove this distortion inside the mixer, and will indeed amplify the distortion problem. Careful microphone placement is very important here. It is very easy to overload a capacitor microphone, prior to feeding it to a microphone channel. Most capacitor mics have an attenuator at the microphone head to avoid overloading the preamplifier inside the microphone shell. Some models have acoustic attenuators, which will reduce overload or input level.

It is equally important to avoid overload distortion on the inputs of microphone channels by using the input attenuators to reduce the gain of the channels. Only location experience can tell you where to set the input sensitivity; it cannot be judged by simple calculations. Given a mixer with three input sensitivity levels, the obvious safe setting is the middle position, halfway between the two extreme settings. Often a line level feed from semi-professional equipment may fall halfway between a microphone input at its minimum level and a line level at its minimum level setting. In this case you could select the attenuated microphone input level, which would probably allow you more flexibility of levels. Remember that you may experience high input levels in locations such as factories and airports; be prepared to adjust your mixer sensitivity accordingly.

Aim to have your faders about three-quarters of the way up their travel, allowing the rest of the fader to give you some extra gain. The main overall fader should be at its unity level, with the facility to add some overall gain to your total mixed output, if required. It would be too late when you find your faders at the backstops and need to reduce your main overall gain control. The inexperienced operator, when mixing a music show for the first time, inevitably finds that he or she has decreased the input levels on the microphone channels, needs to bring up the main gain controls, and then has nowhere to go. At some time this happens to all sound mixers or balancers but, given experience, the sound mixer should always have spare capacity on the faders on all channels. Only occasionally should you find yourself at the top of the faders fighting for level when a real emergency occurs.

It is not within the scope of this book to cover the total concept of mixing audio, as it is often a matter of personal choice and one that can take many years to master. Choice of microphone, too, is often personal; you can often get the same result from a varying range of choices. Suitable further reading is suggested in Appendix A (p. 183).

CHAPTER 13

The Nagra recorder on a film location

With the introduction of the Nagra recorder it became possible to record high-quality audio on location and synchronize this with the pictures. Prior to this, the audio tracks were recorded on **stripe film**: 16 mm film with a magnetic stripe down each. One stripe was used for the recording; the other was a balancing stripe on the other side to even out the film path and help winding on to the spool. Slung underneath the camera, or integrated within it, was a set of audio recording heads; the recordist used an external preamplifier/mixer to record onto the tracks. This system recorded the tracks in sync with the pictures, but required careful setting of the film loop within the camera.

The main problems with this system were the umbilical cord from the external mixer unit to the camera and the poor speed stability within the system, which caused very poor audio quality. This made music recordings impossible, or certainly of poor listening quality. A further problem with the combined magnetic system was the restricted audio bandwidth that resulted from the narrow track widths on the film. The introduction of the Nagra audio recorder, running quarter inch tape, eliminated the problems of the combined system. It used the full track width of the quarter inch tape, allowing a better frequency response, and could operate at higher speeds, giving a further improvement on the frequency response.

Initially, the Nagra system had a **sync lead**, which was a lead carrying a synchronizing pulse from the camera to be recorded on a separate track on the Nagra recorder. This pulse track followed the camera's speed variations. Back at base a transfer of the audio tracks was made, controlled by the location-recorded pulse track, to 16 mm or 35 mm film. Normally 16 mm was used in broadcasting studios; 35 mm was rare in television work except for prestige productions. This early system included a **silent turnover** circuit, which was simply a few frames of film 'flashed', and an audio tone pulse sent to the Nagra recorder and recorded on the normal Nagra audio track. This allowed synchronization without the normal clapperboards. The next improvement was to use a crystal-controlled motor in the camera and a 50 Hz crystal pulse generator in the Nagra recorder. This did away with the sync lead and allowed the sound recordist to 'roam free' and be in the right place to collect the sound tracks without the fixed connecting cord.

The introduction of **timecode** to film saw the introduction of the timecode Nagra, which had a timecode generator replacing the 50 Hz pulse generator. It is also possible to have both types of system on current machines. Timecode working allows the vision tracks to be synchronized electronically with the audio tracks, and can do away with the traditional clapperboard for synchronization. Under traditional film techniques, an assistant film editor placed the clapperboard in visual sync with the pictures by matching the visual identification on the clapperboard with the audio identification on the transferred audio tracks. This can now be achieved electronically by transferring the film to videotape and matching the timecode on the audio and video. When using a timecode Nagra it is usual to 'jam sync' the Nagra timecode recorder to the generator in the film camera. However, on some occasions the reverse is necessary, with the camera locking to the Nagra recorder.

No definitive standard has been laid down for the recording of timecode on film, and so several different methods are currently in use. Many people ask, 'What is the need for timecode in film?', as manual editing of film, using edge numbers and clapper marks has been used for many years without problems. The answer to this question is the need to transfer film onto videotape, which has no sprocket holes, edge numbers, or visible clap points. Timecode can be likened to the edge numbers on film that locate each frame; timecode identifies each individual frame of video picture. The sprocket holes in film identify the individual frames of picture; the control track in a video signal is the video version of these sprocket holes.

Two different recording media for timecode in film are currently in use: a magnetic strip along the side of the film, and optical recording on the film itself. The Nagra IV-S TC was developed to be compatible with both types, provided the final product is an SMPTE/EBU longitudinal timecode. There are various methods of optical recording of timecode, such as block matrix and barcode. The problem of recording and reading timecode on film is outside the scope of this book; we are concerned here with the compatibility of the IV-S TC with all other systems.

To use the Nagra IV-S TC with film, the procedure to follow is almost identical to that for video, except that the continuous need to make a SET FROM EXT each time a camera stops is not necessary, as the colour framing problems that occur in video do not occur in film.

Working in the UK presents no real problems with timecode, but if you are shooting in the USA, or using equipment from the USA, you should take great care to use the appropriate timecode system, as they are different. The Nagra recorder is capable of generating the American 'drop frame' system, and this is switchable within the recorder. Many horror stories are told of recordists who have sent material to the USA and discovered sync problems when attempting to synchronize or assemble the material.

Before the introduction of timecode it was only necessary to record at the correct frame rate on the camera and recorder; if this was wrong, it could be simply converted in the transfer. Sadly, this is a little more difficult in the timecode field.

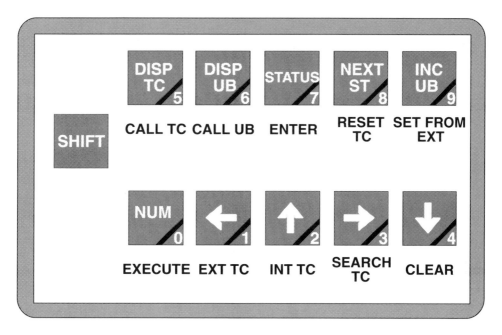

Figure 13.1   The digital entry keyboard of the Nagra IV-S TC recorder.

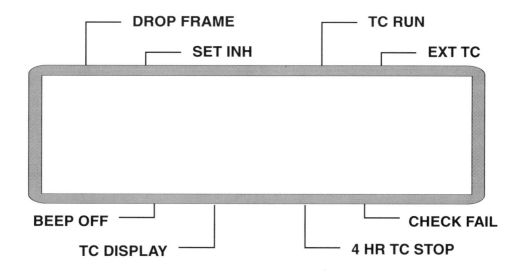

Figure 13.2   The liquid crystal display of the Nagra IV-S TC recorder.

As the Nagra IV-S TC timecode machine is a little difficult to set up, and first-time users have to resort to the handbook, a simplified set-up procedure is shown in Figure 13.3. (Excerpts from the Nagra IV-S TC handbook are printed with the kind permission of Nagra Kudelski (GB) Ltd.)

NAGRA IV-S TIMECODE RECORDER: SIMPLIFIED OPERATING INSTRUCTIONS

Early Aaton film cameras with the Origin C master timecode clock had an RS232 serial interface system, which does not work correctly with some timecode Nagra machines, and entails the machine having a sub-board type QSIA fitted: this is a

> **Direct function**   : Simply press the key
> **Numeric function**   : First press the NUM key (a direct function) – "00000000" will be displayed
                                        Then press the desired numeric keys followed by a 'shifted function'
> **Shifted function**   : First press the SHIFT key (a toggle function)
                                        Then press the desired shifted function

To do the following	Follow this key sequence...
> **Start the generator**	NUM...1...0...1...SHIFT...EXECUTE
> **Set the generator**	DISP TC...NUM...[hh : mm : ss : ff]...SHIFT...ENTER
> **Modify the generator**	SHIFT. .CALL TC..[use arrow keys to modify].SHIFT..ENTER
> **To increment user bits**	SHIFT...CALL UB...INC UB

The numeric codes indicated on the LCD display are as follows...

000 - No operation	100 - Record Run Mode	200 - System reset
001 - Beep on speaker	101 - Clear "Record Run" mode	
002 - Beep on phones	102 - Disable setting	
003 - Beep on	103 - Enable setting	
004 - Beep off	104 - Permanent memory	
005 - Reset UB	105 - 3 days back-up	
006 - Set ext TC	106 - Date Mode (UB dd mm yy)	
007 - Set ext UB	107 - UB free use	
	108 - Cont jam sync	
	109 - 5 fr error limit	
	110 - Auto ext set mode	
	111 - Exit auto set mode	

Timecode frame rate standard selection is inside the recorder and the status is indicated on the LCD

These instructions should be used in conjunction with the drawings of the Nagra 1V-S Timecode keyboard and LCD display in Figures 13.1 and 13.2.

Figure 13.3   Simplified version of the operating instructions for the Nagra IV-S TC recorder. (Courtesy Nagra Kudelski (GB) Ltd.)

'piggyback' board to be installed internally on the timecode circuit. The software in the timecode Nagra must be version 1.7 and beyond, in order for the option to function. (This can be seen by looking at the last line of the STATUS menu on the keyboard.) This allows communication between Aaton timecode cameras and the Origin C Aaton master timecode clock. With this option, the internal clock of the Nagra IV-S TC can be set from the Origin C and vice versa. The internal generator of the Nagra must, however, be in the DATE UB (numerical command 106) mode, as the Origin C does not accept FREE UB. Although the above machines are mostly modified by now, watch out for them, and the older Aaton film camera.

It is possible to synchronize DAT machines with film cameras, and usually with only clapperboards, as the DAT machines are as stable as the crystal-controlled Nagra audio recorders. Timecode-capable DAT machines are available, and a few four-head machines have been introduced, descriptions of which are included within this book. Early DAT machines did not allow the monitoring of the audio off tape, which was always possible on the Nagra, and this made sound recordists a little hesitant to use the machines. However, this has improved with the introduction of the Stellavox, Fostex and Aiwa/HHB four-head DAT machines, as they have off-tape monitoring facilities.

Set-ups on DAT machines with timecode are often very fiddly, and require the operator to read the handbook carefully. Battery usage is usually high, and requires the recordist to carry many spare batteries. It is not unusual for a recordist on drama productions to back up the DAT machine with a Nagra ana-logue recorder for safety reasons. Many recordists question the advantages of using digital machines, as when Dolby SR noise reduction systems are used throughout the shooting and dubbing of a production a highly satisfying result can be achieved using purely analogue techniques. This is often put down as a reactionary attitude.

Much of the pressure to use timecode editing and recording systems comes from the video side of the industry, although the tried and tested film techniques are returning on some locations. The high costs in video editing suites are making traditional methods often cheaper, even though they require more manpower.

SYNCHRONIZATION WITH VIDEO ON LOCATION

The video system of recording has started out by using tracks on the actual videotape. Usually four tracks are available: two analogue and two FM tracks (which can only be recorded with pictures). As this is a combined system, it suffers from the same problems as early stripe film: the lack of mobility for the recordist and, to some extent, a restricted audio response, although this is not quite as bad as with the early film system.

The Nagra timecode recorder is perfectly happy working with film cameras and video cameras, and so can be used as a separate audio recorder. Of course,

DAT timecode machines can also be used with video, as can non-timecode machines; however, non-timecode DAT machines require the use of clapperboards to allow synchronization with the picture.

Synchronization on the standard tracks is automatic, as they are recorded in a fixed position on the tape, and in editing can be simply transferred at the same time as the pictures, or later in a different place when recorded as wildtracks. However, sync should be checked frequently, as it has been known to be shifted by anomalies of sound head placement on some video recorders in the past.

The introduction of digital audio tracks on video will improve the audio quality, but they will be an integral part of the videotape and recorded alongside the video signal on the same tape. This will still restrict the movements of the sound recordist and crew.

Separate sound systems are useful on video locations to save time when recording wildtracks or atmosphere tracks, as they allow more freedom of movement for the sound crew, and also do not tie the camera down as a recording machine and hold up the location shooting.

Within the video editing suite, the editor has complete freedom to use the audio tracks, which are controlled alongside the video by the timecode track. There are some restrictions on the use of FM: they have to be recorded with a picture track, because they are an integral part of the video signal. This makes them almost unusable, apart from transferring down as an original track, and being used as an analogue track in real terms.

It is possible to use, on locations, a DAT synchronizing system that is similar to the Aaton film system. This system, called Clockit, puts a timecode burst on the normal audio tracks on the camera and DAT recorder's turnover. This burst of timecode is regenerated back at a transfer suite and recorded to a separate tape, or other system, for synchronization with the video pictures.

Audio guide tracks are probably recorded on the video camera's built-in camera mic to assist in editing. The quality of these recordings usually makes them unusable as main tracks.

USING THE NAGRA IV-S TC WITH VIDEO

All video recorders interlock their timecode generators, in both phase and speed, with the synchronizing signal supplied by the video camera. In order to align the timecode signal and the image while complying with the requirement for **colour framing** of the image, it is always necessary to use the timecode signal furnished by the video system master clock. As a result, each time the video camera is switched on, the timecode generator is moved by one, two or three frames, depending on how many frames the video system needs to move to get into the next eight-field sequence of video framing. This would cause an additive error with sync on the free-running Nagra recorder, which has no colour-framing sequence.

In theory, the timecode need never move more than two frames; however, in practice a video system always moves the generator forwards. Experience has shown that the scanning and timecode generator circuits in some 'professional' video cameras are very unsophisticated. Jumps forward of up to 17 frames in one go are possible, and the amount of jump in code is unpredictable. Because of this effect, it is necessary to **jam sync** the internal generator of the IV-S TC each time the video camera is started. Despite the fact that the internal generator on the IV-S TC is accurate to one frame in 8 hours, as the video timecode is changing at the start of each take, a **jam sync** must be made to prevent cumulative errors in the timecode throughout the production.

For the above reasons, the Nagra timecode machine is equipped with an **auto set** function to minimize the amount of keyboard manipulation on each take while working with video. Provided you remember, then working with video without permanent cable connections is possible.

WORKING WITH A CABLE LINK WITH ONE OR MORE CAMERAS

This working mode is normally only used when the internal generator of the video camera does not allow **free-run** (or real-time) timecode to be used.

First, switch on the camera(s), set all their timecode generators (if there are several cameras), and check that the **gen locks** have been performed correctly. Then connect the IV-S TC to the timecode output of the camera or video that has been chosen as the master. Check that all the frame rates etc. are the same (using the **status** mode and **next ST mode** on the IV-S TC), modify where necessary, and make sure that the automatic error detection/correction on the IV-S TC has been selected. Finally, press **shift** followed by **ext TC** and start shooting.

Free-run or real-time working

This is when a camera's or recorder's timecode is set to the 'time of day', and each shot is referred to the actual time of day. This type of working gives disjointed code but refers only to the time of day. It allows many rolls of tape within one day, and does not require separate roll numbers on the timecode; however, it is usual to have the date within the timecode user bits.

Record-run working

This is when a camera or recorder has set its timecode at '00.00.00.00.' and the timecode is continuous from zero until the end of the tape, with each new tape starting at zero but with a different tape roll number for each tape. This type of operation gives a continuous code on tape, with each tape identified by its individual roll number. If the internal generator detects a problem with the incoming timecode, Error 02 will be displayed.

Drop frame

In video, the timecode generator is locked to the video signal. In other words, the timecode and the video image advance at exactly the same rate. For black and white television (monochrome) in the USA, the frame rate is 30 frames per second. However, the American colour television system does not actually use a whole number of frames per second; the National Television Standards Committee has fixed its frame rate at 29.97 frames per second (or more exactly 29.970 026 17 frames per second). This means that a signal measured at 30 frames per second would have a delay of 0.03 frame each second. Thus, at the end of 1 hour of recording, the cumulative timing difference between a clock and the code recorded on tape would be 108 frames or 3.6 s.

In order to restore the timecode reading and make it correspond to real time, the television industry in America has developed the **drop frame** compensation system. The problem is to find a way to lose 108 frames per hour. The solution adopted by the NTSC was not to count the first two frames (00 and 01) at the start of each new minute. If the calculation is now made, 120 frames are lost each minute. However, 12 frames too many are omitted during 1 hour's recording. In order to recover these 12 frames, it was decided to count the first two frames every tenth minute.

To summarize, when using the drop frame mode, the NTSC system eliminates the counting of two frames each minute, except in minutes 00, 10, 20, 30, 40, 50:

Passage of minutes	Passage of tenth minute
hh.mm.ss.ff	hh.mm.ss.ff
12.45.59.28	12.49.59.28
12.45.59.29	12.49.59.29
12.46.00.02	12.50.00.00
12.46.00.03	12.50.00.01
12.46.00.04	12.50.00.02

This mode thus permits the recording of timecode that advances at the same rate as the clock. All calculations of the duration based upon the compensated code will be corrected, except for the fact that the standard is not exactly 29.97 and the drop frame will accumulate an error of 75 milliseconds per day.

USING THE NAGRA TIMECODE RECORDER FOR SYNC PLAYBACK

Music videos are a very regular item in TV productions, and the production of a 'clip' often requires, like many other types of programmes, picture recording during the playback of the already recorded audio. The editing of such a programme includes the tedious task of manually synchronizing the pictures and sound. This usually has to be done without the aid of slate points, as they cannot possibly be recorded on the already recorded sound track. Secondly, there may be dozens of identical takes, all corresponding to the same piece of music. The use of the timecode Nagra and its timecode facilities can overcome these problems.

First, the **mix master** of the audio is obtained, onto which timecode can easily be striped using a centre track timecode studio machine, such as the Nagra T-Audio TC, or equivalent machine by another manufacturer. That machine can now be used as a main editing and synchronizing reference while the Nagra IV-S TC plays back a copy of the original (containing the same timecode). The transport of the IV-S TC is resolved to the timecode generator of the video recorder. This is done for two reasons: to ensure that the sound is replaced each time, and to ensure that the sound timecode is in phase with the video signal and hence the video timecode as they are recorded onto the videotape. The sound timecode is also fed to one of the audio tracks of the video recorder, thus giving the video two timecodes, one being the reference for the script and the other being the sound synchronization. As both are synchronous to the video, colour-framed edits and synchronization are always possible.

To play back a previously recorded timecode tape, put the main function selector in either of the two **playback** positions; the 'off-tape' timecode is then fed to the timecode output, the LCD display. Putting the meter switch in the **TC/Pilot Playback** position, it will then indicate the 'off-tape' level of the timecode signal.

TIMECODE CLAPPERBOARDS

The timecode clapperboard was introduced to take the place of the old manual clapperboard used with crystal sync systems on film. With the introduction of timecode some form of board that carried timecode in its own housing and could run sync to the timecode of the camera had to be devised. The current popular timecode clapperboard is the Clockit Master Slate ACD101. This unit contains a state-of-the-art software-based timecode generator and reader. The generator is driven by a very accurate crystal oscillator giving better than 1 ppm accuracy (one frame per day). The slate is compatible with other Clockit units, such as the ACL Lockit video camera synchronizer, ATM Clockit Timecode burst unit for audio recorders (both DAT and quarter inch), and the Ambient Clockit controller.

The clapperboard unit can be set by the Aaton camera's ASCII command, or jam synced to any external timecode. Hand setting of the unit is quick and easy. The slate can be used as a stand-alone unit, where its accuracy will be better than most units it is set by, or as part of a Clockit-driven system where the overall accuracy of all the units can be further tuned by a Clockit controller to give system accuracy better than 1 ppm.

The slate can function as a reader of external timecode, and its display can be advanced or retarded by up to seven frames. Reading code from a video or film camera can be useful to give information to interested parties such as production assistants or script editors. The display of the clapper unit has seven different brightness levels, which can be set by pushbuttons. The slate's internal timecode generator can be jam synced with external timecode. It can be set by ASCII (Aaton Origen C) or by hand. In the hand-setting mode the user bits can be changed but will not affect the overall timecode generation; this allows roll changes with changes of roll number noted in the user bits. In other words, once the time of day and date have been set it is good for the whole day. When using the unit intermittently, as in normal clapping mode, the slate will run for several days from one set of batteries.

A typical system for locking timecode with external recorders is outlined in Chapter 18, in the section on using RDAT recorders on a production (see p. 169).

Figure 13.4   Clockit timecode clapperboard used for film and video location work.

CHAPTER 14

Working with video equipment on location

Video equipment has reduced the possibility of the sound recordist being close to the source of sound, thanks to the 'umbilical cord' between themselves and the camcorder and their audio mixing equipment.

This was not a problem with film operations, as the standard Nagra recorder was crystal controlled and capable of separate operation, quite remote from the camera. This allowed the recordist to hide behind walls or cars, or track alongside artistes on the 'long end' of lenses, obtaining the closest sound quality possible. Another distinct advantage was the ability to 'split the difference' and reduce the range between a radio mic transmitter and receiver, keeping a healthy signal strength at all times. Prior to crystal sync on Nagra recorders the same situation occurred in film operations as in current video working, with a sync lead – the equivalent of the umbilical cord – between the portable mixer and the camcorder. A great sense of freedom was felt by all recordists when this cord disappeared, and many new techniques could be used that improved the audio quality and made reliable radio mic operation possible.

The situation in video has been improved by the introduction of timecode RDAT machines 'jam synced' to the video camera. However, production companies seem reluctant to use these methods, because of the higher cost of laying back these tracks in sync with pictures in post-production. Another restriction on the introduction of these techniques is the current high cost of re-equipping or hiring such recorders.

Since crewing reductions have been introduced, some production units also appear to be reluctant to use sound sweetening or dubbing to smooth out audio quality. In fact it should be given greater priority nowadays, as the recordist is not always able to present tracks as smoothly as in the past. Directors and producers, when faced with post-production, spend most of their time in video editing, with its related high costs; they often make little allowance for the niceties in treating the audio aspects of the production. Outside facilities often have minimal audio equipment, and most of the edit suites' acoustic treatment leaves a lot to be desired. Video equipment noise masking the audio during edits makes it very difficult to assess the real audio quality.

Film shooting allowed much more careful planning, owing to the high cost of film stock and processing and the need to keep the shooting ratio low. Traditionally it was expected that the audio would be dubbed and carefully track-laid. Another advantage was that at the transfer stage, where the quarter inch tape was transferred to 16 mm fully coated film, another 'independent ear' was present, which could judge quality and spot any technical problems. Video production, with its low stock costs, has promoted a much higher shooting ratio, with little time allowed for planning on location. There is no transfer process until the actual edit, which may well be up to a month after the shoot. Any technical problems may not be noticed until then. So a recordist must be competent on location to avoid problems if possible, and keep the director fully informed if a problem *does* occur, so that the scene can be reshot or rethought if necessary. If there is any remaining doubt about quality the director should be informed, and should ensure that this information is forwarded to the editor or transfer area operator.

Many camerapersons and operators are now recruited from studio or outside broadcast operations, where fixed sound rigs are the norm and all positions are covered by either fixed or mobile mics with operators. Their judgement on sound operations may have been coloured by these former practices. Similarly, directors and producers brought up with outside broadcast or studio operations often fail to plan properly for single-camera operation, and expect coverage to be there for audio, having been used to it in the past. Most outside broadcast operations have preplanning meetings, as do studio programmes. Perhaps the exceptions in studio programming are current affairs programmes, which normally have fixed interview positions with permanent microphones available.

You should always carry a kit of microphones that is adequate to cover all situations on location, bearing in mind the limitations of single-person operation. With the introduction of stereo, it would seem prudent that the production team inform the sound recordist about the stereo requirement, so that suitable microphones can be placed in the kit prior to embarking on the shoot.

Under conditions where you have to resort to working a small mini-boom or fishpole over the head of the artistes, there are severe limitations in controlling audio levels because of the lack of hands! This situation puts you in a position where you have to set an average audio level, or rely upon an audio limiter within the mixing unit to control levels. Neither method is ideal, and the dynamic range of the audio will suffer in consequence. Any limiter within the mixer should be of the highest quality and not suffer from unreliable level control or undue 'pumping' of the audio signals.

If the director requires the sound to be split across two tracks, the inclusion of a stereo mixer is vital. There is an increasing use of this facility, with the mix of the two channels being made at the edit. It would be extremely difficult to cope with this situation with a mono mixer, and would require that one channel was set at an arbitrary level on the camcorder and handled by the automatic gain control, which is not a very satisfactory arrangement. On a recent occasion a recordist was in the position where a director was asking for inadequate coverage of audio. The use of split tracks allowed him to place the director's requested mix on one track and his additional mix on the other. In the final edit a mix of both was used, which justified the recordist's original decision on location.

When gathering sound on location, your aim must be to produce the best possible sound for the situation. However, the umbilical cord between the sound mixing unit and the camera means that you will have to move the audio equipment constantly as the camera changes position, and this will probably require continual recabling to the sound sources unless you are using radio microphones. Compromises are inevitable; it is not possible to achieve the same excellence that can be achieved in the studio, with its acoustically treated areas and lack of synchronization problems. Bearing in mind the background levels on most locations, and the often unsuitable locations chosen for financial (not artistic) reasons, the task of achieving good audio quality on location is not getting any easier. This suggests perhaps that the sound recordist's skills should be more highly valued.

On film drama productions post-synchronization used to be the answer to all location sound problems, but it is rare to commit to 'post-sync' under current situations, and 'going for it live' is becoming standard, Again, this requires careful planning, with positive decisions made on all fronts. Wildtracks often covering wide-angle dialogue shots can solve some problems, but radio mic usage is becoming more common.

Much of the criticism levelled at drama audio obtained by the use of radio mics is its lack of ambience and false perspective. This ambience cannot be created with atmosphere tracks at the dubbing stage unless long dubbing sessions are scheduled. On location, if you are not able to obtain a more 'open' sound quality, the best way is to feed in at the time of recording a subtle amount of the 'open' microphone, to add space to the final mixed track from the camera angle. This must, however, be added with caution. Questions are always asked on the use of radio microphones in stereo as to where to place these microphones within the stereo image. The only option would be to shoot in M/S stereo and place the radio microphones down the middle on the mid channel. At least the audio tracks can be used, using only the mono component, and a location recorded atmosphere added if in difficulties with stereo image.

LINE-UP AND USE OF SONY BETACAM EQUIPMENT

Initial set-up on Betacam 5 Series recorder with BVV 5 camcorder back

1. Select zero-level tone on mixer unit, PPM4 or −4 V/U or from external generator if no mixer is used. If the recording is stereo or split track it is customary to identify track 1 with pulsed tone to EBU spec.

2. Switch on camcorder supply.
3. Select line input on input switch.
4. Use sockets on rear of unit channels 1 and 2.
5. Check that Dolby C is selected, if required, and is the company standard.
6. Select LNG (longitudinal analogue tracks).
7. Adjust input gain control to read −4 dB on the V/U Meter for relevant track 1/2 or 3/4 (FM tracks can be selected by monitor select).
8. Select to gang longitudinal tracks to FM tracks 3/4, or record separately, setting individual levels.
9. Select monitor circuit to E to E or playback (remember playback is *not* Dolby encoded and has timecode breakthrough). You will only hear a monitor circuit if the recorder is in the laced-up position.
10. Select timecode to Record Run and preset to required roll number. If needed, enter information in the user bits.
11. Check that gain control is *not* set to Auto on one or both channels.

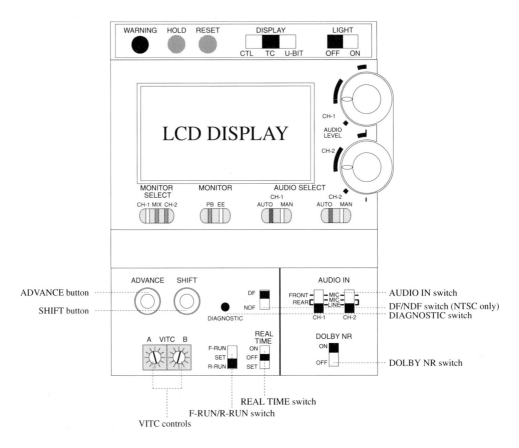

Figure 14.1 The side panel layout of a Sony Betacam recorder, showing the settings used for external mixer unit working.

Beware of the auxiliary level control on front of the Sony 7 camera, designed to be used by the cameraperson. This has an audio gain control on the front of the camera that controls Channel 1, even at line levels. Some recordists fit a plastic knob over this control to stop it being knocked by the cameraperson; this also applies to the controls on the top of the camera for audio gain. There is a Sony engineering bulletin (E-BVP-126) that relates to a modification to disable the front control.

The adjustment details apply to the Betacam 200/300/400 Series camcorders, except that tracks 1/2 and 3/4 are coupled together within the recorder, and only two input sound XLR sockets are available on the rear of the camera. There also is less of a problem with the preset audio gain controls for system audio levels. In a redesign they have been recessed further into the bodywork of the camera, but still need protecting in some way to avoid accidental movement.

Betacam track placement on tape

Below are actual track placements on the half inch Betacam tapes of the audio and other tracks. Reading from the top of the tape:

Band 1: audio track 1
Band 2: audio track 2
Band 3: video helical tracks
Band 4: control track
Band 5: timecode

The FM tracks are recorded simultaneously with the video tracks and layered beneath at a different azimuth. Good separation is available on Betacam, unlike the earlier U-Matic video machines, on which track 1 suffered from breakthrough from the video signal, and track 2 was the commonly used track for the main recording.

LOCKING CAMERAS WITH TIMECODE ON LOCATION

Two-camera operations are becoming increasingly popular on location for cost-saving purposes, but they present difficulties for the recordist. The main problems are:

- The need to feed two cameras with an audio output. This is not a problem with the SQN4 mixer and other mixer units, as two separate outputs are available, independently buffered from each other. It is advisable to be able to monitor both cameras.
- The need to feed timecode to both cameras and lock them together.

Locking two cameras can be achieved as below if no vision mixing unit is involved:

1. Feed external video from master camera (camera 1) to Genlock Video In on slave camera (camera 2).
2. If using external timecode feed this into Timecode In on master camera.
3. Feed Encode Video Out on master camera to Genlock In on slave camera (camera 2).
4. Feed Timecode Out on master camera to Timecode In on slave camera (camera 2).
5. Switch *all* cameras to Jam Sync to External Code. If only lock to camera 1 is required, items 3–5 are applicable, with camera 1 being the master timecode source.

SUITABILITY OF THE CAMERA MICROPHONE PROVIDED ON CAMCORDERS

The usual camera mics provided built in as standard are placed in a position where zoom servos and grunts from the cameraperson can often be heard. The mics are not adequately windshielded, and an auxiliary windshield, such as the specially produced Rycote Softie product, is advisable. A more satisfactory way to obtain good sound from the top of the camera is to construct a microphone mount to screw into the accessory socket on top of the camera. A suitable mic, for example, would be the Sennheiser ME80 capsule or other high-quality rifle mic with a Rycote Softie windshield. The ME80 can be internally powered, or you can use the camera phantom power supply. An attenuation of about 15 dB on the microphone input will overcome the automatic gain control on the recorder if this is placed into circuit for automatic level control operation. Other microphones of the dynamic or phantom power types can be used, with 48 V powering provided from the camera microphone socket itself.

The Panasonic MII equipment follows a pattern similar to Betacam equipment and can be set up in a similar way, although controls in some cases are placed in a different position. Familiarity with Sony equipment makes understanding the MII equipment simple. The level meters on the Panasonic MII equipment respond in a different way from Sony Betacam equipment, indicating higher peaks if set in a similar way to Betacam. The results on viewing the meters look correct if a standard set-up is done with the V/U meter at −4 dB for broadcast zero level. On watching the meters move it would appear that the operator is over-recording the signal. Playing back the recorded material indicates satisfactory level control; these misleading indications are only a question of meter ballistics.

CHAPTER 15

Relationships on location

THE SOUND RECORDIST'S RELATIONSHIP WITH THE CAMERAPERSON AND DIRECTOR

Since the early days of location recording the sound recording has always been placed second to the moving image. The sound assistant has nearly always been available in the past to enable the sound recordist to be more flexible, and to allow him or her to concentrate on the tight control of audio levels and intrusive background levels. However, the 1990s have seen the reduction of crews to levels that were previously common only on news and similar programmes, which were happy to allow a somewhat lower audio quality to be transmitted.

Much of this reduction in crewing size has come about since the UK government turned its attention to the broadcasting industry in 1990. This has reduced programme budget sizes, which has had a knock-on effect on the crewing size of productions. It tends to mean that the sound recordist now has to cope with situations from a more static recording position. The fixed cable to the video camera reduces the recordist's mobility, and hence restricts the coverage that he or she can get from the location.

The relationship between the cameraperson, recordist and director is now probably more important than it was in the past, when the sound recordist was the go-between between the sound assistant or boom operator and the director. Much of the planning is now done prior to the recordist's being involved on the location, which rather puts him or her in a predetermined situation.

Traditionally, the recordist seemed to be the one who was regarded as a bit of a 'nuisance' for requiring retakes on scenes or inserts, even though he or she may well have had problems recording suitably high-quality sound, owing to lighting difficulties or high levels of background noise. It is a relatively simple task to achieve a suitably composed picture, with the right background, and with artistes coming from extreme distances to a foreground position. However, it is not always possible to fit artistes with radio transmitters, either because of poor preplanning, or because of lack of time and warning. Indeed, without forward planning, the necessary equipment may not have been ordered and be available for use on location.

This means that forward planning and discussion with the director and the recordist is now of prime importance to avoid difficulties on location. With the advent of video, the reduction of film as a medium, and the increased pressure for faster location shooting, decisions have to be made more quickly by the sound recordist. Working single camera 'on location' requires different disciplines from the studio situation. There must be a much closer relationship between the cameraperson and the recordist, and an understanding of each other's problems. The relationship between the recordist and cameraperson now seems to be of utmost importance although the present trend of choosing a recordist by consulting the cameraperson must be a questionable way to employ the right person for the job, bearing in mind the constant changes of personnel.

In the broadcast industry many producers and directors saw the term 'technician' as one that raised 'hackles'; many recordists had long arguments with producers to point out that most members of crews see themselves as an integral part of the production team and not a separate 'technical team'. In the past, the cameraperson had a much closer relationship with the recordist, but this decade has seen this relationship start to break up. The search for a cheaper or more cost-effective way of shooting has seen the role of cameraperson and recordist extended into other areas; this allows less time for close working relationships, as both parties have their time taken up in keeping 'higher-tech' equipment to specification or working a 'second role'.

The introduction of video has perhaps introduced a form of 'technocrat' style operator on location. This may see the return of previous splits within the working system, rather than the creation of overall teams. The smaller team does mean an all-round increase in the physical effort that all members have to apply, leaving less time for artistic effort.

The film industry, with its almost hand-crafted and closely checked systems, did not allow too many technical faults through the net. In most areas, technicians and operators knew each other well, and could judge each other's capabilities easily. Indeed, the current criticism of the video sound operation by the film industry in general is that there are a lot of technocrats as operators, which would suggest a lack of artistry in this area and more concentration on a 'technical exercise'. Also, video equipment requires a closer eye kept on it; it is more complex, and the audio control knobs are often flimsy. The video equipment currently in use is constantly changing, as is the compatibility of units and the basic interconnections.

The current trend of fragmentation within the industry has seen many newcomers with no known track record. Although one could in the past be critical of the union for many of its practices, at least there was a certain amount of checking into individual 'track records' or competence. There is a need for some sort of certification in the future, and moves are being made in that direction both by the industry itself and by the Institute of Broadcast Sound. Recently a system of NVQs (National Vocational Qualifications) has been worked out covering all aspects of the sound person's role in broadcasting. See Appendix 3 for the telephone number of Skillset, who control the broadcast NVQ prospectus.

The inability of the sound crew to operate independently, without feeding audio to the audio recording section within the camera, and the constant need for battery changes and system realignment for various reasons, may have put new worries in the mind of the production crews. The introduction of stereo has also introduced some confusion for location production crews.

A great deal of trust had to be put in the film crew on location, as their judgements were not evident until the rushes session, but at least it was a joint viewing, with self-appraisal in 'open court'. Under current shooting situations, 'We can sort it out in the dub' and 'The labs will correct the colour' have been replaced by 'You can equalize the audio in the dub' and 'The edit suite has a colour correction unit and DVE'.

In many cases the video system does not really have the latitude for error that film had, and correction – on all fronts – is not quite as good as one would expect. Many location monitoring systems are inadequate for judging both audio and vision quality. This must surely mean that the crew have to pay closer attention to technical quality.

Directors seem to assume at times that telling the cameraperson what they require is enough, and that this will be passed downwards. But with the increasing pressures on the cameraperson under present situations, alas, the information does not always filter downwards. The recordist must now insist on being in on briefings, and on working in harmony with the production team towards a more integrated operation, which includes the compromises that bring a tighter-knit product.

In judging how to cover a particular situation, the recordist needs to know what area of the action scene needs sound coverage. It is easy to assume that the picture being taken is a simple wide shot. However, it may be that the camera is focused on a foreground subject and it is this subject that requires sound coverage. Alternatively the camera may be 'zoomed in' on a distant subject, who would perhaps require radio mic coverage. It is important on all occasions for the recordist to discuss with the director or cameraperson whom they see as the important contributors within the action area or perhaps do his or her own detective work if this information is not forthcoming. The solution is not to cover everyone in shot with their own personal microphones, as you will very soon run out of channels and of fingers or hands to work with, especially on a stereo production. On every occasion the wisest choice is to use the minimum number of channels.

Most locations are not acoustically as good as the studio, and the 'spill' between microphones can give unpleasant coloration of audio quality. It would be much more satisfactory to cover all mobile participants on a rifle microphone and the interviewer on his or her own personal mic, either radio or hard wired, allowing you to leave the interviewer's channel open and 'ride' the mobile rifle mic, which is where you will encounter the unpredictable levels of sound. This is even more necessary under single-man audio operation. Generally, it is safe to assume that your interviewer is at constant level. Under these unpredictable situations, splitting the tracks could well be justified, allowing questions to be omitted at the edit stage and also re-balanced within the editing session. However, this could not be attained under stereo M/S twin channel recording situations without extra recording channels.

Many directors could be educated towards allowing extraneous noises to finish before calling 'cut'. On many occasions a passing car or overflying aircraft, if left to run, could be trailed over the 'incoming' track on the edit and make what would seem an unusable track perfectly acceptable. Over 30 years of recording I have met only two directors who used this technique; on one occasion a director managed to get together a five minute drama sequence, perfectly cut with overlaps, and no obvious disturbances. Indeed, a presenter on a documentary merely saying perhaps 'On this windy day' or 'More jets' could save hours of shooting time and location waiting time. In the USA, and now in the UK, it is not unusual to rewrite scripts to suit weather conditions; so it would be not unreasonable to place two or three words into a script or piece to camera to justify a natural audio interference. Listeners are well aware that traffic, wind and aircraft exist in the twentieth century.

Perhaps the 'illusion' created by feature films and TV drama in the past has not kept up with twentieth century reality on locations and the current speed required on television productions. There is, alas, no magic microphone that filters out these audio disturbances. Picture disturbances can, of course, be framed out of the shot, but that 'little man' with his pneumatic drill, who seems to tour the world seeking out film crews, can be just 'out of shot' waiting to start his performance.

If you stray from conventional track layouts, you must make a note of the layouts, and inform the editor. On too many occasions, in the 'heat' of the edit, it is found in the dubbing stage that because of poor communication an editor had not been aware that he had this option available or had used a track that was not the one destined for transmission. This problem can be overcome by good documentation from the location to the editor.

CREW RELATIONSHIPS WITH ARTISTES AND THE GENERAL PUBLIC

Making the interviewee feel at ease is part of the role of the recordist and assistant. That nice smile from you can at times make a very 'hair raising' occasion a little easier. A short explanation of why you are actually fixing that mic, where you are fixing it and what it is doing will perhaps take their mind off the situation and help to break the ice.

Although you may not feel it necessary, it is as well to advise the interviewee that bumping the mic will cause a problem, and about the need for a reasonable voice level. Too many interviewees forget that they have a microphone fixed to them, particularly when it is a radio microphone.

With hard-cable microphones, the subject often darts off, forgetting his cable and severing that vital plug from its socket. The subject may even trip over the cable during the operation: you should always be aware of potential hazards such as this.

INFORMING INTERESTED PARTIES OF PROBLEMS

If there is any technical doubt about audio quality, it really is better to stop a take there and then. There is really no shame in either making a wrong instant decision, or a technical fault popping up on you while on location, or even during a studio recording. Before shooting starts, it is always worth checking the status of the video equipment, as faults seem to creep up on you, and controls *do* get knocked.

There is also an absolute requirement that some form of 'audio return' is established via replay from the camera, even if this is an **electronics to electronics** check (E to E). This E to E return is not an absolute replay, but does determine that the audio signal has gone through the electronics within the video recorder, and is reaching its recording destination without distortion.

You cannot assume that something connected earlier will stay untouched or not be readjusted by accident during the day. Much current video equipment, because of its design for single-operator use, has a large number of 'on camera', single-man audio presets. At present there do not seem to be any video units designed to handle both picture and sound satisfactorily. As the design is obviously aimed primarily at the cameraperson, who is thereby also acting as the sound operator, the controls for audio are always in positions where they can suffer from accidental adjustment.

Unlike the monitoring system on the Nagra recorder used on film locations, the video equipment cannot supply a true A/B comparison, but only an indication that audio has reached the recorder itself. The playback facility on Sony or other video recording equipment, although a true audio replay of the original recording, is not Dolby C encoded on most camcorder replays, and has timecode breakthrough present on the circuit. This is not the case with external replay adaptors, as they have a Dolby C encoder within their replay circuits.

The camera systems now seem too good for their recorders; the audio system is just a compromise, but with digital audio tracks promised, this may improve. The current narrow audio tracks have extreme limitations, needing careful attention all the way to the final edit. Unfortunately, this close technical attention to the audio signal all the way to transmission does not always happen on every production, except on 'in house' situations, or within large broadcasting organizations where technical specifications are tight and close audio follow-ups can usually be maintained.

Digital systems of audio recording supply a truly 'transparent' interpretation of the sound quality on location. They are not degraded on transfers and editing, unlike current tracks, which can often suffer from Dolby mistracking and incorrect head alignment of the analogue heads in the edit suites or transfer suites. These problems arise partly because, outside broadcast organizations, routine maintenance is not scheduled, and audio maintenance is given a low priority.

GENERAL LOCATION DISCIPLINE

It is important to be aware of location discipline at all times. It is the recordist's role to inform unit management that the local noise level or crowd noise is getting out of hand. On long location drama shoots, crew members often think that whispering is all right while recording is in progress, but in reality it is not. The recordist should make his or her presence known, and occasionally shout to warn crew members and passers-by that quiet is essential on the location. This sometimes provokes the general public into being noisier, but it usually does the trick. It is certainly worth informing the director that you are not happy about the noise level on location, if you have done all in your power to reduce these levels, as generally people do react to their orders.

On film operations there is usually the clapperboard to attract attention and warn all participants that a take has started. There is no such audible indication on video, as clapperboards are not used. It is important to keep out of actors' and interview participants' eye-lines, although video restrictions often put you exactly in the eye-line. It is equally important to keep physically out of shot and be aware of camera angles.

CHAPTER 16

Location considerations for audio productions

DRAMA PRODUCTION

For the recordist, covering drama is very similar to other forms of recording, but it is usually better planned, and there is often more time to gain a good product. However, drama in the 1990s is being produced and shot under much faster conditions, with much smaller technical crews.

The initial stages of drama productions generally allow the recordist to be in on the planning and location 'recces'. It is helpful to have a copy of the script, so that you can judge how much dialogue you will be required to record on the particular location. The director will always be able to give you an idea of how the action will be shot. It is as well to sound out the director's feelings on radio microphone coverage, as some directors are 'anti'; they prefer open sound, and will adjust shooting accordingly. Other directors will assume that you will use radio microphones for shots that are difficult to cover with conventional boom techniques.

The following description of a typical recce situation of a film location will indicate the technicalities that the recordist should be aware of. The recce crew arrived at a small restaurant location, where the script indicated that two actors would be sitting at a table. Dialogue between the two was clearly scripted, but that was about all that could be gleaned from the script, as no other stage directions were given. On arriving at the location and talking over the scene, the director informed the crew that there would be a small orchestra playing in the corner, and a gypsy fiddler, who would walk behind the two actors during the dialogue playing his violin. At the same time the dance floor would be full of dancers.

This artistic requirement, requested by the director, prompted the following decisions by the location recordist:

- The orchestra would have to be pre-recorded, as the shoot was single camera and would be shot out of sequence. A pre-recording session would have to be booked prior to the shoot.

147

- The instruments would have to be muted, as the musicians were in shot most of the time; direct audio from the live instruments would spill on to the dialogue tracks, which should be free of musical content.
- A location loudspeaker replay unit would have to be supplied with a 50 Hz pulsed tape, and an operator would have to be provided for this replay, as well as some form of radio transmission of the music to the mobile violin player, with cabled earpieces for the other musicians, so that they could mime to the track recorded in the morning.
- A pulsed replay tape of the chosen music should be made up from the pre-recorded session in the morning.

These items were not obvious from the script, and could not have been gleaned without a recce and discussion on location. However, they were all supplied, and the whole sequence recorded, without any major problems. Muting the violin was a bit difficult, but was done by an efficient props department. The piano's hammer section was removed to allow the pianist to hit the keys without the piano making any audible sound. The dancers were given a short burst of music prior to the take and danced from then on without music, remembering the tempo from the cut point onwards.

Another occasion that could have caused problems was a drama situation that required dialogue during a village dance while the floor was full of dancers. On this occasion it was decided to pre-record the band, but record the drums separately on their own dedicated track. This enabled the recordist to maintain a drum rhythm, from which the dancers could gain their dance movements. As there were many inserts of different tempos, all the various tempos were available in case the director should decide to use a different tune. Recording the drums separately was a distinct advantage, as during the pre-record session one number was omitted and the director was able to use the rhythm-only track to film to, and add music to it afterwards. The pre-recorded drum track had no ill effects on the actual location recordings when mixed back with the original pre-recording.

If the location recce is essential before embarking on drama shoots, so too is reading the script. Some production teams feel that the recordist should keep a detailed track of the words on location; however, some recordists prefer to know only in a general way what the dialogue is intended to be, relying on what they actually hear coming through the headset to judge the quality of the dialogue. After all, if the recordist does not understand what is being said, the listener at home has little or no chance, script or no script. Normally the script supervisor on location keeps track of the actual words.

It is advisable to have a headphone feed of dialogue for the production assistant or script supervisor, as well as the director and boom operator. This will enable them to follow the script more closely, and allow the boom operator to judge his or her own performance. Included in the boom operator's feed could be a talkback feed from the sound recordist, which could either be separate or interrupt the supplied programme dialogue feed. The occasional feed of audio may be required by autocue operators. They need to follow the person 'in vision' very closely so that they can keep the words in front of the artiste or presenter and allow the prompter operator to judge the performers' speed.

Recordists soon become aware that actors speak at a much higher audio level than the general public; they can produce dialogue levels that can grossly distort any microphone. To deal with these levels, you generally have to be quite fast on the faders, but fast drops in fader level can sometimes change the background level. An experienced boom operator can help the recordist in his overall level control by loosening off the position of boom microphones.

The main problems occur at the lower voice levels, when intimate scenes are being acted out. Generally an actor can lift a bit on voice level, but often complains that it spoils the artistic effect they are trying to achieve. Some negotiation can be tried with the director as to shot size. This more suitable position can preferably be obtained by using a tighter-angle lens from further away, rather than bringing the camera closer to the subject, as this can often introduce camera noise to the soundtrack, even on video recorders when they are composite units. The problem with noise from film cameras is usually more extreme and depends on the blimping system supplied and the mechanical condition of the camera itself. Difficulties often occur when the recordist requires the actor to give more voice, or perhaps delay a line to allow a microphone to reposition. It has always been protocol to ask the director if this is all right and then approach the actor yourself.

During the preplanning stages it is worth while discussing post-sync, checking whether there is any allowance in the budget for this eventuality, and what the director's feelings are regarding post-sync. Post-sync is normally scheduled within an artiste's contract, but not always.

Another essential thing for a recordist is to know the artistes' names, as often the only reference on location is the script names of the character portrayed by the actor or actress. As direct contact is often needed by a recordist, a complete list of participating artistes should be obtained from the production team.

Some discussions with the costume department could be an advantage; often, in period dramas, some provision within the costumes can be made for radio mic heads and transmitter pouches. It is wise to inform the costume department if a need for extensive radio mic usage is foreseen, as it could affect the choice of fabrics on the production. It is also possible that the costume department can help in fitting the radio mic transmitters to the artistes. Many artistes prefer this anyway. Some of the larger broadcasting organizations train their costume staff in the placing of radio microphone transmitters and their heads, which is useful to the sound recordist.

Boom operation, which is an important part of the gathering of audio on drama, is covered elsewhere in the book (see pp. 88 and 97).

If you have any doubt about a line of dialogue, you should inform the director and make a wildtrack of that line available. It is better to record the line as soon as possible. It is often more difficult to have the time put aside for such niceties at a later stage. Beware of actors improving their performance on wild-tracks. Try for a few takes at differing speeds if you are in any doubt; often an artiste will tend to slow down their delivery on wildtracks, feeling that a more precise performance is required. It is essential to supply location atmosphere tracks for the editor to lay under cuts or use where wildtrack dialogue is inserted, to help smooth over audio transitions or cuts in the final dub.

When recording wildtrack dialogue where artistes are walking and talking it is better to record two separate tracks, one covering the feet only, and one of the dialogue recorded statically, as it is unlikely that the synchronization on the wildtrack of the feet will be correct; they can be 'fitted' separately at the edit. Similarly, if dialogue is required from a moving vehicle it is better to record the vehicle separately from the dialogue. Situations often dictate that these options are not open to you, because of shooting pressures, but you should at least try to achieve this. Any atmosphere of a moving vehicle behind the dialogue will make it difficult for an editor to shorten or lengthen the dialogue to fit it to the appropriate pictures.

When making microphone choices it is always as well to look further into the scene at the action that is to come. On a particularly difficult shoot, which entailed dialogue from a moving tractor, the recordist made a decision to use radio microphones, as it was impossible for a boom operator to follow the action. This worked well until the second part of the action, which was a fight sequence that ended up with one actor falling in a river. The whole sequence was coped with well with fast fader dips, using radio microphones for the general coverage, including the fight sequence, but the last few words had to be wildtracked on the personal mics, and then the mics were removed for the fall into the river. The change in atmosphere caused by removing the radio mics was covered by a balancing atmosphere rifle mic, which was established and used during the radio mic sequences to give a 'looser' perspective. The balancing wildtrack was used on the edit to fill any holes in the final mix.

It is always worth having 'action' vehicles checked for interference suppression if they are old-fashioned or period vehicles; often they are not suppressed, and cause interference on the radio mic transmissions.

Ideally you would use the same type of microphone all the way through a drama production, but this is not always possible. If you have to make any changes in the type of microphone, this is better done on a complete change of scene or location, to avoid any obvious jump in quality. The listener's perception of changes is not usually as acute on transitions between scenes. Dubbing mixers can usually find a suitable equalization setting that does not cause any undue quality change when different microphones are used within a scene, but it is extremely difficult to achieve this mid-scene without seriously affecting the whole scene, as the dubbing mixer will generally have to correct the scene to the lowest common denominator.

One thing to watch for on all locations is intrusive repetitive background noise such as clocks, or even budgerigars! If possible, remove them from the set;

otherwise, when the dialogue is cut together in an edit, it is extremely difficult to keep the rhythm of the background clock correct or remove the budgie. Domestic appliances such as refrigerators cause their own problems, and can usually be shut off for the length of a take. Modern ventilation systems often cannot be switched off during shooting.

One problem that a recordist did not really notice until the duty electrician pointed it out was a system of white noise within an open-plan office, which was meant to stop people from overhearing each other's conversations. As white noise tends to mask conversations, the recordist was having great difficulty in getting clean dialogue. Once the system was switched off all was well, and good tracks were obtained. It is interesting to note that none of the office personnel were even aware that the system was in use, so it is highly unlikely that a recordist would notice such a system or indeed be advised of its existence.

LOCATION ACOUSTIC CONSIDERATIONS

With the high cost of set design, most production companies choose actual locations as the cheaper alternative. Locations are rarely as good as the studio, which most production people, and many new location technical people, are used to. However, there is a lot to be said for the reality that such situations give to a drama production. For long-term shooting, acoustic treatment can be applied to locations, but in general, locations offer very little opportunity to use these forms of additional treatment or to improve acoustics.

The location recordist has to aim for the tightest possible sound pick-up, to avoid the problems of poor location acoustics. It is always possible to add reverberation later if required. Portable acoustic screens can be placed against **dead walls** (areas that are not within the camera shots), or areas not being used for shooting. They can help to reduce any unwanted reverberation and help generally to 'deaden' the set acoustically. (The much cheaper alternative would be carpet underlay fixed to the reflective surfaces.) However, transport to locations is not always available for such luxuries; nor would these extra requirements be provided unless mentioned at the planning and budgeting stage of the production and included in the overall costing of the production.

One location chosen on a drama production that springs to mind was an unused factory of modern construction. It had a plastic roof, which on the recce was fine, but when it rained the resulting noise sounded like peas hitting a drum. This problem was cured by laying plastic grass on the roof; this dispersed the rain and allowed the unit to continue shooting. This was a fairly expensive operation, but so would the loss of shooting have been, as the production unit were to use this location for two months. The moral of this tale is that even if a method of sound insulation is unconventional, if it does the trick, then use it.

If soundproofing or damping with acoustic screens is too expensive, polystyrene sheeting is often adequate, as are heavy curtains or drapes on all the dead walls. As the angle varies, so can the position of any acoustic treatments, usually during the lighting re-rig. It is well worth discussing at the planning and budgeting stage your requirements for your own temporary acoustic screens, as it may well be possible for some provision to be made in the budget, as well as any other extra sound requirements you may need.

The designer on a production can often help the recordist with the choice of draping on the set and the provision of floor coverings to improve the acoustics of a set. On one occasion a set of 10 Downing Street was built within an aircraft hanger. It proved perfectly acceptable for the visuals but was totally useless acoustically. The design department provided a translucent white fabric false ceiling, which reduced the working area and improved the acoustics of the set generally, so that the location recordist was able to use the set with good results. The cameraman placed his lights above the false ceiling, positioned to shine through the fabric.

DOCUMENTARY AND CURRENT AFFAIRS PRODUCTION

The documentary and news areas are difficult ones for the recordist, as it is easy for the camera to present a picture, but not so easy for the recordist to present suitable audio tracks to accompany the pictures supplied by the cameraperson.

The mode of operation in documentaries and allied productions is less clear than in drama production. Planning on documentaries and news is often fairly light, except perhaps for profile-style programmes or musical documentaries, where the planning is usually very thorough. The recordist has to use different techniques, and in general a much wider range of equipment must be available. Radio microphones are often used in preference to the usual fishpole or boom operation. With the reduced crew size, the recordist is often stretched to the limits to cover the various camera angles. The basic ergonomics of coping with mixing, pole operating and being attached to a camera in the video situation is a lot for a sound operator to deal with.

If planning *is* possible, it should be careful. If a director is actually on the shoot, his or her needs should be discussed before commencing the operation, as so many unexpected situations can occur, unlike most drama productions. It is unlikely that the recordist will ever have the opportunity to recce any locations, nor will there be any choice on location venues, except perhaps that alternative choices could be given for master interview situations. Little time is allowed for the supply of wildtracks or buzz tracks, but the recordist should supply these wherever possible, as they are invaluable for the dubbing or sweetening process, should this be available.

The current trend for 'fly on the wall' documentaries puts the recordist in some difficult positions when using current video equipment. Without a separate sound system the recordist is generally governed by the camera position, and must obtain the audio from that position if there is no sound assistant. As these types of documentary are usually audio led, this puts more emphasis on the audio track being of the best quality. Unit discipline is important, but unfortunately it is often fairly lax in these situations. Unless the recordist has some other form of recording equipment available, the governing factor using video is that the camera must be running to obtain the soundtracks.

Certainly a recordist could supplement the camcorder with a separate RDAT machine to record when the camera is still running, but this requires high discipline on the side of the production crew and camera crew when making their moves or giving instructions. There is certainly a case to be put for the use of film on these kind of documentaries; at present it is still more flexible than video.

The future will bring the acceptance of professional timecode RDAT machines, which, alongside locked timecode, can give results as good as film audio quality. The reason for the current lack of interest is budget considerations, not technical ones. Although the small four-head timecode RDAT machine has really only just arrived, any other methods would be more time consuming and more costly on the budget, as the two have to be synchronized after the event. Auto conforming of audio with video using timecode is becoming a more common practice, but only on certain programmes.

News and current affairs have in many cases been downgraded to a lesser role. They are often covered by multiskilled operators, sometimes retrained from other jobs. Many news items are now covered by the once old-fashioned hand microphones, and often the crew is one person only. It is difficult to see how quality control can be achieved by one person, who has probably two other jobs to do at the same time.

When recording 'snatched' dialogue, some personal microphones are better at picking up two-way conversations than others. Reporters or interviewers should be aware of dynamic control on their own voices, and use lower voice levels when trying for two-way interviews under hidden microphone operations. This allows the recordist to increase the level on the microphone channels to allow for the further distance that the interview subject may be from the microphone.

PLANNING AND LOCATION SURVEYS

Prior to any location work or studio work, planning meetings are normal. In this changing industry, in particular on the independent side, these opportunities for planning locations are becoming less frequent. Often the locations are chosen without reference to the sound recordist or supervisor. Indeed, it now seems to be the 'norm' that recordists are not involved in the early planning of the production, being seen as personnel who can be picked up after the planning stage. This can sometimes be an extremely short-sighted attitude, as many problems can be overcome at an early stage and hence costs reduced.

Many areas need to be looked at on location: in particular, the location background noise, and the acoustics of rooms in which action or interviews will take place. It is unlikely that time will be available on documentary shoots to visit any locations, as this is not normal practice.

If post-synchronization time is allowed in the budget, you may be able to use unsuitable sound locations that are visually acceptable and post-synchronize the dialogue afterwards. This can allow the production team more artistic freedom on the shots they take. It is usually better to record such dialogue as soon after shooting as possible; artistes may well be booked up well ahead on other shoots. When considering post-synchronization it is essential to have the artistes' booking periods at hand, as you may need to book recording sessions within their contract times, to save a return at a later date to record the sections. Also, after the event, artistes may well have been playing different parts and not be as adept as you might think at getting back into parts that were recorded months before.

Equipment choice is normally up to the recordist, but the costing is generally the responsibility of the producer, who will give the final word on hire of extra equipment. The recordist needs to discuss all requirements and advise the production unit of the costs of existing and extra facilities that, in his or her opinion, are required.

It is usually the responsibility of the sound recordist to arrange the communications on a location. Drama shoots often require up to six **walkie talkies**, with the capability of second-frequency operation for separate cueing for artistes, etc. The recordist is usually responsible for the charging of the units and their efficient operation. Care must be taken in the frequencies chosen for walkie talkies; on one occasion on a drama shoot the location unit managers were transmitting on the same frequency as the nearby studio, and were breaking into the remote studio talkback system. Much location shooting takes place close to studio bases for cost reasons, so it is essential to have a choice of other frequencies. In addition to normal radio communications, a loudhailer is often useful for crowd control and artiste control. Communications on audience shows and outside broadcast locations are normally resident in the OB units, and so would be available, including radio talkback.

Public address systems are often hired in for the event, complete with operator, to leave the sound crew free to do their own tasks.

Microphone stands should be tied securely to something if an audience is present, or if the microphone stand is overhanging an audience. Safety ties should be placed on all overhanging equipment where the general public and other crew members are likely to be below. All operators should be aware that their actions can cause accidents if equipment is not placed in sensible places or if warnings are not given of the presence of the equipment. It is general practice in studios and on locations not to rig above crowds or indeed other workers, but to do this work with the area underneath cleared and everyone warned of such an operation.

An inventory of equipment should be taken on a large location to ensure that on the de-rig you still have all the equipment you started with. In particular, some method of signing out walkie talkies is advantageous, as they do seem to get left in odd places by crew members who are busy doing other tasks.

Live locations generally need the sound engineer or recordist to feed to either BT lines or radio link vehicles, or even portable satellite units. These units normally accept their feeds of audio at zero level. There may often be a reverse feed of audio from the studio for cueing purposes, but on small locations this may be taken by an 'off air' feed of the live programme. TV companies often use portable radiophones on an open line for talkback to the studio, so some sort of earpiece attachment to a portable phone would be useful. Systems are now available that attach to a mobile phone and allow an in-vision presenter or participant to talk back to a remote location and conduct an interview. Under these circumstances the two ends are recorded separately and edited together in one place to make a composite interview.

HIRING EQUIPMENT

It is not uncommon to get a better deal for a long hire with hire companies, but it is advisable if you are freelance that the production company that employs you deals with such bills. Usually hired equipment is reliable if it is from an established company, and you have the advantage of being able to get a replacement quickly should you have any technical breakdowns.

It is usually the hirer's responsibility to arrange insurance on such equipment, and the penalty for the loss of equipment is often high. Often the hirer has to pay the normal charges until the equipment has been replaced, which can be very expensive. It is essential that insurance is sorted out immediately. Obligations on insurance for equipment should not be taken on lightly; they should be handled by your production company.

Careful checks should be made on incoming hired equipment, and an inventory compiled, which can be checked against the equipment returned at the end of the shoot to the hire company so that any losses can be advised. Even small items within kits should be logged, as often they are expensive and easily misplaced on a hectic shoot. When returning equipment to hire companies, take care that the equipment is not placed in the transit cases wet. This can cause problems on the equipment in future, and is not good practice. It is also not good practice to return equipment in a dirty or dusty condition; cleaning the equipment protects other users from problems.

The hiring of radio microphones for overseas shoots is worth considering; even with upcoming European frequency allotments, using UK radio microphone frequencies overseas is a veritable minefield – and often illegal. Hire companies are usually aware of the suitable frequencies for different countries and can advise accordingly. The other aspect that should guide the recordist towards hire is the speed of replacement of faulty equipment: something that is highly desirable if you are overseas. There can often be a situation where a completely different set of frequencies can be required within one country, and these can be obtained as and when required, if arranged with the hire company as part of the contract. Check before you take radio microphones or walkie talkies overseas, as some countries have an outright ban on their use.

CHAPTER 17

Stereo location production for television and film

The 1990s saw the introduction of stereo sound to television in the UK, and coverage is now nearly complete nationally. The BBC invented the Nicam stereo system, which is almost the equivalent of CD quality, but Independent Television beat them to the post with a national service, despite the BBC transmitting programmes in stereo for many years prior to the ITV national service.

There are now guidelines on identifying tapes containing stereo material. **EBU stereo tone** must be placed at the front of rolls containing stereo information. This is 1000 Hz tone on both tracks, with the left track pulsed for 0.25 s every 3 s; the left track is usually track 1 on the Betacam system, the right track being track 2. Both tones from the same source are in phase coincidence.

One basic problem with stereo for television is the physical width of the TV screen and the placement of the speaker systems on current TV receivers. Already one major TV company has nearly transmitted a programme that had an audio phase reversal on one channel of the stereo. If it had not been noticed, listeners in stereo would have noticed a confused stereo image, but little more. However, it would have resulted in the 'centre of image' announcements being lost completely to the mono listener. I suspect the broadcast company's phones would have been ringing constantly with calls from mono listeners, if the transmission had proceeded out of phase with no central dialogue to the majority audience. However, an alert videotape operator who was monitoring the programme in mono prior to transmission noticed the error and rectified the problem. The transmission area within any company listening in stereo would probably be unaware of any problems in mono unless they had suitable phase-indicating meters available.

The problem of screen size and speaker placement in the home restricts the width of stereo image that the recordist or dubbing mixer should create. The further towards the extremes of the stereo image the sound source is placed, the less information is added to the mono central image. Hence erring towards 'just off centre' is better for imaging of main dialogue, considering screen size and stereo compatibility. This is similar to what happens in cinema, although most dialogue is 'pan potted' to the required place in the picture area from a mono dialogue track. This is supplemented by electronically panned 'wild' mono effects and, on occasions, stereo A/B sync recordings.

Many broadcast companies have recorded programmes in M/S stereo under studio conditions, and have been successful in their results, but conditions are much more controlled in the studio, with multi-boom operation possible. However, it is doubtful if a studio discussion programme would benefit from a stereo transmission, where the person speaking is nearly always cut to centre screen. One stereo quiz programme made by a contractor was very confusing as far as dialogue was concerned; the only benefit from the stereo was for audience reaction.

Sports events *are* enhanced by the introduction of stereo, and as these events are usually live, they can be easily dealt with by intelligent placement of stereo rifle mics or crossed pairs of microphones, with the in-vision presenters placed within the image where required. This assumes that suitable 'stereo sound in sync' circuits are available for network transmission. As these events, when edited, are generally 'straight cut' in the edit suite, no great problems are presented for transmission.

LOCATION RECORDING FOR STEREO

Location recording in stereo is in general new to most independent broadcast operators, and has evolved over the past few years; the BBC has set the lead by assuming all its output to be stereo. In general, operation is not too different from mono, but great care must be taken over the following points:

- careful line-up of the analogue or digital recording system;
- checks on system phase;
- careful logging of stereo material;
- passing information to the editor and production department with regard to track layouts.

When lining up systems like quarter-inch tape, take care over head alignment, as any weave or misalignment here can cause problems with a shifting image in stereo. Digital equipment, because of its design, does not suffer from this problem.

THE SOUND RECORDIST ON LOCATION

The sound recordist's aural judgement

In judging how to place the microphones for a particular situation you have to take into account many problems. Most of all, how can you place your microphones in such a way that you will not interfere with the picture, but still obtain satisfactory sound?

If we consider how we all hear and judge sound, we will see how important the recordist's role is. Human beings have considerable advantages over microphones. We have sight to point us at the object we want to hear; we have two ears; and we have a brain to tell us to ignore the sounds that we do not want to hear. The microphone has none of these advantages of sense, vision and rejection of interfering noise. It has no sense at all: only the guidance given by the operator. The sound recordist is the microphone's brain and only he or she can 'tell' the microphone where to be to pick up the best sound, or to reject unwanted noise. Stereo adds another dimension; it adds the other ear to an audio source and helps the listener to reject unwanted interference.

It is important that you do not judge sound by level meters alone, but rely also on your own aural judgements. Many sound sources output dynamically higher sound outputs than others: for instance, a harpsichord and other musical instruments. In general, all music sounds dynamically louder than speech. It would therefore be wrong to the listening ear to mix all these sounds at the same meter levels, as dynamically they will sound different. There will be many occasions when you will be unable to view your level meters, and will have to mix the tracks aurally. Indeed, all recordists have had occasions when their metering systems have failed, and the aural balance has really not been far off one that uses level meters as the only check.

It is perfectly acceptable to allow some participants to have softer voices if this is what they have in real life; do not be tempted to lift the level of every participant to the same overall. On location it is better to allow an even background than continual fast level lifts, which generally cause noticeable 'bumps' in background levels and make life difficult in the edit. You should be aware of background levels and mix your tracks accordingly, being careful not to cause unwanted background level jumps.

One thing that is important in these days of smaller crews is always to carry some alternative microphone with you to cover sound in a 'crash' situation. You will often embark on a shoot for which you have been told no sound will be required, only to find that sound *is* needed; or the interview that was not going to happen does happen. You rush back to your vehicle to get a spare microphone, but on your return you are told, 'We just missed a great interview'. Always carry a spare set of batteries, and a spare microphone, even if it is only a personal mic and one spare cable. It can be a life-saver.

There seems to be a tendency within the music industry, and to a certain extent within broadcasting, to use extremely 'bright' microphones on music, or to use a great deal of equalization to obtain a bright sound quality. It is good for all sound balancers to place themselves regularly in front of an orchestra and listen to the real acoustic sound. On many occasions you can get caught in the trap of using 'over-bright' microphones on orchestral music, perhaps by the lead given from the recording industry. It is interesting that conductors generally prefer a less 'bright' top end response than we often give, although as recordists we know a certain amount of this 'bright' response will be lost in transfers.

For the recordist on the road the inclusion of a high-quality dynamic mic, with its good overload capability, is a worthwhile addition to the kit. Many occasions occur when this type of microphone could cover a brass band or choir and adequately cope with the dynamics and cover a wide spatial area. Some very suitable microphones are the Electrovoice RE20 or 668, though of course equally suitable types are available from other manufacturers.

Audio acceptability levels

In general, the acceptability of the soundtracks on location is the sound recordist's decision. Finding your own acceptability level comes with experience, of course, but sometimes it can be difficult. There are no general rules, apart from the fact that dialogue should be clearly heard, without undue interference from external noises. The general quality acceptance level is different between types of programming; it is usually higher for drama than documentary, although the combination of drama documentary gives more leeway.

The sound recordist's art is to gain the best-quality sound, despite surrounding interference. We could consider all interference with the end-product as noise, and the product as the signal, and so equate it to a signal-to-noise ratio. On location a road drill, traffic, wind, or other external interferences are the noise, and your subject talking to camera is the signal: the closer the microphone is to the subject, the better the signal-to-noise ratio. Indeed, the more microphones you open up, the more signal and noise you add. If you include the spill between the microphones, and the extra noise added by the additional microphone, it does tend to loosen off the sound picked up, with indirect sound clouding the image you wish to create.

We have to live with the sounds of the twentieth century, but if the offending noise is clearly seen in shot then it is more acceptable than if it were out of shot. The listener will not be too distressed on seeing a bus passing and hearing it, but will wonder where that bus actually is if the camera is looking from a main road to a country scene. Under these circumstances it is justified to retake the scene for sound purposes. Often a director can be persuaded to reframe the shot to include the intrusive noise source, but sometimes may need to leave the frame as it was originally intended. The sound recordist's preference would be for a different location, but sadly such alternatives are decreasing.

As you are closer to the audio being recorded, and hence more aware of background noise, you will often have to complain before anyone else notices. Your closed-ear headphones cut you off generally and allow you to concentrate more on background levels. Often you may require another take when the previous take seems satisfactory to everyone else; only you know the pick-up of your microphones and their directivity. Experience will tell you that if you really did hear the dialogue that was being spoken, then it is all right. If time allows, then do it again, but if no real improvement can be gained it is a waste of shooting time.

For commercial production and cinema release it is quite normal at times to have the location as guide track only and post-synchronize the dialogue. The usual exceptions are locally produced commercials and lower-budget cinema releases.

One occasion when a poor-quality recording was used with some effect occurred while a crew was filming a documentary in Australia. The interviewee was a farmer from the American Deep South who had settled in Australia; he expressed a severe racial trend 'off camera' but never gave his true feelings on camera. It was decided to try a bugging situation, with a radio mic in the sound recordist's shirt, but it proved to be very badly placed. Also, the quality of radio mics was poor at that time. Because of the heat, and the difficulties of getting near the subject, the quality of the recording was, to say the least, diabolical. During the recording the subject let out all his hatred for his farm labourers, and his real reasons for settling in Australia.

On hearing the material the recordist was adamant that it was not of transmission quality, and should not be used. However, when the programme was transmitted these tracks *were* used; they sounded really bad, and full of echo. Naturally, the recordist felt betrayed, and wondered why the material had to be used, and not just voiced by the commentator. Next day, on entering the studio, the recordist was approached by colleagues, who said, 'The sound on that farmer was amazing. How did you get that amazing effect?' They also said it really did sound like a demented man. The reply was that there was no secret; it was just badly recorded.

Perhaps this shows that sometimes the location recordist can be wrong, and a creative editor can use a piece of sound in a way that will make it acceptable for a programme. There is certainly some mileage in the recordist's not rejecting material completely, as sometimes there really is only one bite at a piece of material, and a second bite can often have less real impact. If the production team is aware that a piece of audio is not up to standard, and the editor is informed, then perhaps it can be used in a different way. It is a fact of life on documentaries that if a piece of material is absolutely essential for a programme, it will be used anyway, quality or no quality.

Equalizing audio on location

In the past it was accepted practice within the BBC and other organizations on ENG assignments to 'fix' EQ, and discourage the application of heavy EQ on location. Since more independent access has been allowed, such tight control cannot be achieved with productions using outside crews and facilities.

Equalization should be used with great caution, as should the use of limiters and compressors, for the following reasons:

- Equalization can be applied much more accurately back at the studio or dubbing suite.
- Monitoring via headphones does not give an accurate judgement of bass response. Spill through the side of headphones often gives the wrong impression of background levels.
- Once audio is equalized on location it is difficult to replace lost quality without the addition of noise.

Most portable mixer units allow bass cut to be applied, but great care must be taken, as the ears are surprisingly good at 'getting used' to a particular EQ. This is often not noticed until a new voice or situation is presented and the recordist is at the point of no return, having applied increasing amounts of EQ. A few portable cut units exist: these not only supply phantom power and T-power but have more flexible slopes for bass cuts. A combination of these units and the minimum cuts on the mixers is usually satisfactory and not too severe.

CHAPTER 18

Technical considerations for stereo studio and location productions

THE A/B STEREO SYSTEM

The A/B system of stereo is what most of us know as **left/right** or X/Y stereo. In basic terms there is a time difference between the left and right signals, which represents the different time of arrival (TOA) at each ear from a fixed sound source. As the signals arrive at different times, the **phase** of each signal also varies. In general, the difference in signals is more noticeable at higher frequencies because of their shorter wavelength.

Phasing is more noticeable at frequencies in the lower range. At frequencies above about 1 kHz, time and amplitude differences become more noticeable. This gives our ears a sense of direction. Level differences are approximately 3 dB at 1 kHz and rise to around 30 dB at 10 kHz if the sound frequency is directed to one particular ear. If we were to 'pan' our head and get the sound source central, the

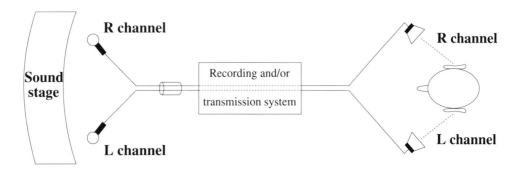

Figure 18.1 A typical stereo system.

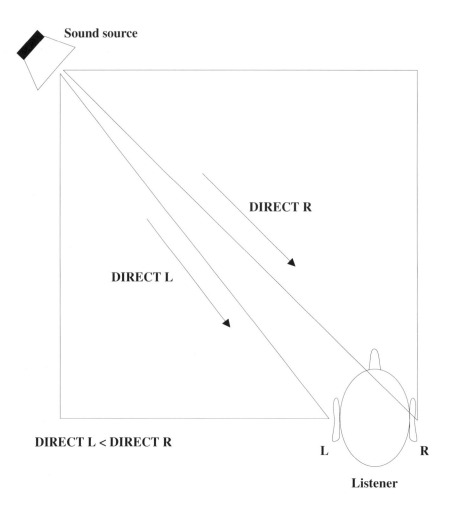

Figure 18.2 Diagram of time of arrival showing different timings of the signal reaching the ear.

ears would receive the same intensity of sound and phasing of the sound waves. As the average head measures approximately 16–16.5 cm between the two ears, these timing differences are extremely short – about 63 ms. In general listening rooms, the speakers would be around 8 ft apart, and the best listening position would be an equal distance between the two speakers in an equilateral triangle.

On location, many methods can be used for recording stereo images. There are two favoured microphone techniques: the crossed pair and the spaced pair. In both cases two identical mics are used. In the **crossed pair** system, the two microphones are above each other and angled towards the edge of the stereo field that you wish to create, overlapping in the centre. Usually these microphones are of a cardioid type, and would generally help to reduce background interference behind the stereo area and give a tighter image.

When a more spatial feel is required you can use the **spaced pair**. This is usually two omnidirectional microphones spaced several feet apart. The method can cause phasing problems, and often gives a 'hole in the middle' effect. You can use cardioid microphones for the spaced pair, but it needs care. Dubbing mixers in the film industry seem to prefer spaced pairs for their effects tracks, but it is not a practical proposition for TV shooting given the shooting time restrictions, and the current size of crews. Spaced techniques are suitable for large-screen productions with Dolby centre speakers, such as we have in the cinema.

Single-point microphones, with the two capsules above each other, are popular for effects shooting. Some have an 'end fire' capability, whereby you do not need to hold the microphone in a vertical position when pointing to the source of sound. Over the past few years dubbing mixers in film and TV have been a bit critical of single-point stereo microphones such as the Neumann RSM191, as phasing problems seem to be evident when used with Dolby surround stereo.

A current trend is to use two microphones by Sennheiser, or other manufacturers, 'piggybacked' in one windshield used as an M/S pair (see below); the M signal is received by a short rifle microphone, and the S signal by a figure-of-eight microphone (either dynamic or condenser). The two signals are fed into separate channels on the recorder and matrixed later in the dub or transferred to A/B stereo. However, it would not be difficult to matrix prior to the mixer unit or within the mixer unit and record in A/B stereo. The advantages are the same as single-point M/S microphones, but single-point systems are often switchable to A/B, and are adjustable by altering a simple switch to change their stereo width or image size. This system would still be susceptible to wind noise on the figure-of-eight microphone, and so would require adequate windshielding.

THE M/S STEREO SYSTEM

Under the M/S recording system the central image information or **mid** image is recorded on one track of the recording medium, with the **side** information, which is the stereo difference signal, recorded on another track. The difference signal is the one that provides the stereo image information. The mid signal can be assumed to be similar to the mono signal, and in the stereo rifle mic system this is a short rifle mic similar to the ones currently on location. So for recording dialogue, there is no difference from current mono techniques, except perhaps more concentration on the stereo image orientation.

The microphone units for the difference or side signals are usually either two separate elements, placed either side of the microphone, or a single figure-of-eight pattern microphone placed above a central mic. There are some problems with windshielding the side elements, and usually some low-frequency response correction is applied. It is usual to have adjustment on the amount of side signal from a remote control unit, which effectively alters the stereo image width. The M/S signals can at any time be converted to an A/B signal by feeding the signals through a suitable matrix with little or no loss.

At the mix-down or dub stage, the signal can be converted to A/B and handled all the way as a standard stereo signal, or treated as two separate signals, by feeding the mid signal into one channel and the side signal into two separate channels on a mixer. The two side signals are panned left and right on the mixer; one of the side signals must be phase-reversed at the channel input. The effective width of the image can be altered by adjusting the amount of side signal added to the mid signal in the mix. This can be a useful technique when riding edits and altering perspectives in drama productions. You could of course totally dispense

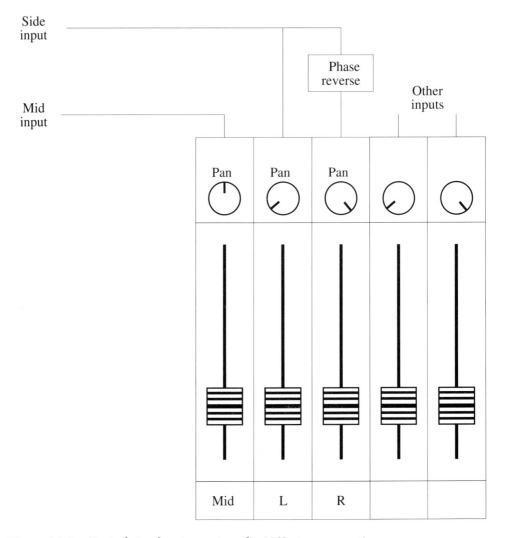

Figure 18.3   Typical simple mixer set up for M/S stereo operation.

with the side signals and add your own more appropriate effects as an A/B signal. It would therefore seem that the M/S system offers far more flexibility, artistically speaking, but it seems to meet a lot of opposition in some television dubbing theatres.

One problem with M/S recording systems is the marking of tapes and the transfer of same. It is easy not to notice that a recording is M/S unless it is marked correctly, so therefore it would not be treated accordingly, and probably assumed to be A/B stereo or even twin-track mono. There is a requirement that documentation must clearly state that a recording is M/S and that the signals are M/S and not A/B stereo, and this information must be advised on location to the production department as well as clearly stated on log sheets attached to the sound or picture rolls.

At the edit stage the editor can edit as in mono, paying little or no attention to the image. As long the difference signal is placed on the same separate track all the time, and the mid signal on the same separate track in the edit, the stereo information will be carried forward, assuming correct orientation of the left and right image as recorded on location. The difference signal or stereo image can be matrixed in the dub or sweetening stage, and the composite stereo A/B effect will be obtained.

ESTABLISHING THE STEREO MODE OF OPERATION

Before embarking on stereo location work it is essential that you are aware of the style of stereo operation the company employing you requires, and its internal technical requirements for editing and dubbing. Many companies in the broadcast field will not accept M/S productions without prior notice; others, the BBC in particular, request M/S stereo input. It is therefore essential that you establish the technical situation from the start of shooting, to avoid problems at a later stage in the editing of the location or studio material. There is certainly no problem in converting M/S recorded material to A/B at a later stage, but it can be time-consuming, and is best avoided if the company does *not* require an M/S input from you. (See Appendix 5 for a list of broadcast companies' current requirements for stereo operation.)

As well as checking the actual mode of operation it is wise to check that companies or facilities houses have the right hardware to play or transfer the material, as often outside facilities are limited. Broadcast companies are normally better equipped, having a wide range of transfer equipment with sophisticated facilities available for dealing with all audio and timecode signals.

Location track layouts are often dictated by the companies, and the logging sheets should clearly state the recorded track layouts for stereo. The BBC, for instance, often require that *nothing* is recorded on the second track if a production is mono. However, there is often a requirement on location to place an interviewer on one track and the interviewee on the other; without suitable warning this track configuration could easily be confused at the receiving end as some sort of stereo recording.

POST-PRODUCTION CONSIDERATIONS

On location, you must always be aware of the implications of your actions in post-production; wherever possible, you should ascertain how the material is to be handled at the post-production stage. Often production teams are unaware of the sound side of post-production, being more picture-orientated generally. If you can, seek out the eventual editor of the programme and perhaps the dubbing mixer; it will make for a much smoother, trouble-free operation. Often, prior to editing, material is viewed on low-quality systems, which have poor sound-monitoring circuits. This can give a wrong impression of audio quality, and may hide any problems there may be with location equipment or location audio quality. An initial check with the editor at the start of production should prevent any problems.

The supply of adequate wildtrack material as well as atmosphere tracks is essential to any kind of shoot, as the editing procedures will inevitably cause holes in the background atmosphere on the original recorded material. Good location 'fill' atmospheres will help to smooth out such problems. Where separate audio shooting is made from the picture, some way of tagging this material to the picture timescale is advisable. In film operation this is easy, as any track (wildtrack, dialogue etc.) that is applicable to a particular shot or sequence can carry an 'X' after the shot number. It is also possible for video with timecode using 'time of day'. When recording wildtrack dialogue for dramas it is wise to record it at different perspectives to give the editor a choice of perspectives to use.

Costly errors have been made on productions where consultations with post-production have not been made, so contact is essential to use these facilities to their fullest extent. In many cases the proper use of post-production can save costs for the location exercise, but the wrong assumptions about post-production can be equally expensive after the event.

USING RDAT RECORDERS ON A PRODUCTION

RDAT is already being used for location work. It offers the advantage of high-quality separate recordings. Separate sync systems are available, as are timecode recorders with off-tape monitoring. There has been a reluctance to use separate systems as the 'norm', because of the extra cost and time in post-production, and the inevitable visit to the dubbing suite. However, as edit suites become more stereo conscious, the RDAT machine, which follows video, is becoming more common.

Film production techniques are usually seen as a backward step, but can be used successfully with video. The good old-fashioned clapperboard can be used only for the separate audio sequences and standard practices used on other occasions. Many new sync systems are being used in the edit process, including Audiofile and other digital 'off lay' facilities. All are usually timecode synchronized and controlled by the edit suite's edit controller unit.

Location systems using a cable timecode burst on the RDAT machine, or a radio-transmitted timecode signal placed at the start of a take, are also very successful. The code bursts can be regenerated back at base and transferred with continuous code to a suitable machine for locking to an edit controller.

DAT Clockit burst unit ATM 101

This unit, built by Ambient in Germany, was designed for the Aaton sound recordist or for Betacam backup and additional recording in DAT quality. The idea is that, as in documentary film making with a normal camera and Nagra set up, the recordist is free to carry on recording as long as he or she needs, and is free to record ambiences, voice-overs and so on without having the camera turned on. On documentaries, the camera can move its position without disturbing the audio recording, as a burst of timecode has been placed at the start of the audio recording that is identical to the camera's current timecode.

The unit consists of an SQN 4S stereo mixer on which is mounted the Ambient burst clock. The external DAT recorder is given an automatic burst of timecode when switching to record. Powering is also supplied for the Technics SV260 (now out of production) and the Sony TCD10 Pro Dat. The recorded code burst is regenerated back in the transfer, and is of course in sync with the camera's timecode on the sync take. The timecode reference can be useful to attach wildtracks to particular takes at a later date.

Lockit ACL201 portable timecode and video sync generator

This unit is a self-contained timecode and video sync generator. It gives about two days' battery life on a new set of batteries. Internal DIP switches select the timecode and video formats. Crystal change for NTSC working is via an internal switch behind the backplate. A red and a green LED indicate generator sync and battery condition. The unit has timecode and composite sync outputs in the standard video formats, settable with internal DIP switches. The unit can be jam synced to external timecode or set by Aaton ASCII.

This unit is primarily used to sync video cameras, which not only take on the timecode of the unit but are also gen locked to the timecode. The camera is then truly locked to the timecode. Using this unit with gen lock will make all cameras run at exactly the same speed. By using the sync from the Lockit crystal the Clockit modules can then feed timecode to external audio recorders.

Fostex, Sony, Stellavox and HHB now have available location DAT timecode recorders and studio DAT timecode recorder players that are capable of being

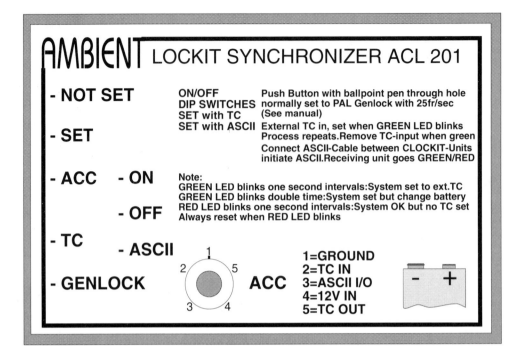

Figure 18.4 Lockit ACL201 synchronizer unit.

brought under edit control. These machines generally have four heads, allowing off-tape monitoring, lack of which is the disadvantage of the domestic and earlier models. These units are much more expensive.

Two recently developed systems are the ADAT and Hi-8 System recorders produced by Alesis, Fostex and Tascam. All systems are eight-track digital and capable of timecode operation. They are probably more suitable for edit suite operation than location, but their small size will make them useful for location music recording, and also for complicated dialogue situations, where many variants are required in sync with picture. However, a suitable mains supply should be available to power these types of recorder.

The eight-track DAT machines are extremely useful in the track-laying areas for post-production, allowing track laying to be done outside the dubbing areas, as well as the sync foleys (footsteps).

Another portable audio system that has been introduced is **digital compact cassette** (DCC), which is a digital system recorded on standard audio-style cassettes, which may replace the standard quarter-inch non-sync machine. Currently these machines seem to be making no headway in this direction, nor in the domestic field.

Sony and other Japanese manufacturers have introduced the digital **minidisk** system. These are smaller than compact disc units but are capable of similar

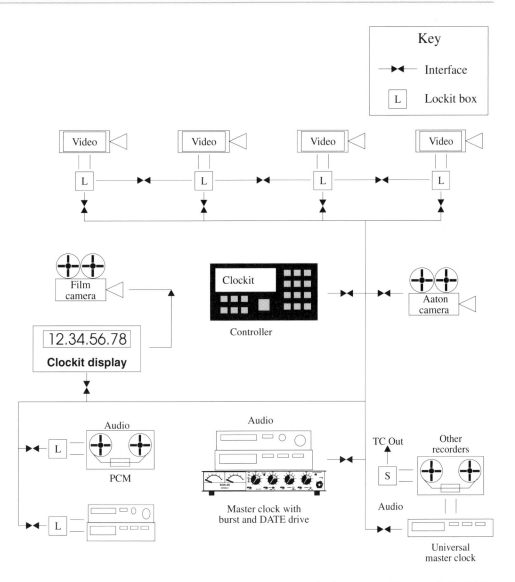

Figure 18.5 Typical system diagram using a Clockit controller and ACL201 synchronizer unit with external recorders and cameras.

audio quality. This system has proved to be slightly short on specification for broadcast use, but may find its way into the system with modifications.

USING RDAT RECORDERS ON LOCATION

The introduction of RDAT recorders for use in the field has opened up the possibilities for high-quality audio recording on location. However, RDAT machines suffer from a number of problems as regards location shooting. Their battery usage is heavy, so that a lot of replacement batteries need to be available on location. The use of external high-capacity batteries can help to achieve longer recording times. When the record button is pressed, the actual start of the recording is delayed by up to 3 s. The recordist therefore has to anticipate the start of recording, or has to advise the production crew to cue a little later. This does not present too much of a problem for a recordist who is experienced with the equipment. Some of the smaller types of RDAT machine have extremely small controls, which are difficult to see in adverse lighting or weather conditions. Some doubt has been expressed on their durability under adverse conditions, but results so far have been good, with few failures.

Domestic models lack a real monitor (off tape) of the actual recording, unlike the Nagra, HHB, Fostex and Stellavox recorders used professionally, with their 'off-tape' monitoring systems. The cheaper and earlier domestic models presented problems as there are only indications of low battery and level in the control monitor area. On one occasion a recordist using domestic RDAT had all indications that everything was being recorded, by the programme numbers advancing up towards 22, but a head clog had occurred early on and no audio had been recorded. On playing the tape on a larger Panasonic machine, the machine indicated that the heads needed cleaning by reading the error rate on the already recorded tape. Perhaps this facility should be extended to the higher-quality portable recorders.

Manufacturers of RDAT machines recommend cleaning the heads fairly regularly, although this is not usually the practice for rotating heads. It seems fairly sensible to do so prior to a long session, and does not appear to do any harm. Cleaning tapes are available quite cheaply. The only real check on domestic machines is to play back a recording.

Line-up on DAT machines seems arbitrary, but to match up with broadcast levels and keep the semi-professional meters in line across the dynamic range, a set-up level of about −12 to −15 dB, with reference to broadcast zero-level tone, seems to be correct. The early PCM701 digital processors had a line-up mark at this point on their level meters.

Some of the newer machines have self-diagnostic systems to advise the operator of any electronic problems, but it is almost impossible to remember all the diagnostic codes while you are in the field. A recordist working with a high-quality broadcast machine in a South American jungle was presented with an error reading on his machine. On checking the manual, which he happened to have with him, he was advised to return the machine to the dealer for repair. Unfortunately no such dealers were available in those jungles!

In the past, with analogue equipment, it was possible for the recordist to keep his equipment going and do first-line maintenance; it would seem that with current digital equipment a spare machine is essential.

ADVANTAGES OF USING RDAT AS A LOCATION SOURCE

There are a number of advantages:

- Extended recording times, with over 2 hours available, and 4 hours in LP mode on some domestic machines.
- The capability of sync operation and the possibility of operating separate from the camera. On documentaries and music programmes this would allow the extension of audio recording beyond the end of the camera's tape length.
- The extended frequency response of digital, with a 'transparent' transfer possible all the way to the dub, now that digital tracks are available on the video edit machines. This would also be helped by the fact that, along the chain, no system 'noise' should be added.
- The better interchange of material, with no head alignment problems between equipment to worry about as in the analogue system.
- For film operations the automatic track numbers on DAT can be easily tied up with shot numbers where the clapperboard system is used. The 'actual time' facility on a DAT machine can be used as an indication of which tracks to transfer.

DAT equipment can be useful in the field, as quite a substantial reduction can be made in the weight of equipment carried, but this tends to be countered by the extra batteries that are required to keep the professional machines running to meet location timescales. Over the first few months of operation with DAT equipment, it was found to be impossible to charge enough batteries to cover a typical 12 hour day, with machines giving only 2 hours' duration on batteries and the typical re-charge time being 12 hours.

Some companies and recordists are now carrying external batteries of about 30 amp-hour capacity, but the size and the weight of such batteries seriously restrict mobility. One way around the problem of battery use on smaller domestic-style machines is a heavy-duty battery like an Sony NP1B, or similar, which is suitably reduced to 6 V or whatever voltage the RDAT machine requires. This battery can supply a mixer unit, and has an emergency switch to power the portable RDAT when the machine indicates low battery. Up to 5 hours' running can be achieved with this modification on some domestic machines. It is also useful to have a multibattery charger unit constructed, which will charge up to four batteries at the same time. These two additions to any kit can take away the worry of battery failure in the field, which is probably the biggest problem.

The better headroom on digital machines has helped to avoid massive overloads on recording in the field. The recordist can generally err below maximum peaks and therefore never approach gross distortion on the recorded tracks. Although this is an advantage for the recordist, it is causing some concern for dubbing mixers, as there is a tendency for less level control on location, which was necessary in the past on analogue systems to avoid overload. It should still be the recordist's role to keep their sound levels within a reasonable dynamic range on most productions. In the broadcast system, despite the introduction of digital, there is still a transmitted dynamic range of only about 22–24 dB, which is quite restricting, and requires the recordist to do a great deal of level riding on location.

SUPPLYING WILDTRACKS OR BUZZ TRACKS

Wildtracks are usually recordings made non sync as a background cover, or separate recordings of dialogue to replace previously made sync recordings. Wildtracks can help in the final dubbed or completed item, and are invaluable in smoothing out edit bumps, or in sweetening in the final mix. These tracks are laid at the edit or run in at the final dubbing stage.

Usually it is better to record a wildtrack at the fader level settings for the original mainstream dialogue or interview. This technique allows the editor to cut in the wildtracks direct, at levels relevant to the original interview or dialogue level. This technique makes for a far smoother operation when the programme is dubbed, or assembled requiring less fader manipulation. It is a fact of life that editors rarely ride levels on wildtracks, or on many occasions just edit in the cut-aways direct at the original recorded levels. It is difficult to match levels without A/B comparisons. This is certainly true of film editors but sadly not always so with their video counterparts.

The acoustics of most edit suites are often unsuitable for audio monitoring at low levels, because of whirring video machines and the intrusion of air conditioning systems. This often leads to subtle differences in audio quality being missed.

Exceptions to the rule on wildtracks apply with, for example, shots deliberately taken to 'wallpaper' a story, such as aircraft, fast traffic, atmospheres, choirs performing, and voice-overs. When recording dialogue wildtracks they should, wherever possible, be recorded with a neutral background. The background should not be intrusive to the scene over which the dialogue is finally placed in the edit.

It is possible that part of an interview may be edited out and used over other locations. It is advisable to enquire if this is likely, either before or after the interview. You can always record these sections on a suitable location with a neutral background, so that they can be used over any scenes. The main problem with using sections of interview that were recorded on location is that the location background may not be appropriate to the pictures or the scene over which the wildtrack is to be placed.

It is no problem to re-record a piece of voice-over after shooting has finished, and it saves an editor a great deal of time in laying matching wildtracks in between the sections of inappropriate dialogue wildtrack to smooth out the tracks. The major problem in the edit may be that perhaps the location wildtrack has inappropriate background: for example, bird noises may be present on it, but the scene the dialogue is placed over is a room interior, where birds would not be appropriate! The reverse situation – using an interior-recorded wildtrack – is not as bad, provided there is not too much reverberation or room acoustic on the recorded track.

One case in point was a programme in which the main interview was recorded outside, but had very loud cicadas or grasshoppers present on the tracks. This presented a problem in any case, if only as a distraction. However, when sections of this interview were edited over other sections of the film, the background was intrusive. As there was no separate wildtrack of the intrusive noises, every time a wildtrack voice-over was added, the cicadas came and went. Overall, the illusion of smooth transitions of sound was totally disrupted, and as the voice-overs already had background as part of the track, the editor could not place a suitable atmosphere track over scenes.

This might well have been a situation where the director did not inform a recordist that he used his material in this way. Alternatively, the recordist may well not be used to working like that, and assume that all the material is going to be used only as 'in vision' material in the final edit. A discussion on how material is to be used is worth while before shooting commences, so that the recordist can give appropriate cover. The recordist normally has to prise this information from the production team, although the production people may well expect a recordist to do wildtracks without being asked. Most problems arise because inadequate shooting time is allowed, and re-recordings and wildtracks are seen as niceties. Most productions are vision orientated, and no one really worries about audio until the final stages of the production. So as a precaution it is always advisable to record an appropriate wildtrack for cover.

Because of the close proximity to the required sound source on radio mics it is often better to mix in a small amount of the local background atmosphere with the radio mics to give more life to the tracks. This helps to cover up some of the 'nasties' of radio mic operations. A small amount of added atmosphere to the close radio mic material helps to loosen off the sound and improve the audio per-spectives. This technique must be used with caution, as overdoing the levels that are added can produce problems for the recordist, and is often frowned upon by dubbing mixers.

In PSC (portable single camera) and news operations it is often a short period of time before the item or programme hits the air, so as much help as possible must be given from location to assist in the smooth editing of the programme.

You should inform editors of the way you have recorded your tracks, the layout of tracks, any problems on tracks, wildtracks recorded and what they are intended to cover.

Wildtrack cover of dialogue in drama production is *not* merely a technical exercise, as some directors seem to think; it is a cover to allow freedom of choice of perspective, and allows a director to have a choice of dialogue quality. The recordings should be taken soon after the original sync take to ensure the same location background.

Voice-overs and wildtracks under the present video recording systems, using Betacam and other forms of video recording equipment, must be recorded over **colour bars** or **colour black** level. This is to maintain synchronization in the edit suite and ensure that correct speed is maintained at the time of recording and playback. Colour bars are the standard video test signals; they contain synchronization signals, which must be present on tape when audio is recorded. Colour black level is simply a signal containing all the synchronization signals required for the video recording system, but the screen is black. It is preferable to record on colour bars, as they attract the editor's attention, and could warn of a voice-over recording or sound wildtrack. Often colour bars appear at the end of a tape roll to indicate the completion of a roll.

The appearance of portable RDAT recorders on the scene has changed the attitude towards wildtracks and sync shooting, with DAT being an available separate sync sound recording system. DAT recorders and the Nagra analogue recorder will both hold sync against video recorders, provided a suitable sync mark or clapper is placed on the picture source and sound source at the beginning or end of a take. However, they should be referenced to the colour signals syncs.

CHAPTER 19

Leaving the nest

This chapter takes a brief look at leaving the established broadcast organization and meeting the 'real world'. Since 1989 the changes within the broadcast industry have seen hundreds of sound engineers going out to find work in the freelance sector. Many operators found the change from 'steady' employment within a broadcasting organization to be a bewildering experience. It need not to be so.

A recent programme on BBC Radio 4 took a look at the decision to go freelance. It expressed the view that the potential freelancer should price himself at more than he would be paid if employed by a company, taking into account the following points:

- the cost of equipment, and running and repairs of the units;
- insurance of equipment, and public liability insurance;
- purchase of car and running costs;
- advertising one's services;
- accountant's costs;
- the need for profit to offset the risks of equipment purchase and repairs and leaving a permanent staff secure position.

PURCHASING EQUIPMENT

The decision on equipment purchase is a difficult one, as the changes are so rapid in all fields, but certain equipment is safe to buy for location work:

- a portable stereo mixer unit;
- two or three personal microphones;
- a stereo microphone, either a composite microphone or separate microphone units;
- a mono rifle microphone;
- a portable cassette machine for transcription purposes;
- a lightweight fishpole;
- high-quality headphones;
- two radio microphones;
- a collection of stereo cables and single mono cables.

When it comes to digital equipment, the field is so fluid that it seems unwise to commit yourself at this stage, except perhaps to buy a low-price DAT machine for wildtracks etc.

Many clients will want you to use equipment hired or owned by themselves, but such equipment is seldom adequate for the recordist, and is often of dubious quality or indeed untested. A sound person's ability and flexibility can be sadly reduced by inferior equipment, or equipment that does not have adequate flexibility. You should insist on using your own well-tried and tested equipment, even if this means reducing your price. In most cases a recordist's customized equipment saves time, gives a more professional result, and even looks more professional. Remember that inevitably, as recordist, you will be responsible for the final sound product. No amount of blame put on the equipment will satisfy the client, be it his equipment or yours.

Radio microphones present their own problems, because of frequency allocation and the high price of such units. Most broadcast companies have a specification on frequencies for their own areas, and dictate the correct frequencies to be used. With the current licence restrictions and constant frequency changes, you need to take great care in your decisions on radio mics, both on the type and on the frequencies used. On balance the scales must tip towards hire on these items.

PRICING YOUR PRODUCT

Pricing your own time and equipment can be difficult. It is generally based on the local freelancers' rates and union rates for the job. It is expected that equipment is charged extra, and stock and batteries on some occasions will also be charged extra. Do not forget the high price of batteries to run equipment; the cost is a charge to yourself, on top of what you receive for your daily rate.

As a starting point, it is often a good idea to find the basic rate that the client wants to pay for your services and equipment by asking what rate he or she usually pays. Pleasant surprises often come your way if you approach your sales pitch like this. Once a daily rate has been established you should decide how many hours this covers, and agree this with your client. It is unusual to find overtime as a part of an agreement, and more usual to find 10 hours or longer as the normal expected working day. It is common for an operator to have a rate for 8 hours and a rate for 10 hours, with an extra hour's rate at the rate divided by the contracted or agreed number of hours. Overtime unfortunately has become a dirty word, and buyouts are becoming common. It would therefore seem wise to have prepared a schedule of rates that include these options. Most companies are now aiming very low on rates, and with the influx of more hungry workers to the freelance field, rate cutting is not unusual.

You need to consider costing your own travel, and including it in your quote, usually based around the agreed national rate set by the broadcast companies.

However, there is often objection to these rates, and some negotiation may need to take place to agree a suitable rate for such travel.

ACCOUNTING AND BILLING

The use of an accountant, and his or her advice, is a must for all freelance operators. Seek the accountant's advice on the correct way to conduct your financial affairs. All the allowable expenses that you can claim will be clearly put forward in front of you, and this will allow you to have a clearer view of the situation. In general, the tax authorities deal fairly with the freelance operator, but there are grey areas with regard to working with broadcasters with their own equipment; this can apply also to other production companies. If you supply equipment and services, you will normally be taxed under Schedule D, but where the employer supplies the equipment, as broadcast companies do, the tax arrangement is often PAYE. A very good booklet on these matters is supplied by the TV and film union (BECTU); see Appendix C for the phone number.

The use of a home PC for accounting and billing, which should include a customer record and costing, is essential, not only to make the task easier but to keep you aware of current debts and indeed profits and losses. Many suitable software programs are available at under £100 that will do the job adequately.

You need to bill your clients swiftly, and if possible have some idea of their creditworthiness prior to taking on a job. The union publishes in its monthly magazine a list of clients that it advises you avoid. This does not of course mean that everyone else is a reliable client. Although you may be reluctant to chase up your invoices, with new clients it is expected that you will. Leaving invoices to roll without chasing them up is unwise, as a lot of clients – including some broadcast ones – wait three months before payment. Over these periods, remember that you will be expected to pay your own way.

On some long-term contracts the clients are prepared to 'up front' part of your payment, and pay from then on in stages. It is worth going for this option to pay your own invoices, while you are away.

It will be your responsibility to pay your own tax and National Insurance. Some freelance operators have a separate account, and place a certain amount into this for tax payment when it arrives. It will not be unusual for you to receive a very large tax assessment that sends you – clutching your throat – to your accountant, only to find that this always happens if your first year's accounts have not been submitted to the tax authorities.

FINDING THE WORK

There is no set way to find the work – or indeed to keep it. Most freelance operators will have contacts in the industry before going freelance, and most broadcast leavers will team up with colleagues who are in the same boat. The best way to keep the work is by doing a competent day's work at a reasonable price and, at the start, not to refuse anything that comes up, no matter how inconvenient.

The television union (BECTU) publishes annually a regional directory of freelance operators in all fields; inclusion in this directory for union members is free. It is also possible to advertise in other directories at a reasonable cost. *Broadcast* magazine has a section for advertisements for operators, and it seems to be quite well used.

You need to visit people, circulate yourself, and make your face and personality known. It is my belief that networking beats a mailshot. So many times, as if by magic, a job comes along after a visit to a potential employer, only because you have shown your face.

There is a lot of trust within the freelance industry, and a very good grapevine, so it is essential to be generally honest, to present a good image for the client, and to work with enthusiasm. Remember that the production is the client's pride and joy, and deserves your closest attention, even though it may be boring you to death!

Diversification is also essential when you are a freelance; often the 'other job' is the one that brings in the cash. Have a look at other areas that you have experience in and which are allied to your job, and pursue them as secondary areas. With the flooding of the freelance industry with redundant workers from the BBC and ITV, the traditional job areas are spreading. The area of the sound recordist has been seen as an easy area to hit by operators in other areas, who offer their own traditional role, plus the role of sound recordist. This seems an unsatisfactory way to operate, but is a fact of life in this changing industry.

KEEPING UP WITH STANDARDS OUTSIDE THE BROADCASTING INDUSTRY

One difficulty when leaving an established broadcasting organization is keeping up with the changing technical standards and requirements. So many changes occur over short periods of time that you will not always be able to keep up with the changing specifications or, indeed, the tools of the trade.

Companies do not print a technical requirement for their location work, only a requirement for the completed product. This document requires that all equipment should be up to broadcast standards, and includes a section that gives the companies and regulating authorities the right to check outside equipment for technical standards and give their approval. The overall technical quality is covered in the document issued, but this applies to the actual videotape supplied for transmission, not the recorded original.

In Appendix E (p. 199) you will find an assembled list of preferred practices for location recordings supplied to broadcasting organizations, which were current

Magnetic /DAT Report Sheet

Date:
Sheet No:
Client:
Production:

Roll No:

Your Company Address
and Phone Number

Recorder Make:

Sample Rate

44.1 Khz / 48 Khz
Tape Speed 3.75 / 7.5 / 15

Sync: Xtal / Wild / Video / Int

Status: Master / Copy
Stereo: A/B / M/S
Mono
Noise Reduction:

Location:
Location Details
Sound Engineer:

TRANSFER

16 mm
Quarter Inch
Betacam
DAT

Scene / Slate	Take	Footage Timecode	Mono Stereo	Channel 1	Channel 2
PRINT CIRCLED OR MARKED TAKES FOR TRANSFER					

Figure 19.1   A typical sound report sheet.

in 1993/94. It is always wise to check with the company for which the material is intended as to their technical standards. Seldom is the production team fully briefed on the final audio technical specifications. Briefings on the post-production requirements rarely seem to filter down to the production representatives.

The paperwork that goes with your sound product is always an essential item, and can do no harm if overdone. It should include a contact number for yourself should problems occur or in case there are any queries of a technical nature.

APPENDIX A

Further reading

Aikin, Glyn (1992) *Sound Recording and Reproduction*, 2nd edn, Focal Press.

Aikin, Glyn (1994) *Sound Techniques for Video and TV*, Focal Press.

Borwick, John (1992) *Microphones: Technology and Technique*, Focal Press.

Bushby, Alex (1993) *A–Z of Film, Television and Video Terms*, Blueprint.

Mansfield, John (1994) *Narration and Editing: Sound for Television*, BBC Television Training.

Miles Huber, David (1992) *The Microphone Manual*, Focal Press.

Nisbett, Alan (1992) *Technique of Studio Sound*, 4th edn, Focal Press.

Nisbett, Alan (1993) *The Use of Microphones*, 4th edn, Focal Press.

Rumsey, Francis (1989) *Stereo Sound for Television*, Focal Press.

Rumsey, Francis (1990) *Tapeless Sound Recording*, Focal Press.

Rumsey, Francis and McCormick, Tim (1994) *Sound and Recording: An Introduction*, Focal Press.

Zaza, Tony (1993) *Sound Recording Techniques for Film and Video*, Prentice-Hall.

Zaza, Tony (1994) *Mechanics of Sound Recording*, Prentice Hall.

APPENDIX B

Glossary

Much location work is surrounded by jargon and technical terms, all of which is rather confusing to the newcomer to locations and studios. Some terminology is universal to studio and location operators, but with the influx of video equipment a large amount of terminology has 'hung over' from the early days of TV and film. Some of these terms are listed below. A few new buzzwords have developed with the introduction of video, and are included here.

Parts of this glossary are edited extracts from *A Stereo Glossary* compiled by the Institute of Broadcast Sound, and are used by kind permission. Extra items have been added to make the glossary more suitable for this book.

A leg and B leg The two signals carrying a stereo signal. The A leg is the left signal and the B leg the right. Sometimes referred to as X/Y.

A/B mics Term often used for spaced mic techniques, or to distinguish mics producing outputs consisting of left and right signals from an M/S stereo signal.

Amos Atmosphere track of location recorded wild or with camera.

azimuth error Error due to the gap in the playback head (or original record head) not being at right angles to the travel of the tape. The effect of azimuth error is to reduce high-frequency response or, in severe cases, introduce a comb effect (phasing) in the derived mono signal.

balance control Adjusts the relative levels of the A and B legs in a stereo signal,

allowing an accurate positioning of the centre of the stereo image. Sometimes found on loudspeaker circuits as well as input channels.

barney Soft cover placed over a film camera for noise reduction.

bars Camera colour test bars for line-up purposes.

binaural Two-channel audio, to be heard on headphones, which attempts to mimic sound the way the ears hear it. A typical mic arrangement for binaural is two small omnidirectional microphones spaced about 9 in apart with some sort of dummy head (or even the operator's head) between them.

bird Satellite terminal or dish.

bit Short for 'binary digit'. Digital/PCM systems use pulses that indicate either 'on' or 'off' state. Each piece of data is known as a bit. In audio systems the dynamic range is determined by the number of bits used to measure each sample: in general, the higher the number of bits, the better the system.

blimp Similar to a barney but a 'total' cover of camera and lens, which should considerably reduce any camera mechanical noise. Usually has a hard outer case.

Blumlein pair The original coincident microphone arrangement invented by Alan Blumlein at EMI, using two figure-of-eight microphones at 90 degrees.

boom A studio mechanical crane with adjustable arm with tracking pram, usually used for drama production. Enables operators to reach far into sets with the microphone. Rarely used outside.

box, the Usually refers to the control room in studio situations where the director and production personnel are situated.

buzz track Similar to *wildtrack*, but usually the atmosphere that prevailed at the time a scene was recorded. Also a special optical sound test track, on 16 mm or 35 mm film, for alignment of PEC sound head.

cans Headphones.

cardioid microphone Microphone with a heart-shaped polar response. Useful for rejecting sound from the rear.

centre track timecode Timecode signal recorded in a guard band between audio tracks on a quarter inch tape machine. The code is used for synchronization with pictures.

coherent When two signals are coherent, identical in phase and level they will add when combined. The sum of the signals is usually 6 dB higher than each.

coincident pair Stereo mic technique using directional microphones placed very close together at an angle.

coincident stereo Form of stereo that uses level differences between legs to create the position between the loudspeakers on replay.

companding System that compresses the dynamic range of a signal when processed on the input and expands the signal on the output. Usually used as a noise reduction system.

compatibility Many listeners to stereo television broadcasts listen in mono, and it is essential that the derived mono sound is satisfactory. Compatibility implies that the acoustic and relative levels sound similar in mono and stereo.

crossed pair See coincident pair.

crosstalk The degree of breakthrough between two channels. Crosstalk for stereo FM and LP disc should be better than −20 dB. Tape systems should deliver −40 to −50 dB. Crosstalk in a digital system should be undetectable.

dailies US term for rushes.

data compression System that discards unwanted information in a digital system, allowing other signals to mask this removal. Dramatically reduces the amount of information to be recorded or transmitted. Used in the NICAM system, minidisk, hard disk editing systems and compact disc.

delay When mixing the output of a distant stereo pair with close-positioned panned mics, some blurring of definition can occur because of the extra time taken for the sound to get to the distant mics (approximately 1 ms per foot). Use of a delay line in the close mics can give an equal delay to improve the mixed sound.

desk Audio mixer unit.

dipping in Usually when a boom operator is just entering shot at the top of frame.

drop in Switching recording machine from play to record while running to make an electronic edit.

dropout Momentary loss of sensitivity in a recording medium (tape). This can cause a drop in level or an image shift when affecting only one channel of a stereo recording.

dry A dry signal is one without reverberation.

dual sound-in-syncs Encoding system to convert a stereo audio signal to a digital stream to be inserted in the line sync pulse period of the transmitted video signal.

dynamic range Difference between the loudest and the softest sound in a recording system or a recorded signal.

eye-line Line between the camera and the artiste or the line between an artiste and the subject they are watching.

figure-of-eight microphone Microphone with a response pattern that resembles the figure 8.

floor Usually describes the studio area where recording is taking place. Can also be used on locations to describe the set.

foldback Audio returned (usually on speakers) to the action area, feeding sound that is either outside the studio or location, or is pre-recorded and relative to the action.

foleys Footstep tracks, usually for drama productions; recorded 'in sync' to pictures within a dubbing suite or by an external specialist company.

FX Sound effects or video effects.

gag Usually describes a windshield for a microphone.

gain Amount of extra amplification inserted to increase signal level.

ganged When two devices (e.g. faders or potentiometers) are tied together so that they operate identically from the same control knob.

GLITS tone BBC identification tone that identifies both legs of a stereo signal, interrupting the A leg once and the B leg twice. The pattern is such that any phase problems would be noticed and any reversal of the legs would be noticed.

guard track The space between tracks on a tape recorder, or a track left unused on a multitrack recorder between programme sound and non-programme sound, such as timecode or a click track.

guide track Recording made to guide or help an editor to lay in post-recorded sound to original location track.

headroom Amount of safe working area above maximum peaks that a system allows. Also the amount of space above a picture.

howlround Acoustic feedback, usually caused by a microphone being too close to a loudspeaker source, or by feeding the same signal back on to itself.

hybrid Usually applied to a telephone balancing unit for feeding audio down telephone lines and recording from the same lines.

image Perceived location of a single source within the sound stage. An image can be narrow or wide. It may be precise or blurred.

left On the left as heard from the control desk. This will often be the performer's right but will coincide with camera left.

M signal Represents the sum signal obtained by mixing A and B legs together equally and in phase, usually attenuated by 3 dB (in the BBC). 'M' does not stand for mono, but for mid or middle (originally the German word Mitte).

M/S Term referring to the two signals *middle* and *side*, which form another way of recording a stereo signal. The two signals are recorded on separate channels.

M/S microphones This technique obtains the M and S signals directly from coincident microphones. Typically, the M signal is from a forward-facing cardioid, but it can be any polarity, depending on the width and acceptance angle required for the mic pair. The S signal is obtained by a sideways facing figure-of-eight mic. Apart from some practical advantages in television work, in some applications they can produce better-defined central images than A/B stereo mics.

matricing Technique of combining signals into different form for recording, processing or transmission. The common forms of matricing are: $A + B = M$; $A - B = S$; $M + S = A$; $M - S = B$.

middle and side See M/S.

monaural Sometimes used to mean monophonic, but actually means listening with one ear!

monophonic Conventionally, the description of sound derived by a simple mix of the A and B legs of stereo.

monophony Sound engineered to a single channel.

multi Multicored sound cable capable of feeding many inputs or outputs.

NATSOF Natural sound effects recorded in sync with picture.

Nicam 728 Digital transmission system designed by BBC Research Department and used as the television stereo transmission system in the UK and some other countries.

omnidirectional microphone Microphone sensitive to sound from all directions.

on the fly Effects or music played in as the recording tape runs in real time. Not previously laid on tape.

P to C Piece to camera: an item delivered straight to camera from a reporter or participant.

pack shots Close-up shots of products or items specifically mentioned in dialogue.

pad Attenuator for reducing signal levels.

pan-pot Contraction of 'panoramic potentiometer': a control that takes a mono signal and divides the feed to the A and B legs so that the image may be moved fully left or right or any place between.

panel See mixer panel.

phasing The result of the selective cancellation of some frequencies or, more often, the mixing of two nominally identical signals with a short or varying time delay between them.

pot Shortened version of potentiometer or fader/level control.

POV Visual 'point of view' of a character or observer of a scene. For instance, if an actor in a play has seen a murder, the camera takes his or her place and 'looks' at the action as it was seen by the participant.

processor (stereo) Device installed in some sound desks for adjusting the offset and/or width of a stereo source. One control can adjust the relative levels of A and B. Another adjusts the relative levels of M and S. Often installed in echo return channels to adjust for central reverberation collapse and also reverb width inasmuch as this may affect mono compatibility.

return Signal returning to a mixer desk input from an external unit, either an effects unit or a recording unit.

run Command to tell operator to start equipment and record.

running, rolling and turning over Indicates that either the camera, or the audio recorder if separate, is actually in motion and ready to record. In film it would be expected that both operators would indicate before shooting commenced.

rushes Video or film daily location tapes; magnetic or film stock.

S signal Difference signal obtained by mixing the A and B legs equally and out of phase. S does *not* stand for 'stereo' but for 'side'. It can usefully be thought of as being represented by a sideways facing figure-of-eight microphone (from which it can be directly obtained as in the M/S mic techniques).

scanner Outside broadcast vehicle; also known as MCR (mobile control room).

scope Oscilloscope.

send Usually a signal that is sent from an auxiliary or other output to an external source or piece of outboard equipment.

set Usually describes either a fixed studio scenery set-up, or a location within which the artistes are working.

simulcast Usually used to denote a television and radio simultaneous broadcast.

soft Usually refers to picture being out of focus, or deliberately defocused for effect; can also refer to soft contrast.

soundstage The available width of a stereo presentation; normally the full width between the loudspeakers.

spaced microphones Technique using microphones that are spaced (as opposed to coincident), often by many feet, but may be only several inches. Sometimes called A/B mics. The technique is widely used in commercial recordings (such as the so-called Decca Tree). A group of three mics a few feet apart or an array across the front of an orchestra are sometimes used. Mono compatibility is usually worsened because spacing causes cancellations for some combinations of frequency and direction of source. The technique is most useful in friendly and desirable acoustic environments, and notwithstanding its disadvantages usually gives an equal proportion of direct and reverberant sound in stereo or mono. The imaging is diffuse compared with coincident mic techniques.

speed Indicates on film and video locations that the camera is up to speed and stable, so that recording can commence.

speed of sound The speed varies, but is generally about 760 miles per hour at sea level, or about one foot per millisecond.

spreader Device for taking a mono signal and 'spreading' it across the sound stage to a desired degree. Some, such as the Orban Stereo Synthesizer, achieve this by frequency banding, others by random frequency panning. Others that use delay circuits should be used only with caution because they can produce bad mono compatibility.

square Usually defines audio tone when it sounds distorted.

squawk box Studio intercommunications unit or talkback unit.

squeak Audio frequency run carried out for test purposes to confirm that equipment or incoming lines are up to specification.

stereo ident tone In ITV the EBU tone is used with the A leg pulsed and the B leg constant; in the BBC GLITS tone is used internally.

stereo line-up Level used for setting up systems. In mono, 0 dBu. Line-up for stereo varies between the BBC and ITV: 0 dBu for ITV on the –6 dB system and –3 dBu for the BBC on the –3 dB system, both using A + B for derived mono.

stereo link Usually found in compressors and limiters; links the two units electronically, ensuring that the image does not wander.

stereophony From the Greek: literally 'solid sound'.

strike Remove the set or object from a set or location. Not to be confused with Union action.

talkback Return and forward communications unit used between the director/cameras/sound and all interested parties on a live or recorded production.

TOA Time-of-arrival difference. The ears sense a sound's location by the different times of arrival of the signal to the ears. Speaker systems recreate these timing differences in the home or studio.

vox pops From the Latin *vox populi*; in television refers to quick interviews with members of the general public on current topics.

width processor Control in a stereo channel of a sound desk or a stereo processor that increases or diminishes the relative levels of S to M, thereby making a stereo source wider or narrower.

wildtrack Audio track that is not synchronous to picture, usually dialogue or atmosphere.

wrap Indicates the end of the shooting period; derived from the film industry term in the early days of 'wind reel and process'.

zero level Standard reference level used in broadcasting; equivalent to 0.775 V r.m.s. irrespective of impedance.

APPENDIX C

Television organizations and manufacturers

BROADCAST AUDIO EQUIPMENT HIRE COMPANIES

London

Audiohire	0181 960 4466
Better Sound	0171 836 0033
Dreamhire	0181 451 5544
FX Rentals	0181 964 2288
Hand Held Audio (radio mics)	0181 880 3243
HHB Communications	0181 960 2144
Hilton Sound	0171 708 0483
London Communications Ltd	0171 223 8166
Osborne Sound Equipment	0171 437 6170
R.G. Jones Sound Hire	0181 540 9881
Richmond Film Services	0181 940 6077
Samuelson Film Services	0181 578 7887
Stirling Audio	0171 624 6000

Carlisle

GFE Equipment Hire	01228 44287; 01706 223147

Midlands

Birmingham Sound Hire	01902 751184
Raycom (radio mics and comms)	01789 400600; 01789 400255

The North

Canford Audio	0191 415 0205

Chris Clarkson Audio	01937 574519
Futurist Light and Sound	01924 468183
KGM Studio Specialists	01924 371766
Michael Gaunt Camera Rentals	0113 258 8080
Pro-Vision	0113 242 5296

The North West

Mac Sound	0161 969 8311
Playlite Hire Ltd	0161 232 9510

Scotland

Mcmillan Video Ltd	01241 78411
Tone Zone Ltd	0141 946 0227

MICROPHONE MANUFACTURERS

AKG Acoustics (Harman International Industries)	0181 207 5050
Audio Technica	0113 277 1441
Beyer Dynamics	01273 479411
Bruel & Kjaer	+45 48 14 27 00
Neumann	01628 850811
Sennheiser UK Ltd	01628 850811
Shure (HW International)	0181 808 2222
Sony Broadcast	01256 55011

RADIO MICROPHONE MANUFACTURERS

AKG Acoustics Ltd	01483 425702
Audio Engineering Ltd (Micron)	0171 254 5475
Audio Ltd	0181 743 1518
Beyer Dynamic GB Ltd	01273 479411
Sennheiser UK Ltd	01628 850811
Telex Ltd	01908 690880
Trantec Systems	0181 640 1225

AUDIO SOUND MIXING DESKS

Alice Soundtech plc	01444 248071
Amek Systems and Controls Ltd	0161 834 6747

AMS Neve	01282 457011
Audio Developments Ltd	01543 375351
Audix Broadcast Ltd	01799 542220
Calrec Audio Ltd	01422 842159
Clyde Electronics Ltd	0141 962 7950
Filmtech	01222 342907
Solid State Logic	01865 842300
Soundcraft Electronics	01707 665000
Soundtracks plc	0181 399 3392
SQN Electronics Ltd	01624 824545
Tascam	01923 819360
Tony Larkin Pro Sales Ltd (TLC mixer)	01462 480009

GENERAL AUDIO EQUIPMENT SUPPLIERS

Ambient Recording (timecode units)	010 89 651 85 35
Audio System Components Ltd	01734 811000
Axis Audio Systems	0161 474 7626
Canford Audio plc	0191 415 0205
Futurist Film Developments	01844 238444
Haydon Laboratories (Denon)	01753 888477
HHB Communications	0181 960 2144
Hilton Sound plc	0171 708 1483
KGM Studio Specialists	01924 371 766
Music Lab	0171 388 1953
Nicral (ISDN systems)	01672 810351
Pag Ltd (chargers and batteries)	0181 543 3131
Raper and Wayman Ltd	0181 800 8288
Rycote Windshields	010 453 759338
Shuttlesound Ltd (Electrovoice mics)	0181 809 1515
Stirling Audio Systems	0171 624 6000
Studio Audio and Video Ltd (Sadie)	01353 648888
Studio Equipment (timecode equipment)	01865 891523
Studiospares	0171 485 4168
Tony Larkin Pro Sales Ltd	01462 480009
Wood and Douglas (UHF/VHF comms)	01734 811444

DAT AND TAPE MACHINE MANUFACTURERS

Denon Pro Audio	01234 741200
Fostex (UK) Ltd	0181 893 5111

HHB Communications Ltd	0181 960 2144
Nagra Kudelski (GB) Ltd	01727 810002
Otari UK	01753 580777
Sony Broadcast UK	01256 474011
Studer/Revox	01635 876969
Tascam (Teac)	01923 819630

HARD DISK EDITING SYSTEMS

Akai UK	0181 897 6388
AMS Neve (Audiofile)	01282 457011
Avid Technology	01753 656301
DigiDesign	01415 323 8155
Digital Audio Research	01372 742848
Digital Audio Solutions (Pro Tools)	0171 258 3454
Digital Music	01703 270405
Fairlight Europe	0171 267 3323
Lightworks Editing Systems	0171 494 3084
Otari UK Ltd	01753 580777
Roland UK	01252 816181
Sadie Disk Editor	01313 572 0500
Soundscape Digital Technology	01222 450120
Synclavier Company	0181 669 4265

BROADCAST COMPANIES

BBC Television

BBC Head Office	0171 580 4468
BBC Television Centre	0181 743 8000
BBC Northern Ireland	01232 338000
BBC Scotland	0141 339 8844
BBC Wales	01222 564888
BBC Aberdeen	01224 625233
BBC Bangor	01248 370880
BBC Dundee	01382 202481
BBC Edinburgh	0131 225 3131
BBC East	01603 619331
BBC East Midlands	0115 947 2395
BBC Midlands	0121 414 8888
BBC North	0113 244 1188
BBC North East	0191 232 4141

BBC North West	0161 200 2020
BBC South	01703 226201
BBC South West	01752 229201
BBC Swansea	01792 654986
BBC West	0117 973 2211

Independent Television

Anglia Television	01603 615151
Border Television	01228 25101
Carlton Television	0171 240 4000
Central Broadcasting	0121 643 9898
Channel Television	01534 68999
Channel Four Television	0171 631 4444
GMTV	0171 827 7000
Granada Television	0161 832 2029
HTV	01222 590590
Independent Television News	0171 833 3000
London Weekend Television	0171 620 1620
Meridian Broadcasting Ltd	01703 222555
Radio Telefis Eirann – RTE	+353 1 643111
S4C – Welsh Channel Four	01222 747444
Scottish Television plc	0141 332 9999
Tyne Tees Television	0191 261 0181
Ulster Television	01232 328122
Westcountry Television Ltd	01752 333333
Yorkshire Television Ltd	0113 243 8283

BROADCAST TRAINING, GUILDS AND UNIONS

Association of Motion Picture Sound	0171 402 5429
BBC Broadcast Training (Wood Norton)	01386 45123
BECTU (the broadcast trade union)	0171 437 8506
BKSTS – British Kinematograph, Sound and Television Society	0171 242 8400
BKSTS Training	0171 242 8400
Bristol University Film and TV Dept	0117 930 3030
European Media School	0191 495 3213
Institute of Broadcast Sound	01753 646404
London International Film School	0171 240 0168
National Film and TV School	01494 71234
Northern School of Film and TV	0113 283 3193

Ravensbourne College	0181 295 0324
Royal Television Society	0171 723 8074
School of Audio Engineering	0171 609 2653
Script to Screen Ltd	01943 870238
Skillset (NVQ details)	0171 927 8585

Audio formats with video

1 inch C-format (reel-to-reel)

Two linear audio tracks with Dolby noise reduction type A, plus a dedicated time-code track. This format was the accepted broadcast standard, but is being slowly taken over by the Betacam SP format.

Betacam SP

Betacam cassette up to 90 minutes' duration. Two linear audio tracks with Dolby C noise reduction, plus two FM and a dedicated timecode track. The FM tracks on location are useful as a back-up, or can be used as extra tracks on location only. Because you have to record a picture to record FM tracks they are of little use beyond the original recording stage. The FM tracks are layered beneath the video tracks and at a different azimuth.

Hi-Band SP

U-matic videocassette. Two good linear audio tracks with Dolby C, plus a dedicated timecode track. Timecode not re-stripeable separate from video.

Hi-Band

U-matic videocassette. Two linear audio tracks; no noise reduction. Since the introduction of Hi-Band SP, used much less.

Lo-Band

U-matic videocassette. Two linear audio tracks. Poor audio quality; seldom used professionally, but used quite often in training establishments and universities.

S-VHS

VHS cassette. Two linear audio tracks with Dolby C noise reduction, plus two FM tracks for stereo. Higher quality than standard VHS; used by some broadcast companies for news operations, but being phased out already. Some machines have timecode track.

VHS

Videocassette. One linear audio track for mono, plus two FM for stereo. Standard format for video distribution of pre-recorded tapes. Stereo linear tracks split the standard mono plus guard band, and gives very poor stereo on linear stereo tracks.

Hi-8

One linear audio track for mono, plus two FM tracks for stereo. Some models have a digital track capability. PCM audio on video track. Special timecode track can be converted to EBU timecode on edit controller. Popular for 'sneaky' under-cover shooting in broadcast documentaries.

R-DAT

Rotary digital audio cassette. One set of stereo tracks; 16-bit digital with similar quality to compact disc. Some professional machines have a dedicated timecode track built into subcodes. A very high-quality recording machine, which is fast becoming a part of all recordist's location kit.

ADAT

S-VHS cassette based. A new format based on S-VHS record machine with eight digital audio tracks. 16-bit digital recording. Adaptors allow synchronization to video systems. This unit, introduced in 1992, will see placement in editing and low-cost dubbing areas. A simple remote control is available at present. With the more comprehensive controller available, full control of all parameters is possible, with slaving of many machines possible, giving a greater number of usable tracks.

DCC

Standard Philips audio cassette size, different tape type. This new standard is based on a standard audio cassette, with 90 minutes running time with a break for head direction change at 45 minutes; however, this may be overcome in later models. Two track 18-bit digital (claimed) audio with capability of replay of normal analogue cassette. The system has a new system called PASC (precision active sub coding), which is similar in action to Dolby S. A serial copy management system is present on the system to allow only one digital copy. Could probably be used as a replacement for DAT in the future.

Minidisk

Mini floppy disk. This new format is twin-track stereo 16-bit digital, and is meant to challenge DCC. Maximum recording is 74 minutes. This may take the place of radio microphones on some difficult assignments.

Quarter inch tape

Audio reel-to-reel. Usually two tracks but can be multitrack. With options for noise reduction and centre track timecode.

Cassette

Philips audio. Two linear audio tracks with option for Dolby C, B and HX Pro. Some machines have a 50 Hz pilot tone and timecode option, but are reduced to mono operation by these.

Current technical requirements for broadcast location stereo input to companies

The results of a survey conducted in the summer of 1993 provided the following specifications from the broadcasting companies and organizations for incoming material, in particular stereo recording. I wish to thank all the companies for their assistance in this survey. Until now there was no information available on these working practices for the freelance operator.

BBC TELEVISION

PSC shoots (normally on Beta SP) in stereo.

Record M/S stereo on tracks 1 = M, 2 = S, 3 = M, 4 = S. From performance locations, music concerts for example, A/B is acceptable but should preferably be duplicated on an audio-only medium (e.g. R-DAT) and must be clearly marked. Never mix M/S and A/B on the same roll.

PSC shoots (Beta SP) in mono

Single mono: record on tracks 1 and 3 only. *Dual mono* (two separate mono sources): record mono 1 on tracks 1 and 3, mono 2 on tracks 2 and 4. The tape *must be marked Twin-Track*. Avoid mixing stereo and dual mono on the same roll or cassette. If not possible for operational reasons, *mark clearly and verbally ident*.

M/S stereo

As above, M/S stereo is acceptable and often preferred, but the message once again is *mark clearly*. M to track 1 (and 3 if available); S to track 2 (and 4 if available).

Drama stereo

Generally M/S sync pick-up is preferred. For electronic post-production, mono dialogue with stereo FX is a very poor second. Where film-style post-production is to follow, then the capabilities of the editor and dubbing house will have to be taken into consideration. For Dolby stereo post-production, mono dialogue plus stereo FX is virtually mandatory. So:

- Pick up M/S always.
- Offer stereo for all BBC productions.
- Indicate which track carries the M signal, for those who can *only handle mono.*
- Record simultaneous FX and wildtracks with a stereo pair, not a single space mic. *Mono dialogue/single-spaced mic does not give stereo.*

BBC edit suites are all capable of handling M/S stereo in the following formats: M or A on odd/upper/left/centre; S or B on even/lower/right/edge.

Line-up levels

For clarity it is safest to relate line-up levels to analogue peak. Equipment/systems/circuit line-up is made with tones at −8 dB with reference to peak (i.e. PPM4). Programme line-up − i.e. the tones immediately preceding programme material − uses tones at −11 dB with reference to peak (PPM 3.25, or −3 dB with reference to zero level) for stereo. Derived mono maximum level is peak (PPM 6). (Mono = (A + B) −3 dB.)

Digital recordings are as above, except that for reasons of safety headroom, analogue peak is not the same as digital peak. For 16-bit recordings the EBU recommendation (proposal), which the BBC follow, is for standard line-up at −18 dB with reference to peak. This puts analogue peak at −10 dB with reference to digital peak.

Tape identifications

The BBC internally uses GLITS tone rather than EBU tone for stereo. This positively identifies both A and B legs, indicates correct pairings, and checks for out-of-phase. However, those not equipped with GLITS tone may supply correctly identified EBU tone.

At the start of each programme or recording session, bands of at least 30 s of tones at approximately 100 Hz and 10 kHz are much appreciated. If a noise reduction system is in use (not BBC standard, but acceptable), then its presence and type must be shown on the information areas, and the appropriate line-up signals – again at least 30 s – should be recorded. Appropriate line-up signals in this context mean manufacturer's standards: e.g. Dolby tone (A) or noise (SR).

Finally, accurate log sheets containing slate or shot numbers, programme numbers and/or timecode starts/ends must be provided. Any wildtrack locations and durations must also be indicated.

PPM levels

Where material is not complex – i.e. not a mix of many sources – and is to be carried through a post-production process, then recorded levels should be judged so as to make best use of the recording medium in terms of signal-to-noise ratio, but without significant compression. Compressors and limiters should generally only be used to facilitate clean recordings, avoiding noise or distortion. However, programme material that is partially or completely mixed should be recorded substantially in accordance with the following guidelines:

	PPM
Speech to camera (documentary)	4.5–5
Drama dialogue (general)	3.0–5
Drama dialogue (peaks)	6
Classical music (majority range)	1–5
Classical music (peaks)	6
Classical music lowest:	
not more than 30 s	<2
not more than 10 s	<1
Rock and pop music	5.5
Applause (alone)	5.0
Applause (with music)	6.0

Compressed material is best avoided if the compression will be very obvious. Where desirable or unavoidable, apparent loudness should be the guide. Speech should be recorded so as to sound similar in loudness to equivalent uncompressed speech, and will therefore peak 4–5 dB lower. Operators should remember that the commonest form of compression is that produced by overworked limiters, especially those included in radio mic transmitters for protection reasons.

Obviously the BBC would expect equipment to meet broadcast standards and to be kept to such a standard.

THE ITV NETWORK

Granada Television

Granada Television conforms to all the ITC technical specifications, as do all ITV network companies, but the basic sound rules below apply.

Radio microphones

Prior to any programme being made within the Granada contract area, it is essential that programme makers ensure that they are operating on the radio mic frequencies allocated to Granada Television:

    217.000 MHz   184.800 MHz   201.000 MHz
    175.525 MHz   192.800 MHz   216.600 MHz

Any queries concerning the use of these frequencies within the Granada area and all requests for licences covering other UK areas should be addressed to John Hesketh of Granada Facilities.

Requirements for video post-production

Granada Television requires that all location dialogue be recorded in mono, with stereo effects supplied in A/B stereo. Any input of M/S stereo must be cleared with Granada's Chief Engineer prior to shooting. A copy of Granada Television's technical requirements can be obtained by contacting them. Any queries beyond the technical requirements booklet should be addressed directly to the Chief Engineer at Granada Television.

What follows, whilst not exhaustive, gives an indication of track allocations that are likely to meet the requirements of Granada Television for post-production purposes. If the programme is to be made in stereo, A/B stereo sound should be used: M/S stereo should not be used without prior permission from the Chief Engineer.

Monophonic sound

Dialogue, music, M&E, pure M&E, pure effects, final mix:

    Track 1: mono dialogue (or mono music, mono M&E, etc.)
    Track 2: mono dialogue (or mono music, mono M&E, etc.)

If the two mono signals are identical, they must be coherent and in phase and of equal amplitude to produce a central stereo image. Only one of the signals is used in the course of post-production, to preserve the integrity of the stereo image through the transmission chain, but delivery of two-channel mono can provide a useful backup should signal problems occur. Mono dialogue can be either synchronous speech, commentary/voice-over, etc., or both.

A/B stereo sound

Music, M&E, pure M&E, pure effects, final mix:

Track 1: music left (or M&E left, etc.)

Track 2: music right (or M&E right, etc.)

M/S stereo sound

Dialogue, pure effects:

Track 1 M (left + right): sum signal (mono dialogue or mono pure effects)

Track 2 S (left – right): difference signal

A stereo final mix usually consists of: a stereo M&E plus either mono dialogue or M/S stereo dialogue (where the dialogue is commentary/voice-over only); or a stereo Pure M&E plus, again, mono or M/S stereo dialogue (where the dialogue is commentary/voice-over *and* synchronous speech). A stereo final mix should normally be of A/B type unless there is no music at all. Stereo music should always be recorded A/B.

A/B stereo dialogue is not seen as a practical option and is not recommended. The dialogue format should be decided at the onset of production to avoid a mixture of mono and M/S stereo dialogue, which gives unsatisfactory results. Care must be taken to preserve the mono compatibility of material.

Identification of audio signals

Signal	Track 1	Track 2
Stereo	Interrupted	Continuous
Dual-channel mono	Interrupted	Interrupted
Single-channel mono	Continuous	Continuous

Tone interruptions to last 0.25 s and occur every 3.00 s. Source tones must be accurately related to the ensuing programme material and should be recorded in phase on both tracks at a frequency of 1 kHz and at a flux level of 100 nWb corresponding to 0 dBu (PPM 4).

The ITC Code of Practice requires that the amplitude frequency response and the level difference between the two channels should not stray further than 1 dB between 125 Hz and 10 kHz for analogue tape recorders. Any more than this and the image may be on the move for the more critical listener, and this could have an effect on the monophonic signal. When, say, the left channel has an excessive HF response compared to the right channel, this will result in the apparent movement of the sibilant sounds towards the left loudspeaker.

Central Broadcasting

Generally, Central have no rigid policy on recording stereo, but the following format is their general standard. As a rule, location stereo is recorded M/S, with the exception of complex music or situations requiring complex rigging, where it is more appropriate to adopt A/B. Central's edit suites can cope with A/B or M/S material, and if passed on to sound dubbing its original recorded format will be retained.

Drama recording

Drama is generally recorded in M/S stereo with the possible exception of FX tracks, which may be A/B. In all cases they request that the tape box and recording sheet are clearly marked M/S or A/B, whichever is appropriate, and if possible, a verbal ident should be provided within the line-up tone. The two formats should *not* be recorded on the same tape.

Track layouts

Track 1: always left or M signal
Track 2: always right or S (side) signal
This applies equally to audio or videotapes.

London Weekend Television

At present, LWT have not laid down any fixed rules on stereo input, though they will generally accept both M/S and A/B stereo, but insist on clearly marked boxes and no mixing of formats on the same tape. Their edit suites can cope with both systems.

Border Television

Although a small company, Border can handle material in M/S and A/B format, and would expect the same rules as Central Television.

Other ITV companies

It is always a good idea to call the head of sound of the appropriate company and find out how they wish you to present your material. If possible, obtain a few copies of their sound sheets to give you a clue to what information the company expects. It is as well to remember the rules on radio mic operation, and the technical standards that your equipment is meant to reach. It is rare for the production crew to be aware of required standards from a technical point of view back at base, so this is well worth your checking out. In general, all companies expressed the desire that *all* input of audio was suitably documented, and that different material types (i.e. M/S and A/B) were on separate rolls, not mixed on rolls. As far as the recorded level on tape is concerned, the recordist should modulate the tape to its best advantage from a signal-to-noise point of view.

Digital sound editing tools

There are a variety of digital tools now available for editing of audio data. Professional tools are a combination of computer-related hardware and audio-editing software. The following is an overview of some of the more well-known and widely used tools.

AUDIOFILE

Platform

Proprietary hardware and software.

Functions

Digital editing of recorded audio data onto various optional storage devices, such as magneto-optical disk or Exabyte tape systems. VTR emulation option allows direct control of audio data via video editing systems. EDL software option allows reading and interpretation of industry-standard edit-list formats. Audiofile has optional EBUS interface, which will allow the base unit to become a timeline controller for up to four external devices. Potential link-up to a fully digital console (desk). Large number of audio outputs (maximum 24).

Use

Broadcast audio/film/TV/recording studios.

Unique

The first, most flexible, widest used in broadcast, and most expensive. Not reliant on external computer system.

Overview

Very specialized. Not user-friendly from a software or hardware point of view. Similar in appearance to standard video outboard equipment and older audio tools; allows intuitive access for professionals already familiar with this equipment (e.g. jog and shuttle wheels etc.). Because of its unbeatable integration with film and TV industry requirements for audio syncing to visual equipment, this is a pro tool only.

Cost

£45 000.

Pros

Unbeatable interfacing to film and video equipment.

Cons

Cost; steep learning curve of proprietary hardware and software. Single source of supply support and backup.

SADIE

Platform

IBM 486 or Pentium PC running Windows; Sadie Windows-based editing software; analogue/timecode interface board; SCSI-based storage devices.

Use

Broadcast audio/video.

Unique

High-quality computer-based tool. The specialized digital I/O capabilities of an in-built 32-bit DSP and the outboard interface direct to SCSI storage avoiding CPU drain allows this solution better user performance and higher quality output (24-bit) than similar computer-based solutions.

Overview

Very clever and cost-effective solution from medium-sized British company. Makes the most of a software environment and hardware that most people are familiar with, and therefore has a less steep learning curve than most solutions. The ingenious way that this solution has utilized hardware interface is less cumbersome and offers more performance than others. Highly suitable for broadcast audio mastering; perhaps not quite as flexible for music and video applications owing to limited interfacing options.

Cost

Basic set-up approximately £5000; advanced set-up £7000–£10 000.

Pros

Clever design; reasonable cost; high output quality; well-known software environment gives ease of use and in-built help.

Cons

Single source of supply and backup; limited interfacing to film/video (SMPTE).

DIGI-DESIGN – SOUND TOOLS

Platform

Macintosh LCII or higher, Quadra, Power Mac; System 7; various digital I/O interface boards (e.g. Audiomedia/Session 8); SCSI storage; sound tools edit software.

Use

Post- and pre-production digital audio/video/music.

Unique

In many ways similar to Sadie; however, has extra benefit of a wider interface capability and a slightly more powerful hardware and operating system to run under. This was the first computer-based hard disk recording system to take off commercially and attain market leadership. The ability of this system to interface with video and digital music outboard equipment gives it an edge.

Overview

Highly regarded and widely available solution used by audio, video and music professionals. Reasonable cost today, although previously very expensive. Has added benefit of Macintosh ease of use and higher power/cost ratio; ability to add easily almost unlimited extra SCSI devices gives higher potential record time. Increased number of audio outputs and simple integration with digital video applications such as AVID means that this and similar Mac-based solutions are likely to be prevalent for many years to come.

Cost

£5000 intermediate solution; < £10 000 professional solution.

Pros

Ease of use, power/cost, flexibility, close association with video hard disk recording systems now coming available. Widely sold and supported by various audio/music/video and computer dealers, giving choice of supply and support and maintenance options.

Cons

Steeper learning curve of sound tools software if self-training.

SOFTWARE AUDIO WORKSHOP (SAW)

Platform

IBM 386/486 PC running Windows; 16-bit audio board; MIDI/SMPTE interface board; SAW edit software (Windows).

Use

Small studio/home pro use/mobile pro audio work.

Unique

The first broadcast-standard product to be widely available for anyone to have at home or in smaller studio environments. Because this software uses a widely available and low-cost hardware platform it combines ease of use, reasonable power, pro-quality 16-bit output and extremely low cost. It also gives the potential to be used on laptop or portable computers and therefore become perhaps the first portable hard disk recording system available for on-location use. With newer audio cards, a digital input and output can be achieved.

Overview

SAW software will run on any multimedia-specification IBM PC. Uses many standard 16-bit audio cards (low cost), and utilizes a DAT as backup device. The SAW software is written at a binary level, and it is this excellent software coding that allows it to run on lower-spec and widely available machinery. It allows: four-track stereo manipulation of audio data, 32-bit registering with the hardware, simultaneous record and playback of full bandwidth audio data, looping, reversing and midi and SMPTE interfacing.

Cost

£2500.

Pros

Well-known software environment gives ease of use and built-in help. Well-written software gives low hardware overhead, and clever choice of supported hardware gives pro output at very low cost. Wide availability of supply of software and hardware (mail order); potential for portability.

Cons

Limited interface for video/film (SMPTE only).

APPENDIX G

The licensing of radio microphones in the UK

ASP Frequency Management Ltd is the body that handles radio microphone management on behalf of the Department of Trade and Industry. It can be contacted for full details of radio microphone licensing at the following address: ASP Frequency Management Ltd, Edgcott House, Lawn Hill, Edgcott, Aylesbury, Bucks HP18 0QW; tel: 01296 770458.

Radio microphones fall into three groups, for each of which differing approvals and frequencies apply.

DEREGULATED DEVICES

These must be type-approved to DTI specification MPT 1311 or MPT 1345, and must work on the following frequencies only (maximum effective radiation power 2 mW): 173.800 MHz; 174.100 MHz; 174.500 MHz; 174.800 MHz; 175.000 MHz. These devices may be used anywhere within the UK without a licence.

INDOOR FIXED SITE RADIO MICROPHONES FOR THEATRES, CONFERENCE HALLS, CHURCHES ETC.

Almost 40 frequencies are available, dependent on geographical location (more frequencies are available in London than in other areas). Radio microphones in this group may transmit at higher power levels than deregulated devices. The limit is 10 mW erp for hand-held devices and 50 mW erp for pocket transmitters. They must be type-approved to MPT 1350 specification.

VHF frequencies available

In the band 173.7–175.1 MHz, plus two fixed frequencies of 176.4 MHz and 177.0 MHz. In practice this gives a total of six usable frequencies.

UHF frequencies available

For London use only: up to 12 fixed frequencies in TV Channels 22, 24 and 25. For use in London, Birmingham and areas where the new TV Channel 5 is *not* broadcasting on these frequencies: TV Channel 35 within the limits 583.355–586.835 MHz and 588.300–589.250 MHz. In practice this will give a total of 8–10 usable frequencies. Whole country: TV Channel 69 within the limits of 856.100–859.650 MHz

Licences are required for these fixed site frequencies, currently costing £135 per site (£225 if both Channel 35 and 69 frequencies are used). Licences are available from ASP Frequency Management.

UK GENERAL RADIO MICROPHONES

There are various VHF and UHF frequencies available for general UK use, for both indoor and outdoor work. Radio microphones are of the same higher-power type as used for indoor fixed sites, and must be type-approved to MPT 1350. The frequencies are:

VHF channel	Frequency	UHF channel	Frequency
ML1	191.9 MHz	ML14	854.900 MHz
ML8	200.3 MHz	ML15	855.275 MHz
ML2	208.3 MHz	ML16	855.900 MHz
ML3	216.1 MHz	ML17	860.400 MHz
ML18	860.900 MHz		
ML19	861.750 MHz		
ML20	856.175 MHz		
ML21	856.575 MHz		
ML22	857.625 MHz		
ML23	857.950 MHz		
ML24	858.200 MHz		
ML25	858.650 MHz		
ML26	861.200 MHz		
ML27	861.550 MHz		

Licences are required for these frequencies, currently costing £100 per frequency per year, available from ASP Frequency Management Ltd.

MULTICHANNEL SYSTEMS

To avoid intermodulation problems when installing more than one receiver, or if further receivers are added at a later date, great care must be taken with choice of frequencies.

If a deregulated system is envisaged, then 174.8 MHz should be avoided. The frequency 174.1 MHz should be avoided for Beyer or Trantec systems, but this frequency is usable if a Sennheiser, EDC, or some other manufacturer's system is planned. It is best to ask your particular supplier on this point. Some manufacturers have more refined circuitry to cope with this problem.

If only a single channel use is envisaged there is no problem in using 174.1 MHz or 174.8 MHz frequencies. For a four-channel system the best choice of frequencies would be: 173.800, 174.500, 175.000 and 177.000 MHz. However, if the frequency 177.000 MHz is used, a licence must be obtained for its legal operation, and units need to be approved to MPT1350. This frequency can only be licensed for indoor use.

If fixed site frequencies are envisaged contact your supplier for advice, as intermodulation-free frequencies vary from manufacturer to manufacturer. If a licensed UK general system is envisaged, all ten frequencies mentioned earlier are intermodulation-free and can be used together.

The basic rule on choosing your radio microphones is to get on to your intended supplier and check out your requirements and fit them around the available equipment and frequencies. New frequencies become available so check out with your suppliers prior to the purchase of any systems.

Most broadcast companies would require you to use specific frequencies while working on their productions; a call to their engineering department should give you the required information.

APPENDIX H

Film dubbing chart

Typical Film Dubbing Chart

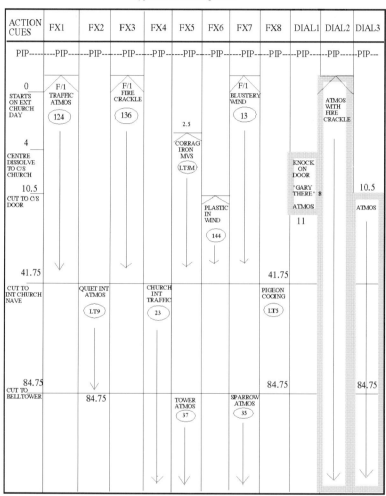

The sheet illustrated above does not reflect all tracks on a major film dub, as extra footsteps (foleys) are recorded either in the dubbing theatre or at an external dubbing theatre.

Further tracks containing the music will be supplied usually by an outside recording studio.

The numbers at the side of the chart and within the chart are film feet; they could also be expressed in minutes and seconds, or timecode.

Obviously there are a great number of carefully laid tracks for the dubbing mixer to use, which gives a fairly fine control over the whole dub.

Index

Page references in **bold** indicate figures, those in *italic* indicate tables.

Aaton, cameras 128–9, 130, 133–4
A/B stereo 163–5, 167–8
  BBC requirements 199
  dubbing 166
  equalization 69
  ITV requirements 203–4
  matricing 31
  television 158, 199, 203–4
Accounting 179
Acoustic guitars
  decibel levels **26**
  dynamic range **26**
  equalization *72*
  microphones 42, **90**
  see also Guitars
Acoustics 1–3
  location recording 151–2, 154
Actors
  voice levels 149
  see also Artistes
Adaptors, balanced input systems 21
ADAT machines 9–10, 170, 197
Advanced Music Systems, digital samplers 101
Aerials, radio microphones 87, 110–11, 113
AFM tracks, Betacam equipment 104–5

Aiwa/HHB, DAT machines 129
AKG, microphones 90–2, 117–18
Alesis, video recorders 170
Amos, *see* Atmosphere tracks
Amplifiers
  aerial amplifiers 110
  audio distribution amplifiers 60, 74–6
Amplitude 1
Analogue audio
  conversions 4–6
  equipment 6
  fidelity 4, 8
  line-up 6
  signal-to-noise ratio 19
Analogue mixing consoles 57–76
  audio distribution 60, 74–6
  audio jackfields 60, 62, 73–4
  audio level checking 76
  auxiliary sends 58–9
  channel inputs 57
  comparison with digital mixing 77
  compressors 63, 65–6
  effects returns 60
  electronic switching 62, 74
  equalization 57–8, 69–73
  group faders 60
  impedance 62–3
  insert points 58, 60
  interfacing 67–9
  limiters 63–5
  lines areas 62

mixer desk **61**
mix-minus feeding 75–6
noise gates 66
outboard equipment 58
pan controls 59
peak-level LEDs 59
phase reverse switches 57
PPM monitor circuits 60
pre-fade listen control 59
reverberation 58, 60
talkback 62
Analogue-to-digital converters 8, 75
Apartments, noise levels **26**
Applause, PPM levels 201
Artistes
  professional relationships 144–5
  see also Actors
Atmosphere tracks
  drama productions 137
  location recording 115, 130, 168, 174–6
Audiences 109, 144–5, 201
Audio
  decibels 23–5
  EBU recommendations 95–6
  editing 98–103
  location recording 135–40, 147–56, 203
  standards 23–4
  stripe film 125
  video recording 135–40, 196–8
Audio distribution amplifiers 60, 74–6

Audio expanders, dynamic range 36
Audio jackfields
  analogue mixing consoles 60, 62, 73–4
  lines areas 62
  normalling 60, 62
  talkback 62
Audio Ltd, microphones 117
Audio mixing consoles 57–78
  see also Analogue mixing consoles; Digital mixing consoles
Audio systems
  electronically balanced outputs 20
  fidelity 3–4
Audiofile system 205–6
  dubbing 104
  hard disk editing 99–102
  LOGIC mixer 102
  operation 102
  optical disk editing 103
  sampling 9, 101
  video dubbing 99, 101
Australia, documentary 161
Autocue 148–9
Auxiliary outputs
  analogue mixing consoles 58–9
  mix-minus feeding 75–6
  post-fader 59
  pre-fader 59

Background noise 144, 150–1, 154, 160–1
Balanced input systems 20–2
  circuit diagram **21**
  common mode rejection 20
  electronically balanced outputs 20
  ground-compensated outputs 20
  location recording 21
  public address systems 21
Balancing 23–37
  drama productions 80–1
  monophonic productions 79–80
  music productions 81–3

news and current affairs 84–5
  studio audio levels 79–85
  see also Equalization
Bands, microphone placement 49
Bass attenuation, portable mixing consoles 121
Bass drums
  decibel levels **26**
  equalization *72*
Bass tip-up, microphones 41–2, 49–50
Basses, *see* Electric basses; String basses
Bassoons, frequency range **55**
Batteries
  cost 178
  DAT machines 9, 129
  location recording 143
  Lockit system 169
  portable mixing consoles 119
  radio microphones 87, 110–11, 113
  RDAT machines 172, 173
BBC
  digital audio distribution 75
  drama productions 81
  dynamic range 27
  equalization 161–2
  high fidelity 5
  listener survey 27
  location recording 116, 161–2
  M/S stereo 167
  multitrack dubbing 101
  stereo television 93, 157, 158, 199–201
  telephone numbers 193–4
  tone line-up levels *37*
  see also Nicam stereo system
Beatles, multitracking 99–101
Bells, equalization *72*
Betacam equipment
  AFM tracks 104–5
  dubbing 106
  EBU tone 157
  limiters 64–5
  portable mixing consoles 121

set-up 137–8
  side panel layout **138**
  track placements 139
  wildtracks 176
  see also Sony; Video recording
Beyer, microphones 52, 117–18
Bibliography 183
Bidirectional microphones
  directional response 40–2
  polar patterns **40–1**
  ribbon microphones 41–2, 49–50
Billing 179
Birdies 113
BITC *see* Timecodes
Bits, digital processing 8
Bongos, microphone positioning **92**
Boom operations
  directional response 45–6
  drama productions 80–1
  image orientation points 97
  location recording 148–9
  sound supervisor responsibilities 108–9
  stereo television 97
  studio floor 88–9
  video monitors 89
Border Television 204
Broadcast sound
  absolute maximum signals 75
  dynamic range 26–8
  electronic compression 27–8
  operating levels 25
  signal-to-noise ratio 27
Bugging, interviews 161
Buzz tracks, *see* Atmosphere tracks

Cables
  balanced input systems 20
  Nagra recorder 131–2
  phase reversal 15–16
  safety regulations 87
Camcorders
  Betacam 137–40
  microphones 140

Panasonic 140
see also Cameras
Cameras
Aaton 128–9, 130, 133–4
camerapersons 141–4
rehearsal 109
Sony 121, 139–40
stripe film 125
timecode locking 139–40,
169–71
see also Camcorders; Nagra
recorder
Capacitor microphones
bass tip-up 42
circuit diagram **51–2**
directional response 38
electret 52
location recording 50–1
phantom powering 51–3
polarizing voltage 51–2
signal-to-noise ratio 20
T-powering 53–4
Cardioid microphones
A/B stereo 165
directional response 42–3,
45
hypercardioid microphones
42, 44–6
polar patterns **41**
positioning 89–92
proximity effect 42
supercardioid microphones
42
Cellos
equalization *72*
frequency range **55**
microphone positioning **90**
Central Broadcasting 203–4
Chains
fidelity 3
side-chain circuits 66
signal-to-noise ratio 19
Channel 4, stereo television 93
Clapperboards
Clockit system 133–4
location recording 146
RDAT machines 173
synchronization 129, 130
timecodes 133–4
Clarinets
frequency range **55**

microphone positioning **91**
Classical music
dynamic range 327
PPM levels 201
Classic FM, minidisk systems
10
Clockit system 130, 169, **171**
clapperboards 133–4
Close-speaking microphones
49
Clothing, personal
microphones 112
Cochlea 17
Code, digital recording 7
Coloration
microphones 89, 143–4
resonance 12–3
Colour bars 176
Colour framing, Nagra
recorder 130–1
Commercials
auto-decompression 36, 66
electronic compression
27–8
hard disk editing 99
limiters 63
recommended PPM levels
36
tone line-up levels *37*
Common mode rejection,
balanced input systems
20
Compression
analogue mixing consoles
65–6
auto-decompression 36
broadcast sound 27–8
commercials 66
gain 63
location recording 161–2
phase 16–17
technical requirements 201
Computers
digital recording 6–10
hard disk editing systems
98–102, 193, 205–9
screen grab **100**
see also Audiofile system
Conga drums
decibel levels **26**
microphone positioning **92**

Contact microphones, direct
inject boxes 49
Contacts 179–80, 190–5
Control rooms *see* Mixing;
Studio recording
Costumes, location recording
149
Cottage loaf response,
microphones 42, 44–6
Crew
location recording 141–6
relationships on location
144–5
Current affairs, *see* News and
current affairs
Cymbals
equalization *72*
frequency range **55**
microphone positioning **92**

Damping
location acoustics 151–2
resonance 12–13
Dart system, digital recording
10
DAT machines
Aiwa/HHB 129
Audiofile system 102
batteries 9, 129
Clockit system 130, 169
Fostex 129
manufacturers 192–3
Nagra recorder 129
off-tape monitoring 9
Stellavox 129
timecodes 129–30
see also RDAT machines
Datastream
digital mixing consoles 77
hard disk editing 99
DCC, *see* Digital compact
cassette
Decibels
definition 23–5
musical instruments **26**
noises **26**
De-essing 66
Difference signals, M/S meter
pointers 31
Digi-design, sound editing
software 207–8

Digital audio distribution 75
Digital compact cassette (DDC) 69, 170, 197
Digital equalization 73
  spectrum analysers 73
Digital hard disks, editing 98–102
Digital mixing consoles 76–8
  comparison with analogue mixing 77
  edit decision lists 77
  LOGIC mixer 102
  pre-set configurations 77
Digital processing 7–10
  analogue-to-digital converters 7
  bits 8
  digital-to-analogue converters 8
  editing 7, 9, 205–9
  ISDN 85
  non-destructive editing 7
  quantization noise 8
  solid-state switching 34
  see also Audiofile
Digital recording 6–10
  code 7
  Dart system 10
  EBU recommendations 9
  fidelity 4, 7, 8–9
  floppy disk recording systems 10
  information storage 6
  sampling 7
  signal-to-noise ratio 19
  video 20
Digital samplers, Advanced Music Systems 101
Digital-to-analogue converters 8
Direct inject boxes
  contact microphones 49
  earth lift switches 68
  equipment interfacing 67–8
Directional response, microphones 38–45, 56
Directories 180
Directors
  dubbing responsibility 107
  relationships on location 141–4

Discrete data 7
Distortion 10–3
  frequency distortion 11
  harmonic distortion 10–11
  intermodulation distortion 11
  resonance 12–13
  spatial distortion 11–12
  transient distortion 11
  volume distortion 12
Diversity systems, radio microphones 110–11, 113
Documentaries
  Australian farmer 161
  location recording 115–16, 152–3
  microphone choice 116–19
  RDAT machines 153
  stereo television 96
Dolby
  electronic noise reduction 19
  location recording 145–6
  Neumann microphones 118, 165
Double basses, *see* String basses
Double ribbon microphones
  acoustic guitars 42
  directional response 42
Drama
  audio level balancing 80–1
  BBC requirements 200
  ITV requirements 204
  location recording 114–16, 147–51, 175–6, 200, 204
  microphone choice 80–1, 116–19, 137
  M/S stereo 166–7, 200
  Nagra recorder 129
  PPM levels 201
  radio microphones 137
  stereo television 96, 200
  video location recording 137
  walkie talkies 154
Dress rehearsals 109
Drop frame
  Nagra recorder 132
  USA equipment 132

Drums
  bass **26**, *72*
  conga **26**, **92**
  decibel levels **26**
  frequency range **55**
  location recording 148
  microphone positioning **92**
  snare *72*, **92**
  tom-toms **26**, *72*
Dubbing
  burnt-in timecode 106
  director's responsibilities 107
  equalization 72–3
  film productions 106–7, **213**
  on the fly 106
  layback 106
  lift off 105–6
  location recording 115
  mixers 107
  M/S stereo 166–7
  music 104, 105, 106–7
  news and current affairs 84, 104
  pre-mixing 106–7
  punch-in points 106
  Sony equipment 106
  sound effects 104, 106–7
  stereo television 105
  treatments 105
  video 99, 101, 104–6, 135
  voice-overs 104, 105
  see also Post-production
Ducking 66
Dynamic microphones 50
  directional response 38
  orchestras 160
  positioning 89–92
Dynamic range
  audio expanders 36
  aural balance 27
  broadcast sound 26–8
  television 79–80
  see also Limiters

Ears **17**
  eardrums 17
  sound detection 2, 17–19
  structure 17–18
  see also Hearing

Earth lift switches, direct inject boxes 68
Earth loops, balanced input systems 21
EBU, *see* European Broadcasting Union
Echo units, phase 16–17
Editing
    audio 98–103
    Audiofile system 99–103
    digital hard disks 98–102
    edit decision lists 77
    non-destructive editing 98–102
    optical disks 103
    quarter inch tapes 98, 101–2
    signal-to-noise ratio 35
    see also Sampling
Effects
    analogue mixing consoles 60
    film dubbing 106–7
    location recording 114
    video dubbing 104
Electrets
    capacitor microphones 52
    personal microphones 47–8, 52, 160
Electric basses
    equalization *72*
    microphone positioning **90**
Electric guitars
    equalization *72*
    microphone positioning **90**
    see also Guitars
Electronic compression
    broadcast sound 27–8
    commercials 27–8
Electronic instruments, sound quality 3
Electronic switching, analogue mixing consoles 62, 74
Electronically balanced outputs 20
Electrovoice, microphones 117
Equalization
    A/B comparison 69
    analogue 57–8, 69–73
    digital 73
    dubbing 72–3
    graphic equalization 70
    high-pass filters 70

hiss 71
howlround 71
location recording 117, 161–2
low-pass filters 70
microphones 46
musical instruments *72*
news and current affairs 84
Nicam stereo system 71
parametric equalization 70
rumble filters 70
voices *72*
see also Balancing; Frequency response
European Broadcasting Union
    digital recording 9
    EBU tone 16, 157, 200–1
    stereo television 95–6, 157
    Switching Centre, Brussels 62
Eustachian tubes 18
Extraneous noises 144, 150–1, 154, 160–1, 175

Faders
    auxiliary outputs 59
    dynamic range 27
    group faders 60
    portable mixing consoles 120–1, 124
    slider-type 121
Fidelity
    analogue equipment 4
    audio systems 3–4
    digital recording 4, 7
Figure-of-eight response
    A/B stereo 165
    location recording 118
    microphones **40–1**, 97
    M/S stereo 165–6
Film productions
    audio quality 136
    dubbing 106–7, **213**
    Nagra recorder 125–35
    Neumann microphones 118
    stereo recording 157–62
    timecode clapperboards 133–4
Fire regulations, studio floor 86
Fish-pole operation, drama productions 81

Floppy disks, *see* Minidisk systems
Flutes
    frequency range **55**
    microphone positioning **91**
FM tracks, signal-to-noise ratio 35–6
Foam, microphone windshields 45–6
Foldback facilities, studio floor 87–8
Fostex, recorders 129, 169–70, 172
Free run, Nagra recorder 131
Freelance working 177–82
French horns
    frequency range **55**
    microphone positioning **91**
Frequency
    A/B stereo 163–4
    definition 2
    distortion 11
    Dolby noise reduction 19
    fidelity 3–4
    hearing 18–19
    hired equipment 155–6
    musical timbre 3
    presence 18
    radio microphones 110–11, 178, 210–12
Frequency response
    microphones 54–6
    RDAT machines 173
    technical requirements 203
    see also Equalization

Gabriel, Peter, Advanced Music Systems digital samplers 101
Gain, limiters and compressors 63
General public, location recording 144–5
GLITS tone 16, 200–1
Glossary 184–9
Granada Television 202–3
Grand pianos, *see* Pianos
Graphic equalization 70
Ground-compensated outputs
    hum 20
    mixers 20

Guitars
    contact microphones 49
    portable mixing consoles
        119
    see also Acoustic guitars;
        Electric guitars
Gun microphones, directional
    response 45–6

Hand microphones
    location recording 117, 153
    radio microphones 112–13
Hard disk editing systems
    98–102, 193, 205–9
Hard knee response, limiters
    64–5
Harmonic distortion 10–11
Harmonicas, microphone
    positioning **91**
Harmonics 3
Head azimuth 34–5
Headphones
    high-impedance 63
    location recording 117,
        148–9, 162
    playback systems 83
Hearing
    aural judgment 159
    fidelity 3
    logarithmic scale 18–19
    phase 14
    sense of direction 18–19
    threshold of hearing 18, 26
    threshold of pain 18, 26
    time of arrival 19
    volume 17–19
    see also Ears
Heart-shaped response,
    microphones 42–6
HHB, video recorders 169,
    172
Hi-8 6, 9–10, 99, 170, 197
High fidelity 3, 5
High-pass filters, equalization
    70
Hi-hats, microphone
    positioning **92**
Hiring equipment 155–6, 178,
    190–5
Hiss 71
Horns, equalization *72*

Howlround
    analogue mixing consoles
        58–9
    equalization 71
    mix-minus feeding 75–6
Hum
    ground-compensated
        outputs 20
    interfacing 67
Hypercardioid microphones
    directional response 42,
        44–6
    gun microphones 45–6
    polar patterns **44**

Image orientation points,
    boom operations 97
Impedance 24
    analogue mixing consoles
        62–3
    headphones 63
    microphones 54, 56
Input devices
    analogue mixing consoles
        57, 75–6
    balanced systems 20–2
    digital processing 8
    see also Analogue-to-digital
        converters
Insert points, analogue mixing
    consoles 58, 60
Instruments, *see* Musical
    instruments
Insurance, hired equipment
    155
Interfacing
    digital compact cassette 69
    direct inject boxes 67–8
    domestic and professional
        equipment 67–9
    earth lift switches 68
    hum loops 67
    microphones 68
    minidisk systems 69
    pro-interfaces 67
    RDAT machines 69
Interference
    microphones 46–7
    vehicles on location 150
Intermodulation distortion 11
Interviews

location recording 144–5
video dubbing 104
IOPS, *see* Image orientation
    points
ISDN 85
ITV
    auto-decompression 36
    digital audio distribution 75
    Nicam stereo system 157
    sound sampling 101
    stereo television 93, 202–4
    telephone numbers 194
    tone line-up levels *37*

Jacks, *see* Audio jackfields
Jam sync
    Nagra recorder 131
    video equipment 135
Japanese equipment
    interfacing 68, 69
    minidisk systems 170–1
    power ratios 24
    VU meters 29
Jargon 184–9
Jingles, Dart system 10

Lavalier microphones, *see*
    Personal microphones
Layback, video dubbing 106
LEDs
    Lockit system 169
    peak-level 59
Licensing, radio microphones
    210–12
Lift off, video dubbing 105–6
Light-emitting diodes, *see* LEDs
Lighting, studio floor 88–9
Limiters
    analogue mixing consoles
        63–5
    Betacam equipment 64–5
    commercials 63
    gain 63
    hard knee response 64–5
    location recording 161–2
    phase 16–17
    radio microphones 111
    soft knee response 64
    technical requirements 201
    television and radio stations
        63–4

see also Dynamic range
Lines areas, analogue mixing consoles 62
Line-up levels 6, 200
Lip ribbon microphones 49–50, 58
Listeners, sound levels 27, 36
Live broadcasting, audio level balancing 79–85
Location recording 114–24
   A/B stereo 164–5, 167–8
   acoustic considerations 151–2, 154
   atmosphere tracks 115, 130, 137, 168
   audio productions 147–56
   autocue 148–9
   balancing 21
   Betacam equipment 137–40
   boom operations 148–9
   capacitor microphones 50–1
   compressors 161–2
   costumes 149
   discipline 146
   documentaries 152–3
   drama productions 114–16, 137, 147–51
   drums 148
   dubbing 115
   dynamic range 27
   equalization 117, 161–2
   equipment 122–3, 155, 177–8
   extraneous noises 144, 150–1, 154
   film productions 125–34
   headphones 117, 148–9, 162
   hired equipment 155–6, 178
   interviews 144–5
   limiters 161–2
   lip ribbon microphones 49–50
   microphone choice 115–19, 122–4, 136–7, 150, 158–60
   mobile phones 155
   M/S stereo 165–8

music 83, 114
Nagra recorder 125–34
news and current affairs 152–3
personal microphones 143–4, 153
portable mixing consoles 119–22, 124, 162
post-production 168
problems 145–6
professional relationships 141–6
public address systems 154
RDAT machines 168–74
reconnoitre 123, 147–8, 153–5
rifle microphones 143–4
safety aspects 154
secret filming 115
signal-to-noise ratio 19
sound effects 114
sound mixing 119–22, 123–4
sound supervisor responsibilities 108–9
stereo productions 96, 157–62, 163–76, 199–204
telephone lines 155
timecode clapperboards 133–4
tone line-up procedure 34–5
video equipment 135–40
violins 147–8
white noise 151
wildtracks 114–15, 123, 149–50, 168
Lockit system 169–71
LOGIC mixer, Audiofile system 102
London Weekend Television 204
Loudspeakers
   foldback facilities 87
   playback systems 83
   resonance 13
Low-pass filters, equalization 70

M&E 107

see also Effects; Music
Magnetic tapes
   Dolby 19
   signal-to-noise ratio 19
Manufacturers 190–5
Martin, George, multitracking 99–101
Matricing, M/S to A/B signal conversion 31
Maximum signal levels 75, 79
Measurement 23–37
   impedance 24
   standards 23–4
   voltage 24
Metering 28–33
   M/S meter pointers 31–3
   peak programme meters 30–1
   slugging 29
   VU meters 28–30
Micron, microphones 112, 117
Microphones
   A/B stereo 164–5
   AKG 90–2, 117–18
   Audio Ltd 117
   balanced input systems 21
   Beyer 117–18
   bidirectional microphones 40–2
   boom microphones 45–6, 89
   bugging interviews 161
   camcorders 140
   capacitor microphones 20, 38, 42, 50–4
   cardioid microphones 42–3, 45–6, 89–92
   choice 54–6, 115–19, 122–4, 136–7, 150, 158–60
   close-speaking microphones 49
   coloration 89, 143–4
   contact microphones 49
   cottage loaf response 42, 44–6
   directional response 38–45, 56
   documentaries 116–19
   drama productions 80–1

Microphones (*cont.*)
  dynamic microphones 38,
    50, 89–92, 160
  Electrovoice 117, 160
  equalization 46
  equipment interfacing 68
  figure-of-eight response
    40–1, 97
  frequency response 54–6,
    116
  hand microphones 117, 153
  heart-shaped response 42–6
  impedance 54, 56, 63
  interference 46–7
  lip ribbon microphones 58
  location recording 115–19,
    122–4, 136–7, 150,
    158–60
  manufacturers 191
  Micron 112, 117
  M/S stereo 165–6
  multi-microphone balance
    82
  music 82–3, 89–92,
    159–60
  neck microphones 112
  Neumann 96, 118
  news and current affairs
    116–19
  noise gates 66
  omnidirectional
    microphones 38–40, 165
  personal microphones 45–6,
    47–9, 117, 143–4, 153
  phantom powering 22
  phase 14–16
  physical features 48–50, 54
  placement restrictions
    48–9, 158–60
  polar patterns **39–44**
  polarity 21
  popping 45–6
  portable mixing consoles
    119
  positioning 89–92
  pressure microphones
    38–42, 46–7
  resonance 13
  rifle microphones 68, 116,
    117, 118–19, 140,
    143–4, 165

Sanken 112
Sennheiser 52, 53, 112–13,
  116, 117, 118, 140,
  165
sensitivity 56
Shure 58
signal-to-noise ratio 19, 20,
  63
Sony 112, 117
sound supervisor
  responsibilities 108–9
spill 89
spot microphones 68, 97
stands 154
stereo microphones
  118–19, 136–7, 165
studio floor 86–7, 89–92
Tram 112, 117
types 38–56, **90–2**
unbalanced 22, 52
unidirectional microphones
  42–3, 45
video recording 136–7
voice 58, **90**
windshields 45–6, 140
see also Radio microphones
Minidisk systems 170–1, 198
  Classic FM 10
  digital mixing consoles 77
  equipment interfacing 69
  Sony 10, 170–1
Mixing
  capacitor microphone
    powering 52–3, 54
  ground-compensated
    outputs 20
  location recording 119–22,
    123–4
  M/S stereo **166**
  phase reversal 15–16
  pre-mixing 106–7
  see also Analogue mixing
    consoles; Digital mixing
    consoles; Portable mixing
    consoles
Mix-minus feeding, analogue
  mixing consoles 75–6
Mobile phones
  location recording 155
  news and current affairs 84
Modulation, VU meters 28–9

Monitoring 23–37
  see also Peak programme
    meters (PPM)
Monitor return, portable
  mixing consoles 122
Monophonic productions
  audio level balancing
    79–80
  technical requirements 202
  television 157
M/S stereo 165–8
  BBC requirements 167,
    199–201
  boom operations 97
  documentation 167
  drama productions 81,
    166–7, 200
  dubbing 166–7
  ITV requirements 203–4
  matricing 31
  meter readings **32–3**
  mixing **166**
  phase 16
  portable mixing consoles
    121
  television 158, 167,
    199–201, 203–4
Multitracking
  Beatles 99–101
  dubbing 104
  musical productions 83
  video dubbing 99, 101–3
Music
  audio level balancing 81–3
  dynamic range 27, 36
  film dubbing 106–7
  limiters 64
  location recording 83, 114,
    203
  microphones 82–3, 159–60
  multitracking 83
  Nagra recorder 132–3
  outside broadcasting 83
  playback systems 83
  PPM levels 201
  public address systems 83
  rigging 83
  sound quality 2–3
  stereo television 96
  tone line-up levels *37*
  video dubbing 104, 105

Musical instruments
  decibel levels **26**
  electronically balanced
    outputs 20
  equalization *72*
  frequency range **55**
  microphones 54–6, 89–92

Nagra recorder
  analogue 9
  cable links 131–2
  DAT machines 129
  digital 10
  drama productions 129
  drop frame 132
  film productions 125–35
  jam sync 131
  liquid crystal display **127**
  music 132–3
  operation 128–9
  playback 132–3
  RDAT machines 172
  real-time working 131
  record run working 131
  set-up procedure **128**
  synchronization 125–6,
    129–33
  timecodes 126, 130–3, 169
National Vocational
  Qualifications, *see* NVQs
Neck microphones, *see*
  Personal microphones
Neumann, microphones 96,
  118, 165
News and current affairs
  audio level balancing 84–5
  dubbing 104
  location recording 152–3
  microphone choice 116–19
  telephone hybrid units 84–5
  video dubbing 106
Nicam stereo system
  digital audio distribution 75
  equalization 71
  location recording 116
  signal-to-noise ratio 35
  studio recording 93
  see also BBC; Stereo
    television
Noise
  city apartments **26**

  decibel levels **26**
  extraneous 144, 150–1,
    154, 160–1, 175
  quantization 8
  white 151
Noise gates
  analogue mixing consoles
    66
  microphones 66
Non-destructive editing
  digital processing 7
  hard disks 98–102
Normalling, audio jackfields
  60, 62
NVQs 143

Oboes, frequency range **55**
Off-tape monitoring, DAT
  machines 9
Omnidirectional microphones
  A/B stereo 165
  directional response 38–40
  personal microphones 47–9
  polar patterns **39**
On the fly, video dubbing 106
Opera, audio level balancing 83
Optical disks, editing 103
Orchestras
  audio level balancing 82–3
  microphones 49, 159–60
  pre-recording 147–8
Outboard equipment, analogue
  mixing consoles 58
Outdoor recording
  microphones 54
  windshields 45–6
  see also Location recording
Output devices
  digital processing 8
  mix-minus feeding 75–6
  see also Digital-to-analogue
    converters
Outside broadcasting, *see*
  Location recording
Overtones, music 3

Pan controls, analogue mixing
  consoles 59
Panasonic, camcorders 140
Parametric equalization 70
PCs, *see* Computers

Peak-level LEDs, analogue
  mixing consoles 59
Peak programme meters (PPM)
  30–1
  analogue mixing consoles 60
  broadcast television 36–7,
    201
  dual-movement 37
  levels 201
  portable mixing consoles
    121
  readings **32–3**
  standards 37
  stereo 31
Percussion instruments,
  microphone positioning
  92
Personal microphones
  Beyer 52
  clothing effects 112
  directional response 45–6,
    47–9
  electrets 47–8
  location recording 117,
    143–4, 153
  placement 48–9
  radio microphones 48,
    112–13
  Sanken 52
  Sony 49, 52
  windshields 112
Phantom powering
  microphones 22, 51–3
  transformers 22
Phase 13–17
  analogue mixing consoles 57
  cables 15–16
  compressors 16–17
  EBU tone 16
  echo units 16–17
  GLITS tone 16
  limiters 16–17
  microphones 14, 15–16
  mixer units 15–16, 122
  M/S metering 16
  processors 16–17
  stereo 15–17, 163–5
Pianos
  decibel levels **26**
  equalization *72*
  microphone positioning **91**

Piccolos, frequency range **55**
Pirating, serial copy
management systems 9
Playback
musical productions 83
Nagra recorder 132–3
studio floor 87–8
Polar patterns
cottage loaf response **44**
figure-of-eight response
40–1
heart-shaped response **43**
microphones **39–44**
Polarity
balanced input systems 21
microphones 21
stereo television 95–6
Pop bands
PPM levels 201
rigging 83
Popping
close-speaking microphones
49
microphone foam devices
45–6
Portable mixing consoles
bass attenuation 121
batteries 119
faders 120–1, 124
location recording 119–22,
162
monitor return 122
peak programme meters 121
phase check 122
SQN-4S Series IIa **119–20**
Post-fader auxiliary outputs 59
Post-production
location recording 168
stereo television 93–4
technical requirements 202
see also Dubbing
Post-sync, location recording
149, 154
Power ratios 24–5
PPM, *see* Peak programme
meters
Pre-fader auxiliary outputs 59
Pre-mixing, film dubbing
106–7
Pre-recording, orchestras
147–8

Pressure microphones,
directional response
38–42, 46–7
Programme material, stereo
television 96
Pro-interfaces 67
Proximity effect, cardioid
microphones 42
Public address systems 154
balanced input systems 21
musical productions 83

Qualifications 143
Quantization noise, digital
processing 8
Quarter inch tapes, video
dubbing 98, 101–2,
105, 198

Radio microphones 110–13
aerials 87, 110–11, 113
batteries 87, 110–11, 113
diversity systems 110–11,
113
frequencies 110–11, 178,
210–12
hand microphones 112–13
hired equipment 155–6,
178
licensing 210–12
limiters 111
location recording 117, 124
manufacturers 191
multichannel systems
211–12
personal microphones
112–13
placement 48
problems 111–12, 178
regulations 112
setting up 111
studio recording 87, 113
technical requirements 202
windshields 112
see also Microphones
Radio recording
limiters 63–4
microphone placement
restrictions 48–9
Rates of pay 178–9
RDAT machines 6

ADAT machines 9–10
advantages 173–4
batteries 172, 173
documentaries 153
interfacing 69
location recording 168–74
portable 176
serial copy management
systems 9
tape tension 9
timecodes 135
video recording 135,
168–71, 197
see also DAT machines
Real-time working, Nagra
recorder 131
Reconnoitre, location
recording 123, 147–8,
153–5
Record run working, Nagra
recorder 131
Rehearsals, sound supervisor
responsibilities 109
Resonance 12–13
Reverberation, analogue
mixing consoles 58, 60
Ribbon microphones
bass tip-up 41–2
directional response 41–2
double ribbon microphones
42
lip ribbon microphones
49–50
Rifle microphones
camcorders 140
directional response 45–6
equipment interfacing 68
location recording 116,
117, 118–19, 143–4
stereo 118–19, 165
Rigging
musical productions 83
pop bands 83
sound rig 109
studio floor 86–7
Rocking and rolling 105, 107
Rock music, PPM levels 201
Rumble filters, equalization 70

Sadie, sound editing software
206–7

Safety
location recording 154
studio floor 86–7
Sampling 7
Audiofile system 9, 101
see also Editing
Sanken, microphones 52, 112
Saxophones
decibel levels **26**
frequency range **55**
microphone positioning **91**
Scale distortion 12
SCMS, *see* Serial copy
management systems
Secret filming, location
recording 115
Sennheiser, microphones 52,
53, 112–13, 116, 117,
118, 140, 165
Sensitivity, microphones 56
Serial copy management
systems (SCMS), RDAT
machines 9
Shure, microphones 58
Side-chain circuits 66
Signal processing
analogue audio 4–6
difference signals 31
Signal-to-noise ratio 19–20
analogue audio 19
broadcast sound 27
chains 19
digital recording 19, 73, 77
Dolby 19
editing 35
location recording 19
magnetic tape 19
microphones 19, 20, 63
Nicam stereo system 35
portable mixing consoles
119
sound level control 35–6
videotapes 19
Silent turnover circuits, Nagra
recorder 125
Sinewaves 1, 13–15
Slugging, meters 29
Snare drums
equalization *72*
microphone positioning **92**
Soft knee response, limiters 64

Software Audio Workshop,
sound editing software
208–9
Solid-state switching, digital
routeing 34
Sony
cameras 121, 169
microphones 49, 52, 112,
117
minidisk systems 10, 170–1
video machines 101, 106
see also Betacam equipment
Sound
basic principles 1–22
level control 34–6, 75–6,
79–85, 159–62
measurement 23–37
metering 28–33
quality 2, 116
reflection 2
waves 1–3
see also Distortion; Phase
Sound effects
analogue mixing consoles
60
film dubbing 106–7
location recording 114
video dubbing 104
Sound recordists
freelance working 177–82
location recording 141–4,
158–62
professional relationships
141–4
Sound report sheets **182**, 201
Sound rig 109
Sound supervisors, roles and
responsibilities 86–7,
108–9
Sound in syncs 75, 93, 95
Spatial distortion 11–12
Spectrum analysers, digital
equalization 73
Speech
decibel levels **26**
dynamic range 27, 36
microphones 58, **90**
PPM levels 201
tone line-up levels *37*
whispering **26**
Spill, microphones 89

Sports events
lip ribbon microphones 50
stereo television 96, 158
Spot microphones
equipment interfacing 68
stereo television 97
SQN-4S Series IIa, portable
mixing consoles 119–22
Stagger-through 109
Standards
audio 23–4
frame rate 132
freelance workers 180
peak programme meters 37
tone 34
Standing waves 12–13
Stellavox, recorders 129, 169,
172
Stereo microphones 118–19,
165
Stereo peak programme meters
31
Stereo recording
film productions 157–62
location productions 136–7,
163–76
phase 15–17
studio productions 163–71
video productions 136–7
Stereo television
A/B stereo 158, 199, 203–4
audio distribution amplifiers
74–5
audio signals 95–6
boom operations 97
drama productions 81
dubbing 105
location recording 143,
157–62
microphones 97
M/S stereo 158, 167,
199–201, 203–4
polarity conservation 95–6
post-production 93–4
programme material 96
sports events 96, 158
studio recording 93–7
technical requirements
199–204
see also Nicam stereo
system; Television

String basses
  equalization *72*
  microphone positioning **90**
Strings, equalization *72*
Stripe film 125
Studio recording
  balancing 79–85
  boom operations 88–9
  dynamic range 27
  foldback facilities 87–8
  lighting 88–9
  microphones 86–7, 89–92,
    113
  mixing consoles 57–78
  noise level **26**
  playback facilities 87–8
  rigging 86–7
  sound supervisor
    responsibilities 108–9
  stereo productions 93–7,
    163–71
  studio floor 86–92
  talkback facilities 87
  television 93–7
  tone line-up procedure
    34–5
  wall box facilities 86
Supercardioid microphones,
  directional response 42
Sweetening, *see* Dubbing
Synchronization
  clapperboards 129, 130
  Clockit system 130
  Lockit system 169–71
  Nagra recorder 125–6,
    129–30
  RDAT machines 173
  video recording 101–2,
    104, 129–30
  see also Timecodes
Synclavier, optical disk editing
  103
Sync leads, Nagra recorder
  125
SYPHER suite, multitrack
  dubbing 101

Talkback facilities
  analogue mixing consoles
    62
  studio floor 87

Talking, *see* Speech
Tambourines, equalization *72*
Tape editing 98
Tape streaming, hard disk
  editing 99
Tascam, video recorders 170
Tax 179
Technical rehearsals 109
Telephone lines
  digital mixing consoles 77
  hybrid units 84–5
  ISDN 85
  location recording 155
Television
  audio level balancing
    79–85
  dynamic range 27, 79–80
  limiters 63–4
  location recording 114–24
  microphone positioning
    48–9, 89
  Nicam digital audio 4
  organizations 190–5
  recommended PPM levels
    36–7
  safety regulations 87
  see also Broadcast sound;
    Stereo television; Video
    recording
Terminology 184–9
Timbre 2
Time of arrival, hearing 19
Timecodes
  burnt-in timecodes 106
  clapperboards 133–4
  Clockit system 130
  DAT machines 129–30,
    169
  locking cameras 139–40,
    169–71
  Lockit system 169–71
  Nagra recorder 126, 130–3
  RDAT machines 135
  technical requirements 201
  USA equipment 126
  video dubbing 99, 101–2
Timpani, frequency range **55**
Tom-toms
  decibel levels **26**
  equalization *72*
Tonander, *see* T-powering

Tone
  line-up procedure 34–6, *37*
  standards 34
T-powering, capacitor
    microphones 53–4
Training 194–5
Tram, microphones 112, 117
Transformers
  balanced input systems 21
  phantom powering 22
Transient distortion 11
Trombones
  decibel levels **26**
  frequency range **55**
  microphone positioning **91**
Trumpets
  frequency range **55**
  microphone positioning **91**
Tubas
  frequency range **55**
  microphone positioning **91**

Unbalanced microphones
  balanced input systems 22
  wiring **22**
Unidirectional microphones,
    directional response
    42–3, 45
Unions 194–5
Units, decibels 23–5
USA equipment
  drop frame compensation
    132
  head azimuth 34–5
  timecodes 126
  VU meters 28–9

Vehicles, interference
    suppression 150
VHS 35–6, 196–7
Vibraphones, microphone
    positioning **92**
Video monitors, boom
    operations 89
Video recording
  audio formats 130,
    135–40, 196–8
  digital 20, 130
  drama productions 137
  dubbing 99, 101, 104–6,
    135

equipment 135–40,
169–70
jam sync 135
limiters 65
professional relationships
142–5
RDAT machines 135
Sony equipment 101, 169
stereo 136–7
synchronization 101–2,
129–30, 135, 169–71
timecode clapperboards
133–4
see also Betacam equipment;
Nagra recorder;
Television
Videotapes
audio formats 196–7
signal-to-noise ratio 19
Violas
equalization *72*
frequency range **55**
Violins
equalization *72*

frequency range **55**
location recording 147–8
microphone positioning **90**
Vocals
decibel levels **26**
microphones 58, **90**
Voice
equalization *72*
microphones 58, **90**
see also Speech
Voice-overs 104, 105, 174, 176
Voltage 24
polarizing voltage 51–2
Volume
distortion 12
hearing 17–19
threshold of hearing 18
threshold of pain 18
VU meters 28–30

Walkie talkies 154
Walk-through 109
Wall box facilities, studio floor
86

Wave propagation 1–2
Weaving 17
Whispering, decibel levels **26**
White noise 151
Wildtracks
location recording 114–15,
123, 137, 149–50, 168,
174–6
Nagra recorder 130
technical requirements 201
Windows, hard disk editing
99–102, 205–7, 208–9
Windshields
A/B stereo 165
camcorder microphones
140
microphones 45–6, 112,
118, 140
M/S stereo 165–6
Rycote softie 140

Xylophones, microphone
positioning **92**